S0-AXO-082

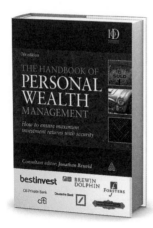

The Handbook
of Personal
Wealth
Management

The Institute of Directors is *the* professional body for business leaders and we have been representing our members for over 100 years.

The IoD is an influential network reflecting the full spectrum of international business leadership from the largest public corporation to the smallest family firm.

With such a diverse membership, a broad portfolio of benefits and services has been carefully designed to ensure that you and your business receive the practical support you need to successfully fulfill your role as a Director.

IoD membership can add real value to your business. Benefits include free access to facilities offered by our prestigious premises in London, the UK and Europe, free business information and advice, professional development, training, conferences and publications to help you maximize your potential. This respected and influential organization works on your behalf, representing your concerns to government, and delivers you professional business support, wherever it is needed.

For more information about the IoD, visit **www.iod.com**.

SEVENTH EDITION

The Handbook of Personal Wealth Management

Consultant editor
Jonathan Reuvid

RECOMMENDED BY

INSTITUTE OF DIRECTORS

LONDON PHILADELPHIA NEW DELHI

This book has been endorsed by the Institute of Directors.

The endorsement is given to selected Kogan Page books which the IoD recognizes as being of specific interest to its members and providing them with up-to-date, informative and practical resources for creating business success. Kogan Page books endorsed by the IoD represent the most authoritative guidance available on a wide range of subjects including management, finance, marketing, training and HR.

The views expressed in this book are those of the author and are not necessarily the same as those of the Institute of Directors.

Publisher's note

Every possible effort has been made to ensure that the information contained in this book is accurate at the time of going to press, and the publishers and authors cannot accept responsibility for any errors or omissions, however caused. No responsibility for loss or damage occasioned to any person acting, or refraining from action, as a result of the material in this publication can be accepted by the editor, the publisher or any of the authors.

First published in Great Britain and the United States in 2005 by Kogan Page Limited
Second edition 2006
Third edition 2007
Fourth edition 2008
Fifth edition 2009
Sixth edition 2010
Seventh edition 2011

Apart from any fair dealing for the purposes of research or private study, or criticism or review, as permitted under the Copyright, Designs and Patents Act 1988, this publication may only be reproduced, stored or transmitted, in any form or by any means, with the prior permission in writing of the publishers, or in the case of reprographic reproduction in accordance with the terms and licences issued by the CLA. Enquiries concerning reproduction outside these terms should be sent to the publishers at the undermentioned addresses:

120 Pentonville Road
London N1 9JN
United Kingdom
www.koganpage.com

1518 Walnut Street, Suite 1100
Philadelphia PA 19102
USA

4737/23 Ansari Road, Daryaganj
New Delhi 110002
India

© Kogan Page, Jonathan Reuvid and individual contributors, 2005, 2006, 2007, 2008, 2009, 2010, 2011

The right of Kogan Page, Jonathan Reuvid and the individual contributors to be identified as the author of this work has been asserted by them in accordance with the Copyright, Designs and Patents Act 1988.

ISBN 978 0 7494 6315 1

British Library Cataloguing-in-Publication Data

A CIP record for this book is available from the British Library.

Library of Congress Cataloguing-in-Publication Data

The handbook of personal wealth management : how to ensure maximum investment returns with security / [edited by] Jonathan Reuvid. – 7th ed.
    p. cm.
  Includes bibliographical references and index.
  ISBN 978-0-7494-6315-1
1. Finance, Personal. 2. Rich people–Finance, Personal. 3. Investments. I. Reuvid, Jonathan.
  HG179.H2549 2011
  332.024'01–dc22
                              2011014947

Typeset by Saxon Graphics Ltd, Derby
Print production managed by Jellyfish
Printed in the UK by CPI Antony Rowe

CONTENTS

CONTRIBUTORS' NOTES

Jeremy Beckwith joined Kleinwort Benson in April 2003 as Chief Investment Officer and is responsible for all aspects of the investment process and investment performance of discretionary portfolios. He introduced Multi-Asset Class investing to Kleinwort Benson and is regularly invited onto Bloomberg TV to give his views on markets and economics.

   Prior to his arrival at Kleinwort Benson, he was a Managing Director and Head of EAFE Equities (non-US equities for American retail and institutional clients) at Merrill Lynch Investment Managers. Before joining the EAFE Team in 1988 he had been Managing Director of Merrill Lynch Global Asset Management, managing the portfolios of high net worth private clients and small institutions from Europe and the Middle East, and also chaired the Global Investment Committee. Prior to 1990, he was Head of Equities for Mitsubishi Finance International and a Portfolio Manager for Manufacturers Life Insurance Company, having started his career in 1983. From 2006 to 2008 he was Chairman of the FTSE Private Banking Index Advisory Board, and was named on the Citywealth Private Banking Leaders List for 2008.

Amy Bennett joined the team at British Bloodstock Marketing (BBM) as marketing executive in June 2010. Her role includes managing editorial content for the website, yearbook and newsletter, as well as supporting the International Development Manager in implementing marketing strategy. Formerly a bloodstock journalist with the *Racing Post* newspaper, Amy has also worked in marketing in the New Zealand bloodstock industry.

   BBM was established in 2007 to promote the British racing and breeding industry worldwide. It is an industry-funded organization that aims to be the first port of call for overseas visitors to the British sales and race meetings, and is available to offer practical assistance and impartial advice to both international and domestic buyers. An active programme of marketing trips to countries such as India, Turkey, Russia, the Middle East and all over Europe means that BBM has forged links with buyers from around 30 countries, as well as assisting numerous visitors to Britain. Working on behalf of the British bloodstock industry, BBM is proud to fly the flag for the British thoroughbred.

Adam Challis is Head of Research at Hamptons International providing full-service support to the business and its clients. In addition to regular monthly and quarterly market commentary, the team offers a bespoke research capability to address the specific residential market requirements of Hamptons International clients in the UK and across its international offices.

   Adam joined Hamptons International in July 2010. He has extensive experience in the public and private sectors of residential development in London and the UK. He is also a regular commentator in the UK press and at industry events, while authoring a number of articles on residential markets around the globe.

Nicole D'Angelo is a Director and Co-Head of Operational Due Diligence for Citi Private Bank's Alternative Investments platform. Nicole has seven years investment management experience. Prior to joining Citi, Nicole was Director of Operational Due Diligence at Gottex Fund Management. At Gottex, Nicole had global market responsibility managing the operational due diligence team and developing the department's processes and procedures across all firm investment methods and asset classes ranging from standard hedge fund equity investments and private lending to direct asset acquisition. Before Gottex, Nicole was an analyst at The Midway Group, a mortgage-backed hedge fund. In this capacity, Nicole worked on the day to day operations of the firm, including compiling the monthly portfolio valuation, NAV calculation and annual audited financial statements, compliance and investor relations. Nicole has a BSc Economics from Fordham University.

Michael Darriba is Director and UK Head of Lending and Credit Solutions, Deutsche Bank Private Wealth Management. Michael has over 20 years of banking experience in corporate lending and designing sophisticated lending structures for high net worth individuals. His career started at HSBC where he spent 10 years focused on corporate banking, and then five years at Coutts & Co. Private Bank before moving to UBS AG Private Wealth Management where he spent nearly six years as the Head of Banking Products in the UK and then the United States. He has a track record in setting up and growing the lending business as well as building partnerships with both internal and external clients.

Mark Davidson is a Director and Co-Head of Operational Due Diligence for Citi Private Bank's Alternative Investments platform. Mark has 11 years of investment management and hedge fund industry experience. Most recently Mark was the Director of Risk Management for Russell Investment's multi-billion dollar alternative investment platform. In this role Mark developed the risk management programme and framework for alternative investment products offered to clients. While at Russell Investments, Mark managed the Operational Due Diligence programme for numerous private investment vehicles, including hedge fund and private equity/private real estate funds. Mark is experienced with private fund vehicle structuring and governance. At Russell Investments he was a member of the Alternative Investments Pricing Committee.

Prior to Russell Investments, Mark was a Manager in the Regulatory Consulting practice of Deloitte & Touche, the audit and professional services firm. During his time with Deloitte, Mark developed and managed the 'investment manager oversight' service line, which delivered operational due diligence services to large fund-of-fund and pension fund clients. Additionally, he specialized in providing operational and regulatory consulting services to an array of investment management clients, ranging from large mutual fund complexes to small hedge funds.

Mark graduated cum laude from Boston College with a BS in Finance.

Tina Fordham is Senior Political Analyst and a Managing Director at Citi Investment Research and Analysis. She has over a decade's experience in international policy analysis and political risk assessment. Ms Fordham joined Citi in 2003 and, as Senior Political Analyst, focuses on the implications of global political developments for companies and investors. Additionally, she is an Associate Fellow at Chatham House and a member of the World Economic Forum's Global Agenda Council on Strategic Foresight having previously served as Senior Adviser in the UK Prime Minister's Strategy Unit and as Director of Global Political Risk at the international consultancy Eurasia Group. Ms Fordham has a Master's degree in International Affairs from Columbia University's School for International Public Affairs.

Stephen Ford is a Director of Brewin Dolphin Limited and his team currently manage assets of circa £600 million on behalf of private clients and institutions making it one of the largest teams within the group. He was made Head of the London office in 2008, sits on the group's Asset Allocation Committee and became a Director of the operating company in October 2009. He holds the Chartered Alternative Investment Analyst designation, is a Chartered Fellow of the Chartered Institute for Securities & Investment and also holds the Diploma in Financial Services. Stephen is also an early bird and can often be heard on Radio 5's 'Wake Up to Money' or the Today programme.

Simon Gibson has 21 years' experience as an Independent Financial Adviser and is a Director at Atkinson Bolton Consulting. Simon's client base is made up of wealthy clients, integrating their financial planning and asset management needs. His expertise covers a wide area of investment management, inheritance tax mitigation strategies (estate protection), broad financial planning, business protection (including key person and partnership/shareholder protection), retirement planning, family protection and tax planning/mitigation for higher rate taxpayers. Atkinson Bolton Consulting was established in 2001 and has a highly personalized approach developing long-term partnerships with both their private and corporate clients. Their personal touch can be seen across all facets of the business, including Employee Benefits. Atkinson Bolton has received many awards, including 'Money Marketing Investment Adviser of the Year 2011' and Runner Up in the 'Money Marketing IFA of the Year 2011'. They also hold Chartered Status. Creating and Preserving Wealth is the mantra of Atkinson Bolton Consulting, and in their tenth year, the company goes from strength to strength.

Ropinder Gill has been Head of Individual Giving of Epilepsy Society, the new working name of the National Society of Epilepsy, since April 2008. Prior to this, she was Head of Legacy Giving at the Children's Society. Epilepsy Society is the UK's foremost epilepsy charity, committed to enhancing the quality of life for people who have this potentially life-threatening condition. Epilepsy Society makes a real and lasting contribution to the treatment and understanding of epilepsy by raising awareness, undertaking medical research and providing specialist medical services, respite, residential care, information and support.

James Goodwin is an MA and MBA who lectures on the art market at Christie's Education in the UK and Hong Kong; Maastricht University and Erasmus University Rotterdam, The Netherlands; HEC and Euromed Management, France; Ca' Foscari University, Italy; and City University and Kingston University in Britain. His research and writing has appeared in *The Economist, Financial Times* and *Wall Street Journal* and has been broadcast on BBC TV and radio, and CNN. His book *The International Art Markets – The Essential Guide for Collectors and Investors* includes 42 country art market chapters and was published in English in July 2008 and in Chinese in June 2010.

Patrick Harney is a partner in Forsters LLP. He is an international private client lawyer experienced in tax and trust planning in the UK, Ireland and New York, and specializes in UK tax planning for non-domiciliaries with particular experience in UK-Irish tax planning and US-UK tax planning from the UK side. He advises high-net-worth individuals on the tax-efficient structuring of property transactions. He is a chartered tax adviser, an associate of the Irish Institute of Taxation and is a member of the Society of Trust and Estate Practitioners (STEP).

Stephen Hershoff is the former Managing Director of Pastor-Genève bvba. He has over 40 years of experience in the diamond business. Beginning in London in the 1960s, he was a dealer in diamonds and other coloured gems. Throughout the late 1960s and 1970s, he concentrated on advising a private client base of international collectors and connoisseurs through his own consulting company. In the early 1980s, he moved to North America to assume responsibility for a company that became one of the four most important gem dealers recommended by the Dow Jones-Irwin Guide to fine gems and jewellery. His previous company, Pastor-Genève, is recognized as one of the most established dealers in the coloured diamond market.

Felix Karthaus is a forestry graduate of Aberdeen University, born in Holland, with almost 42 years of UK forestry experience. Border Consultants (Forestry) Ltd, the UK company he shares with his wife Jane, was started in 1988. Their Baltic company was formed in 1997 and the Romanian enterprise started in 2009. In total, the management base consists of 50,000 ha of forest land and 10,000 m^2 of commercial property. Jane provides a communication service to the Confederation of Forest Industries (Confor) and edits its magazine.

Dianne Laing is a full-time Fundraising Manager for Scottish Native Woods, a post she has held for over five years and one that allows her passion for woodlands and wild landscape to benefit Scotland's environment. As a generalist professional fundraiser, Dianne engages with individuals, community groups and companies to promote the aims of the charity to win support, and she encourages people from all walks of life to become involved as volunteers.

Ian Lane is a partner in the private client department of Davies Arnold Cooper LLP. He is experienced in all aspects of both onshore and offshore tax planning, including wills, trust formation and estate administration. He has experience with the Court of Protection dealing with receiverships and has acted as a receiver for a number of patients at the Court of Protection. Ian also deals with charity formation and charity advice generally.

Clive Mackintosh is a Senior Tax Partner at PricewaterhouseCoopers (PWC) and is leader of the Private Client Practice. Clive joined PwC in 1980 from Oxford University, qualified as a Chartered Accountant in 1983 and became a partner in 1992. He specializes in tax planning for international individuals and families. Clive advises on all areas of personal tax but, in particular, on residence and domicile issues, capital gains tax and inheritance tax as they affect individuals and trusts. Clive's clients include some of the UK's wealthiest individuals and families.

The PricewaterhouseCoopers Private Client Group is one of the largest in the UK. Its team is dedicated to providing innovative tax solutions and strategic wealth management and is exceptional in its breadth and depth of expertise. The team in the UK works as part of an international network located in all major countries around the world.

Adrian Mee joined Mattioli Woods after graduating from the University of Birmingham with an economics degree. He was fundamental in the establishment of the company's broking team which has now developed into the Investment Research and Banking Division, providing key information for investment recommendations to clients.

Adrian worked as an account manager before moving into consultancy after gaining a Diploma in Financial Planning. His core clients are business owners and self-employed individuals focusing on self-administered pension scheme solutions. He lectures regularly on pension legislation at both internal and external events, as well as being an editor for various tax journals on pension planning.

John Pickles is currently senior partner at Moore Stephens Guernsey, a member of Moore Stephens International Limited, which is itself a global accountancy and advisory network with its headquarters in London. The firm's offices in Guernsey were opened in 1974. John joined Moore Stephens in London in 1982 and became a tax partner shortly thereafter specializing in personal taxation and advising high net worth individuals on international tax planning. He relocated to Guernsey in October 1998 and assumed responsibility for the firm there with effect from January 2000.

The Moore Stephens network comprises 630 offices in 98 countries throughout the world regulated by the Guernsey Financial Services Commission in the conduct of trust and company business and regulated to carry out audit work by the Institute of Chartered Accountants in England and Wales.

Jonathan Reuvid is an Associate Publisher at the business and reference division of Kogan Page. Before taking up a second career in publishing, Jonathan held senior management positions in a Fortune 500 multinational and was previously an oil industry economist, investment banker and consultant to SMEs. In the 1980s and 1990s, he was engaged in joint venture development in China for international clients and on his own account. He continues to write on business in China.

Michael Schmeja is Head of FX Sales and Structuring at Citi Private Bank, EMEA. Michael joined Citi Private Bank from Saxo Bank A/S in Copenhagen where he worked as Global Head of Derivatives Sales. Prior to that Michael spent time at the

Royal Bank of Scotland where he covered financial institutions in Switzerland, Germany and Austria on all RX products. Previously, Michael was Managing Director, Head of Foreign Exchange and Money Market for the Private Wealth Management Group at Deutsche Bank, having moved from JPMorgan Chase where he was responsible for FX Spot, swaps, forwards and options in Germany and Austria. Michael was educated at Technical University in Munich, where he read Economics and Agriculture.

Penny Shepherd MBE is Chief Executive of UKSIF, the sustainable investment and finance association. She has over thirty years experience working with financial services, including over fifteen years on sustainability and responsibility issues. She received an MBE in 2000 for 'services to sustainable economic development and socially responsible investment.'

UKSIF is a non-profit membership network with over 250 members. It promotes responsible investment and other forms of finance that support sustainable economic development, enhance quality of life and safeguard the environment.

H John Stollery is Chairman of DiaMine Explorations Inc. He began his career in the early 1960s as an engineer after completing a BSc in civil engineering from the University of Alberta in 1961. In 1965, he received a master's degree in business administration from the University of Western Ontario. From the late 1960s until the early 1980s, he worked as a vice-president and director at Xerox Corporation, specializing in marketing and systems development. After departing from Xerox, he ran two successful transport companies as their CEO, TNT Canada and TST Solutions Inc. Both companies grew significantly and recorded multi-million-dollar sales increases under his tenure. His experience in management and strategic development is an integral component of the direction and guidance of DiaMine Explorations Inc.

Dan Tubb joined Bestinvest after graduating with a degree in economics from Southampton University and trained as an investment adviser. He moved to Unicorn asset management in 2001 where he was assistant fund manager for VCTs and other smaller company funds. In 2006, Dan joined *Analyst* magazine as the lead writer, producing detailed reports on a range of UK-listed companies. During this time, he also set up a marketing and design business which was subsequently sold to a major listed company and helped establish a new investment business. In 2009, Dan rejoined Bestinvest to head up their alternatives department, which includes VCTs.

Stefan Velvick has worked at Charities Aid Foundation (CAF) for 20 years. He has held the post of Trust Senior Client Manager for six years administering trusts for high net worth donors.

Alan Wallace is an Investment Director at Octopus Investments Limited. Alan has more than 27 years of experience making investments into smaller companies. He has a particular focus on deal flow, investment selection, monitoring and portfolio management.

Prior to moving into investment management, Alan had an extensive career that included senior management and marketing roles at a number of companies, including Sara Lee UK Limited, Dairy Crest plc, and Great Universal Stores plc. Alan has a BA (Hons) in Economics. He also studied for an MSc in Management, subsequently graduating with a PhD in Management Sciences from the University of Manchester.

David Warner is Chief Executive of the National Animal Welfare Trust (NAWT). His first involvement with NAWT was when he and his partner re-homed a 23-week-old cross-bred puppy called Truffle. Their second dog, Misti, a cross-bred stray from Wales, joined them from the NAWT a year later. David has spent over 20 years working in the charity sector for a wide range of organizations, including five years as chief executive for the Homeless Network charity. He joined the NAWT as Chief Executive in 2004. The NAWT is one of the top 10 animal rescue and rehoming charities in England and runs centres across the country in Watford, Berkshire, Essex, Somerset and Cornwall. It cares for around 500 animals (primarily cats and dogs) at a total cost of £8,000 per day (equivalent to £16 per animal).

Philip Watson is Head of the Investment Lab EMEA and a Managing Director at Citi Private Bank. He is also a voting member of the Global Investment Committee which defines strategy for the Private Bank. Specializing in portfolio construction and investment strategy, Philip's team provides holistic wealth management and advice tailored to meet clients' financial needs and individual objectives. Prior to leading the team, Philip worked within the Investment Lab as a Senior Portfolio Analyst. Within Citi's Corporate and Investment Bank he has held roles previously within Equity Derivatives, Risk Management and Warrants Trading where he was a project manager during the Y2K assignment. He was recently awarded a 'Top 100' Rising Star rating by the *Financial News* and appeared in the Wealth Bulletin's 40 Rising Stars list in *European Wealth Management, 2008*. Internally, he has been awarded 'Product Head for Europe' Chairman Council's Award for two consecutive years. He is a regular contributor to the media and Citi investment road shows. Philip graduated from the University of Leeds with an honours degree in Ecomonics and French and is a Certified Securities and Financial Derivatives Representative.

Eric Williams is National Head of Private Client for Grant Thornton and Head of Tax for Grant Thornton in Birmingham. He is recognized for his holistic approach to tax planning, reflecting his experience of many different taxes. Eric speaks extensively on tax, both internally and at external conferences, and has a reputation for thinking widely about commercial as well as tax issues so that tax advice is never given in a vacuum. He has been a partner with Grant Thornton since 1995 and has over 30 years' experience of giving practical tax advice to wealthy individuals, entrepreneurs and their companies.

FOREWORD

The task of planning the best use of assets to secure the future for our families, dependents and ourselves is no easier than a year ago when I highlighted this responsibility in my Foreword to the 2010 edition of *The Handbook of Personal Wealth Management*.

The Chancellor's March 2011 Budget has introduced a number of changes to the tax regime for the individual and for companies. The latter are focused on stimulating economic growth and are generally beneficial, but some of the changes to personal taxation are less welcome. Coupled with a higher rate of inflation and rising commodity prices, likely future increases in interest rates, although good for savers, will be an additional burden for borrowers and will intensify the squeeze on disposable incomes. Under these conditions income available for new investment is likely to be constrained for the foreseeable future.

The contents of this new edition address issues of prime concern to investors and to a certain extent reflect the continuing distrust of the more arcane financial instruments and a wariness of the services of the financial community at large. The well-known providers of financial services who have contributed to the book have returned to first principles and sensibly focused on good practice in asset management and risk avoidance.

However, all is not gloom and doom. For those who have succeeded in maintaining income and have capital availability, other authors have updated their previous advice on investment in tangible assets ranging from forestry in Europe and overseas property to gold and coloured diamonds and, more speculatively, from art and antiques to bloodstock and racehorse ownership.

We know that the new climate of cost consciousness will persist for at least the next couple of years and recent international events, in particular the disasters in Japan, have cast a pall on prospects for the global economy. We rely on the informed input of reliable advisers and the annual editions of *The Handbook of Personal Wealth Management* will continue to provide important insight.

Miles Templeman
Director General, IoD

Introduction

As the United States, United Kingdom and most other European economies experience only slow recovery from the financial crisis of 2008, high net worth individuals (HNWIs) face fresh imponderables. Although most banks that were rescued by government funding have returned to profit and those that maintained independence (with a little help from their friends) are reporting 2010 results at pre-crisis levels, doubts linger as to how stable the global financial system really is. Equity markets, although impacted by environmental catastrophe in Japan and its effect on the economy, are relatively buoyant but this may reflect a false sense of security.

While a policy of investment in carefully selected securities remains sound, how safe is it to re-enter the shark-infested waters of more sophisticated financial derivatives? Like their Asia-Pacific counterparts in the aftermath of the financial crisis, European and North American HNWI investors want a choice of suitable products and services that are aligned to their risk profiles and their investment goals. They need to understand better what they are investing in and are demanding better value-added investment advice. This new edition of *The Handbook of Personal Wealth Management* sets out to address some of those requirements.

Defining the HNWI

This seems an appropriate moment to review the definition of HNWIs and changes in their worldwide dispersion. Definitions vary: while Wall Street parlance for a wealthy individual is someone who has at least US$500,000 in liquid assets, private banking business typically defines an HNWI as having investable assets (financial assets not including primary residence) of more than US$1 million.

However, the US Securities and Exchange Commission (SEC) has adopted a different definition of HNWI for regulatory purposes. All investment advisers registered with the SEC are required to file a periodic report, designated Form ADV, stating how many of their clients are HNWIs. In this context, an HNWI is defined as an individual with at least US$750,000 under management with the reporting investment adviser, or whose net worth the adviser believes to be in excess of US$1.5 million. Under the latter definition, the net is widened significantly because the 'net worth' of an individual may include assets held by his or her spouse and the value of a person's verifiable non-financial assets, such as a primary residence or art collection. Translated into UK terms, this would mean that anyone with an unmortgaged residence worth £1 million would qualify.

The HNWI population

The Merrill Lynch Capgemini *World's Wealth Report 2010* adopts the private banking definition of US$1 million in financial assets, excluding 'collectibles, consumables, consumer durables and private residences' for an HNWI and US$30 million for an ultra-high net worth individual (Ultra-HNWI).

The report found that in 2008 there were 8.6 million HNWIs worldwide (a decline of 14.9 per cent from 2007), having a total wealth of US$32.8 trillion (a decline from 2007 of 19.5 per cent). At the same time, the population of 95,000 Ultra-HNWIs had declined by 24.6 per cent and its accumulated wealth by 23.9 per cent. Looking ahead, the report projects a recovery in HNWI wealth to US$48.5 trillion by 2013.

Regional variations

Within the global HNWI statistics for 2009, the Asia-Pacific population of HNWIs rose by 25.8 per cent to 3.0 million, catching up with Europe's HNWI population for the first time. At the same time, Asia-Pacific's HNWI wealth jumped by 30.9 per cent to US$9.7 trillion, exceeding Europe's HNWI wealth for that period. The number of Asia-Pacific's Ultra-HNWIs also increased by 36.7 per cent to 129,600, with their total wealth rising 42.6 per cent in 2009.

The drivers of this strong regional growth are, of course, China and India. Although Hong Kong's HNWI population recorded the highest percentage growth in the world of 104.4 per cent, the heavy decline in Hong Kong HNWI numbers in 2008 was not recouped. The 76,000 HNWIs there at the end of 2009 were still only 79 per cent of the number at the end of 2007.

This edition's contents

Part One

Part One opens with a chapter by Tina Fordham of Citi Private Bank on political risk, a particularly relevant topic for investors in 2011 as the sagas of crumbling autocracies in the Middle East and the Libyan revolution unfold. In the next chapter, Stephen Ford of Brewin Dolphin takes forward from the 2010 edition his analysis of financial investment alternatives, followed by Simon Gibson of Atkinson Bolton who proffers prudent advice on investment strategies for individuals through the 'seven ages of man'.

Moving on from the more conventional financial investments, Dan Tubb of Bestinvest introduces readers to the world of Venture Capital Trusts and their tax advantages. Next, Jeremy Beckwith of Kleinwort Benson makes the case for investing in gold as an insurance policy, either directly or through alternative gold-related securities. Closing this section of the book, Alan Wallace of Octopus identifies alternative investment models for private equity and venture capital.

Part Two

Turning to good practice in asset management, Nicole d'Angelo, in the first of two further Citi Private Bank chapters, focuses on the necessity for operational due diligence in hedge fund review. Michael Darriba of Deutsche Bank Private Wealth Management UK discusses the application of lending to unlock equity, followed by Philip Watson and Michael Schmeja, again of Citi Private Bank, who focus on the management of foreign exchange risk.

Part Three

Part Three is devoted to pension and personal taxation issues. Ian Lane of Davies Arnold Cooper and Adrian Mee of Mattioli Woods guide readers through the complexities of the new pensions regime and changes in tax relief for pensions introduced by the coalition government since May 2010. In a similar vein, Eric Williams of Grant Thornton offers advice to investors on how to cope with other aspects of the new tax regime.

The next three chapters focus on relieving the tax burden for 'non-doms' and UK citizens moving abroad. First, Patrick Harney of Forsters discusses the taxation implications for UK resident non-domiciliaries. Second, Clive Mackintosh of PricewaterhouseCoopers unravels the complexities and UK taxation pitfalls for non-UK-domiciled HNWIs and UK nationals moving abroad. Finally, John Pickles of Moore Stephens offers a dissertation on the exceptional benefits of the Guernsey tax regime and the not inconsiderable complications for expatriates deciding to relocate there.

Part Four

The first of two sections on profitable investment in assets other than financial securities and their management, Part Four consists of three chapters. Felix Karthaus of KMS Baltics briefs readers on the opportunities in forestry and real estate in parts of Northern Europe, while Adam Challis of Hamptons International, a new contributor to the book, defines the many options for direct and indirect investment in residential real estate property outside the United Kingdom. In the third chapter, Dianne Laing updates her 2010 chapter on forestry investment in Scotland.

Part Five

As in previous editions, this part of the book is for HNWIs with a taste for investment in tangible assets which offer degrees of aesthetic satisfaction, sound investment potential or personal involvement. Stephen Hershoff of Pastor-Genève, a regular sponsor and contributor to *The Handbook of Personal Wealth Management*, updates his chapters on understanding and investing in coloured diamonds for current market conditions. Similarly, H John Stollery of DiaMine Explorations, another long-standing supporter of and contributor to the book, has also revised his chapters on the allure of precious metals and Canadian diamond mining.

James Goodwin of Arts Research, the well-known art historian, university lecturer and a Kogan Page author, has brought up to date and added content to his two chapters on art and antiques. In a welcome return to the book, British Bloodstock Marketing's Amy Bennett describes the current opportunities in racehorse ownership and bloodstock investment with potential for high rewards and enjoyment but correspondingly high risks.

Part Six

No edition of *The Handbook of Personal Wealth Management* would be complete without a section on ethical investment. Penny Shepherd of UKSIF sets the scene with an authoritative chapter on sustainable and responsible investing, followed by Stefan Velvick of The Charities Aid Foundation with a thought-provoking account of the help that HNWIs can give to charities during the present tough times.

Finally, two charities have been selected from past contributors to restate their cases for support from the wealthy: the National Society for Epilepsy and the National Animal Welfare Trust.

Acknowledgements

As always, the publishers pay tribute and offer their grateful thanks to the sponsors, advertisers and authors who have contributed in varying degrees to this edition. They are all stakeholders in the book and I hope that readers will find the expert advice and information that they have provided of both interest and practical assistance in the selection of advisers and management of their investments.

Jonathan Reuvid

PART ONE
Investment in the age of austerity

The Importance of Trust in a Private Banking Relationship

Your trust is never blindly handed over. Rather, it is earned by carefully listening and responding to your specific needs, one at a time. Trust is the foundation of our relationship and the basis from which we help solve complex financial challenges for some of the world's wealthiest individuals and families.

As one of the world's global private banks, we have a history of expertise and intellectual leadership that few institutions can match. We understand that you seek to build upon the successes of your hard work. We provide access to investment opportunities with exceptional service tailored to your needs and aspirations to help you build your wealth legacy now and for generations to follow.

For an office location near you and for more information, please visit citiprivatebank.com.

Citi Private Bank

Citi Private Bank is a business of Citigroup Inc. ("Citigroup"), which provides its clients access to a broad array of products and services available through bank and non-bank affiliates of Citigroup. Not all products and services are provided by all affiliates or are available at all locations. In the US, brokerage products and services are provided by Citigroup Global Markets Inc. ("CGMI"), member SIPC. Accounts carried by Pershing LLC, member FINRA, NYSE, SIPC. CGMI and Citibank, N.A. are affiliated companies under the common control of Citigroup. Outside the US, brokerage products and services are provided by other Citigroup affiliates. Investment Management services (including portfolio management) are available through CGMI, Citibank, N.A. and other affiliated advisory businesses. In the United Kingdom, Citibank, N.A., London Branch (registered number BR001018) and Citibank International plc (registered number 1088249) are registered at Citigroup Centre, Canada Square, Canary Wharf, E14 5LB. Citibank, N.A., London Branch and Citibank International plc are authorised and regulated by the Financial Services Authority. The contact number for Citibank, N.A. London Branch and Citibank International plc in the United Kingdom is +44 (0)20 7508 8000. In Jersey, this document is communicated by Citibank, N.A., Jersey Branch which has its registered address at PO Box 104, 38 Esplanade, St. Helier, Jersey JE4 8QB. Citibank, N.A., Jersey Branch is regulated by the Jersey Financial Services Commission.

For more information on the awards, please visit ftbusiness.com, step.org or spearswms.com.

INVESTMENT PRODUCTS: NOT FDIC INSURED • NO BANK GUARANTEE • MAY LOSE VALUE

Citi and Citi with the Arc Design are registered service marks of Citigroup or its affiliates.
© 2011 Citigroup Inc. All Rights Reserved.   761994 03/11

Investors need to raise their political IQ

TINA FORDHAM, CITI

Introduction

After a long absence, political risk has come back into focus for investors, with a vengeance. The trouble is that today's investors typically have little practical experience of assessing it. The boom of the past 20 years, when the world was awash with liquidity, meant little consideration was given to political risk: growth seemed to power ahead regardless of who was in charge. The conventional wisdom of the day was that political risk – not easily quantified at the best of times – could be captured by using aggregated indicators inserted into complex statistical models.

But these methods largely failed to anticipate the recent unrest in the Middle East and North Africa (MENA), perhaps the most significant geopolitical event of the past decade. This has exposed a fundamental flaw in the way political risk has been assessed. Old approaches must be rethought if investors are to be equipped to address the fast-moving and complex politics which will take shape in the post-crisis era. As well as new methodological frameworks, investors need to stay abreast of a wide range of political developments, from elections in the rich world to security and development matters in the developing world, to be ahead of the curve. In short, they must raise their political IQ.

Making sense of these new dynamics and diversifying to buffer the effects of what can be rapid geopolitical shifts will be key to successful investing. Although this won't be straightforward, there are some structured, yet nuanced, ways to approach – and anticipate – these geopolitical shifts.

From 1989 to 2008

The 19-year period between the collapse of the Berlin Wall and the collapse of Lehman Brothers in 2008 will be looked back on as a golden age for globalization and investment. Following the demise of communism in 1989, nearly every part of the world experienced a political opening. Military dictatorships fell in southern Europe and Latin America, there was de-colonization in Africa and democratization spread through much of East Asia. The only part of the globe excluded from these political changes was, in fact, MENA.

These political openings were accompanied by a broad-based embrace of the Washington Consensus, with its adherence to the principles of free trade and open markets. Membership of the World Trade Organization expanded, and growth in what we broadly call emerging markets boomed, opening up a world of possibilities for investors.

The crises of the late 1980s in Asia and Russia were temporary setbacks. With inflation slowing and current account surpluses rising, many emerging markets prospered, attaining investment-grade status from rating agencies, and seeing large inflows of foreign capital. During this period, when financial markets were awash with liquidity, even dramatic geopolitical events such as the 9/11 attacks and the second Iraq war had little sustained impact on volatility, as measured by the Chicago Board Options Exchange Market Volatility Index.

In these conditions, assessing political risk became a component of due diligence, and one which gained prominence as predominately developed-world investors sought information about 'how Russia really works', or how investor-friendly a new Brazilian government led by a fiery trade union activist might be. New analytical tools emerged which sought to distil risk to an aggregate indicator that could be inserted in a financial model to address the elusive component of risk known as the 'fat tail'.

By the new millennium, the prevailing investment view was that there was negligible political risk in developed markets, because they were transparent democracies with independent financial institutions, central banks and regulatory agencies. In other words, the role of the state in the economy and investment environment had become minimal, and changes to the political party in power weren't thought to be significant. Even emerging markets were also gradually perceived as less risky, thanks to improvements in governance and the convergence of economic policy with international standards. But were they really? When the global financial crisis struck in 2008, these and many other myths were exposed.

Political risk returns to the developed world...

During the nearly two-decade period of rapid expansion in emerging markets, the idea that political risk was also present in developed markets – with their elections, independent institutions and high living standards – would have been laughed off by most people. But while the potential for disruptive elections or anti-business, anti-growth policies was lower in developed markets, the global financial crisis changed that, exposing the cracks in what appeared to be stable countries. After an extended period of limited government intervention in business and markets, the state was back.

The measures taken to mitigate the financial crisis in Washington, first by the Republican administration of George W Bush, then the Democratic administration of

Barack Obama – whether corporate bailouts or the fiscal stimulus package – have been enormously unpopular with the electorate, even though most economists may agree that these actions probably kept the US economy, and indeed the global economy, from worsening. In the aftermath of the crisis, unemployment levels remain at post-war highs and public hostility to government and the private sector also remains high. Political risk levels in the United States have increased markedly, as tensions over budgets and regulation, once the province of grey-suited bureaucrats, have become front-line political issues. This is illustrated by the rise of the Tea Party movement, which puts fiscal prudence and, rather counter-intuitively, low taxes as its core principles. Its message resonated deeply with many voters in the November 2010 Midterm elections, and will doubtless influence the political landscape in the lead-up to the 2012 Presidential contest.

The return of the state may have helped stabilize the global economy, but in the process it appears to have unleashed an unease which had lurked below the surface for some time: the middle class's growing sense of anxiety about stagnating and/or declining living standards. The post-Second World War era was remarkable for its steady improvement in living standards and expansion of the middle class. Better educational opportunities, the globalization of economies, free trade, an asset price boom, the lower cost of credit and many other factors combined to give rise to a powerful sense of permanent social mobility – the sense that one's children would enjoy a better quality of life than oneself. For some decades, this expectation was justified. But, for example, in the 10 years before the financial crisis, real wages remained stagnant for the average US worker despite rising aggregate growth levels. In fact, as much as 90 per cent of the phenomenal gains of the boom accrued to just 10 per cent of the population.

In Europe, new austerity policies have severely tested post-war ideals and European Union integration. There was much debate in the years before the global financial crisis about the future of the welfare state, with its emphasis on generous social safety nets, and growing state intervention in business, from cross-border mergers and acquisitions transactions to investment by foreign sovereign wealth funds. Since then, European political risk has soared as the eurozone sovereign debt crisis has unfolded, increasing the likelihood of a eurozone member state default, and pitting debtor states around the periphery such as Ireland, Greece, Portugal and Spain, against surplus states, most notably Germany. This has undermined European unity and contributed to an alarming disconnect between EU leaders and bondholders.

Due to the complex dynamics surrounding the eurozone and the requirement that all agree any mechanism to support indebted members, investors now need to be familiar with European events on a regional level, not just a national one, if they are to have any idea what the future political landscape may look like. In Germany, there will be seven regional elections this year, and general elections next year ; all will be important when determining the timing and extent of Germany's support for long-term eurozone stabilization fund support. The Irish general election on 27 February 2011 was also largely fought over the issue of changing the terms of Ireland's bailout package. It has proven extraordinarily tricky for market participants to triangulate the conflicting messages and assess the likely outcomes, as if different languages were being spoken.

More broadly, across the Group of Seven economies (France, Germany, Italy, Japan, the UK, United States and Canada), austerity policies are only just beginning to bite the proverbial man on the street, despite financial markets' participants becoming more optimistic about the recovery. Herein lies yet another potentially significant disconnect, as a combination of high unemployment, reduced disposable incomes and large-scale public-sector layoffs provides fertile ground for dislocation, social upheaval and protest. This was illustrated in the UK in December 2010, when demonstrations about the proposed phasing out of tuition subsidies for university students turned violent. As many European Union countries begin to experience more onerous debt burdens over the next several years, the tensions between politics, economics and society will become greater.

...and to emerging markets too

The rapid upheaval in North Africa and the Middle East in the early part of 2011 has also shattered illusions about emerging market stability. As recently as January, both Egypt and Tunisia were rated in the top three most politically stable countries in the region.[1] Within a month of those ratings being published, both countries experienced the rise of leaderless, non-ideological national protest movements which forced two of the longest-serving leaders in the region out of power within weeks, in a sort of 'flash revolution'.

These events have inspired protests around the region, including Yemen, Bahrain, Libya, Jordan, Morocco, Oman and Algeria. Not all protests will result in regime change – indeed, we believe the monarchies in the Gulf states have greater potential to successfully negotiate with protestors than the military regimes of North Africa. Nevertheless, the political dynamic within these countries – and the world – has irrevocably altered. What has been termed the 'Arab spring' has unleashed a process of social, political and economic recalibration in the region which will continue for many years. Political apathy has been overturned by what the Middle East's increasingly young and socially networked populations believe is a once-in-a-generation opportunity for change. It will also have implications far beyond the region, as the temptation to try 'people power' grows.

Autocratic regimes may have provided stability in the past, often reinforced by strong security services, but recent events show this is no longer true. Investors will need to re-evaluate political risk and how they diversify to protect themselves from further upheaval. They also need to accept that geopolitical risk more broadly has returned to the fore. Having strong connections to the leadership of vulnerable countries can be an advantage in gaining contracts and opportunities to invest, but when the political environment turns, the exposure to risk is substantial. Associates of the deposed Tunisian, Egyptian and Libyan regimes are already finding themselves, and their investments, under uncomfortable scrutiny.

DM and EM: where the elite meet

There are some obvious differences between developed markets (DM) and emerging markets (EM), not least that in emerging markets stronger growth has, at least in democracies such as Brazil, translated into higher approval ratings for leaders, and therefore enhanced political capital. However, there is a common theme that cuts across both DMs and EMs: anxious middle classes are becoming angrier about the perceived concentration of elite privilege. In the United States and Europe, this is reflected as anxiety about jobs, social benefits and threats from globalization, captured in survey data that show that even members of the 'educated public'[2] mistrust business, government and the media: all elites, in other words. Historically, such an acute divide between the population and the elites hasn't led to harmony; instead, it has helped foment discord and support for revolution. In the developed world, discontent can be expressed through the ballot box, though the current levels of polarization between parties makes policymaking even in mature democracies exceedingly contentious.

Even in the MENA countries, where citizens lack the political and civil rights of the United States and Europe, discontent within the region's new middle classes is at the core of the dispute between protestors and governments. And similar threads can be detected, for example, in China, as evidenced in the public outcry surrounding a fatal car accident involving the son of a leading Communist Party member.[3]

In short, political risk in both the developed markets and emerging markets is increasingly linked by a common thread: anti-establishment sentiment. We believe this is a powerful consequence of another key feature of the post-financial crisis political environment: the globalization of public expectations. What this means is that the old social contracts between governments and citizens appear to have lost their 'glue'. People increasingly want the same things no matter where they live, and they feel entitled to them. The MENA events signal how citizens are no longer willing to accept the old explanations, or repressive tactics, which prevent them from sharing economic opportunities and participating in political life. In the rich world, reversals of living standards are triggering powerful anxiety, and antipathy to elites.

Revolution spotting

How can investors make sense of these fast-changing political developments? One way is to change the tools we use to assess political risk. How can investors think more systematically about where large-scale, revolutionary change might occur? Most protests won't lead to revolutions, but a revolution is certainly the most disruptive outcome, as it typically involves violence and a long and uncertain political path in its aftermath.

Citi have developed a new analytical framework which combines historical risk factors associated with revolutions with the new factors which have emerged in the MENA unrest. Political risk until now reflected the assumptions that sustained aggregate gross domestic product (GDP) growth rates and strong militaries acted as a firewall against change. (Note that the factors below are specifically associated with prospects for revolution, not social unrest more generally.)

Military/authoritarian regime

The military/presidential model can be long-lasting, but less durable than monarchies, which may benefit from greater loyalty from citizens and a willingness to reform.

Youth bulge

A 'youth bulge' (a high proportion of the population aged under 35, combined with large-scale unemployment) is historically the most significant risk factor for revolution.

Ethnic/religious homogeneity

Revolution is more likely to occur where the majority of the country is from the same ethnicity and/or same religious group, which helps them act cohesively. Ethnically divided countries (for example, Lebanon and the former Yugoslavia) are more likely to experience civil conflict than revolution. However, there are exceptions: in Libya tribal differences have largely been put aside to oust the regime.

High corruption

Corruption has been a major galvanizing factor in the recent MENA unrest, uniting populations against elites from government, the security services and business. Concentration of elite privilege – cronyism in plain English – also appears to have been an important factor, not just wealth accumulation.

Suppressed civil liberties

Lack of civil liberties is a key factor for fuelling dissent, especially the widespread use of incarceration and torture.

Moderate media freedom

Perversely, allowing moderate media freedom within an otherwise repressive political climate may permit the proliferation of opposition sentiment and the spread of ideas. Social media can build upon this.

Absence of recent major internal/external conflicts

Wars, especially if over an extended period, often produce 'conflict fatigue', with populations fearful of relapse and scarred by loss of life and dislocation. Societies with a recent experience of large-scale conflict may therefore be less inclined to contemplate a return to conflict.

Leader in office 20-plus years

Ageing leaders in office for decades may be more out of touch with the demands of a young population and surrounded by self-interested elites; they are also likely to control business interests, further reducing their willingness to transfer power.

Beyond MENA – where next?

Having first witnessed the return of political risk to the developed markets in the form of increasing sovereign debt burdens in the United States and European Union and more interventionist government policy, then the return of political risk with MENA's revolutionary fervour and spreading protest activity, investors are now asking where political risk might pop up next, now that Pandora's Box has been opened.

We don't predict that regimes will topple like dominoes, but we do believe that the MENA unrest will be felt beyond the region. But while the incidence of protests and unrest is likely to increase, a cursory analysis according to the principles of the Revolution Risk Sensitivity framework above suggests that Venezuela, for example, doesn't fit the mould. It is led by a populist yet still broadly popular elected leader who maintains genuine, though declining, support. Hugo Chavez's declining personal support could result in unrest, but not necessarily revolution.

Similarly, while Iran exhibits many of the risk factors associated with revolution, the regime has large areas of support; the 2009 Green Movement would need to convert rural populations and the army before its appeal could broaden significantly enough to galvanize the country in opposition. The rapid trajectory of events in MENA suggests that it isn't out of the realm of possibility, but the components for a counter-revolution in Iran aren't yet evident.

As for Russia, it doesn't have a large youth population, but instead has a similar demography to much of Europe. Nor have President Dmitry Medvedev and Prime Minister Vladimir Putin yet overstayed their welcome, enjoying levels of popular approval of 70 per cent that would make them the envy of many Western liberal democracies.

In China, while the authorities will be observing the MENA developments carefully, there is little reason to suggest that there is much interest yet in a Jasmine Revolution, judging by the tiny turnouts at Facebook-advertised events at various McDonald's locations. Still, the Chinese authorities will be even more sensitive than before to the kinds of triggers that could prompt public outrage, whether reversals in real wages, increases in inflation or news stories about party members taking undue advantage of their position. More high-level prosecutions for corruption, for example, are likely.

Investors should take note: the MENA unrest highlights a crucial change in trend. Namely, no country should be regarded as immune to the risk of popular pressures for reform, even long-standing 'stable' regimes. Assessing the public mood in many emerging market countries is problematic because no public opinion data are available, and the pace of change in MENA shows just how quickly people power can move from a ripple to a tsunami. With this in mind, more transparent countries are likely to benefit as investors reassess how to evaluate risk.

The return of political risk won't be limited to the emerging world. There have been heated protests in Madison, Wisconsin and London, England: hardly two hotbeds of dissent in recent decades. Investors need to be sure to track and monitor political developments before they make the front page, rethink long-held assumptions about the components of political risk, and make sure they mitigate their exposure to these kinds of risks – real or potential – in future.

Notes

1 Economist Intelligence Unit, January 2011
2 Edelman Trust Barometer; Pew Center for Globalization and the Media
3 See 'My father is Li Gang', Al Jazeera

Absolute return, hedge funds or structured investments?

STEPHEN FORD, BREWIN DOLPHIN

T he last decade has seen a surge in the number of investment opportunities that aim to deliver cash-plus or equity-like returns on an absolute return basis. The three most popular sectors have been hedge funds, absolute return funds and structured investments. The aim of this chapter is to review how these products fared over the past three years and to see what conclusions we might be able to draw. I am grateful for the assistance of Catley Lakeman Securities, who provided support for this article. I should state at the outset that this is not an academic study and its conclusions should be viewed as an aid for discussion. Clearly, this article cannot encompass all the various structured, absolute or hedge funds available.

Structured investments, hedge fund of funds and absolute return funds – what's the difference?

There is no single definition for these vehicles and while there are many variants, we can define these investments as follows.

Absolute return funds

These are funds that aim to deliver a positive return in all market conditions over a certain period of time, typically three to five years, with a low level of volatility. In the UK, the BlackRock UK Absolute Alpha fund managed by Mark Lyttleton has stood out for both its popularity and consistent performance and therefore we will use this as our 'proxy' for this sector.

IT'S NOT JUST THAT
YOU CAN TRUST US
WITH THE NUMBERS,

YOU CAN TRUST US
NOT TO TURN YOU INTO
ONE TOO.

At Brewin Dolphin, we like to get to know our clients. That's why every relationship begins with you, your investment manager, and a blank sheet of paper. We're independently owned, with no in-house funds to 'push' or 'sell', and our investment managers are free to choose from the whole investment market. So you can rest assured your portfolio will always reflect your own specific circumstances and your own unique wants and needs. But, while we're on the subject of numbers, give us a call on the one at the bottom of the page, we can have a chat, and hopefully you'll find that **the first thing we earn is your trust.**

BREWIN DOLPHIN

Investment Management
Financial Planning
Corporate Advisory

Investments may fall as well as rise and you may get back less than you invested.

brewin.co.uk For more information please contact us on 0845 213 2000 or at info@brewin.co.uk

Brewin Dolphin is a member of the London Stock Exchange and is authorised and regulated by the Financial Services Authority No.124444

Hedge fund of funds

These are funds that invest in a portfolio of different hedge funds to provide broad exposure to the hedge fund industry and to diversify the risks associated with a single fund. The underlying hedge funds undertake a wider range of investment and trading activities than traditional investment funds, and invest in a broader range of assets including short positions (selling securities that the fund doesn't own with a view to buying them back at a lower price) in shares, bonds and commodities so as to generate returns in falling markets.

The Dexion Absolute Trust is the largest UK-listed fund of hedge funds with total net assets of circa £880 million. This trust will provide a 'proxy' for the hedge fund of funds sector and, in our analysis, we have used the share price performance as this represents the investors' experience. As investment trusts can trade at a discount or a premium to their net asset value (NAV), the share price performance may not accurately represent the manager's returns.

Institutional structured investments

These are investments that offer returns based on the performance of underlying investments. Many such products are linked to a stock market index such as the FTSE 100. A typical structured product will have two underlying investment components: a type of debt security which is used to provide capital protection and a derivative (a financial instrument linked to the value of something else, such as a stock market index or the price of another asset, such as oil or gold). This component is used to provide the potential capital growth that investors might receive at maturity. These investments are tradable daily and we have used Auto-calls in our examples. Auto-calls are normally designed to pay a return on a flat market and a defensive Auto-call is designed to pay out even if the market falls.

In looking at all of these investments, we must remember that none is guaranteed and that, if sold, investors will receive the prevailing price and, therefore, the volatility of that price is an important consideration.

How have these investments fared?

One-year experience – issued at 100p on 26 January 2010 at 5,276.85 on the FTSE 100 index

The HSBC Defensive Auto-call offered the chance to earn 8.65p pa if the FTSE 100 index is at or above certain levels on each anniversary. The index level required to trigger a payout decreases over the term and the investment has capital protection, provided that the FTSE 100 does not end below 3,166.11 (60 per cent of its starting level) at maturity, as in Table 1.2.1.

TABLE 1.2.1

Date	Maturity Conditions & Values	Compound Annual Return	If Conditions not met
26/01/11	If FTSE 100 index closes at or above **5,276.85** investment matures for **108.65p**	8.65%	Proceed to Yr 2
26/01/12	If FTSE 100 index closes at or above **5,276.85** investment matures for **117.30p**	8.31%	Proceed to Yr 3
28/01/13	If FTSE 100 index closes at or above **4,749.17** investment matures for **125.95p**	7.99%	Proceed to Yr 4
27/01/14	If FTSE 100 index closes at or above **4,221.48** investment matures for **134.60p**	7.71%	Proceed to Yr 5
26/01/15	If FTSE 100 index closes at or above **3,693.80** investment matures for **143.25p**	7.45%	OR
	If FTSE 100 Index closes at or above **3,166.11** investment matures for **100.00p**	0%	1% of capital for 1% fall in index from outset

This investment (as with all the following structured investments) does carry equity risk: should the FTSE 100 close at or below 3,166.11 at maturity on 26 January 2015, investors will lose the capital protection and participate in the full loss of the FTSE 100 Index from the outset (ie a 50 per cent fall in the index will translate into a 50 per cent loss of capital). The capital protection is dependent on both the level of the FTSE 100 index and the creditworthiness of the issuer (HSBC), as underlying this investment is a senior unsecured unsubordinated debt instrument in HSBC, which enjoys an AA credit rating – just below the UK government's AAA rating. In the event of HSBC's default, investors would also face a capital loss.

This structured investment has a different set of risks from the active strategy found in hedge funds or absolute return funds, which contain a high level of 'skill' risk – ie the manager's investment strategy may work well in some instances and may not work well at other times. By contrast, structured investments can offer a predictable return profile if held to maturity. One of the key questions that investors must ask is 'How would other investments fare if the market fell 40 per cent and/or HSBC defaulted?' The credit crunch can offer some insights in this area and is discussed later.

Performance analysis

The 30-day volatility is derived from the daily price fluctuations, and the higher the score the more volatile the investment. The Sharpe ratio tells us whether a portfolio's returns are due to good investment decisions or a result of excess risk. This measurement is very useful because although one investment can generate higher returns than another, it is only a good investment if those higher returns do not come with too much additional risk. The higher the Sharpe ratio, the better has been its risk-adjusted performance. A negative Sharpe ratio indicates that a risk-free asset would have performed better than the investment being analysed.

We can see from Table 1.2.2 that the FTSE 100 delivered the highest return with the highest level of volatility and the best risk-adjusted performance. An analysis of the Sharpe ratio shows that, after the FTSE 100 index, the structured investment offered the most effective combination of return for the risk taken (as measured by volatility).

The absolute return funds offered the smoothest ride (lowest volatility), although they mostly underperformed UK government debt (gilts), with the exception of the Cazenove fund. Dexion Absolute delivered negative returns with higher volatility than the structured investment, absolute return funds and gilts.

TABLE 1.2.2

Investment Name	Investment Type	Performance %	30-Day Volatility	Sharpe Ratio
FTSE 100 Index	FTSE 100 Total Return	16.51	17.12	2.98
HSBC Defensive Autocall	Structured Investment	8.39	5.12	2.71
Cazenove Absolute UK Dynamic	Absolute Return	6.07	5.64	1.26
iShares FTSE All Gilt index	UK Gilts Total Return	5.13	7.51	
Gartmore UK Absolute Return Fund	Absolute Return	2.96	4.01	2.13
BlackRock Absolute Alpha	Absolute Return	2.14	2.35	0.97
Dexion Absolute	Fund of Hedge Funds	-2.03	10.1	-1.32

SOURCE Catley Lakeman Securities. From 26.01.10 – 21.12.10

2010 was a good year for equities and stable for bank debt (a key component of a structured investment); so our analysis will now move over a two-year period, which encompasses most of the credit crunch.

Two-year experience – issued at 100p on 31 January 2008 at 5,879.80 on the FTSE 100 index

The Citigroup Defensive Auto-call offered the chance to earn 12.50p pa if the FTSE 100 index was at or above 80 per cent of its starting level on each anniversary. As detailed in Table 1.2.3, this investment has at outset factored in the possibility of the market falling 20 per cent, and the investment has capital protection provided that the FTSE 100 index did not end below 2,939.90 (50 per cent of its starting level) at maturity. This investment redeemed on the second anniversary and, during its life, Citigroup was rescued by the US government.

Again, there is real equity risk should the index close at or below 2,939.90 on 31 January 2013. Furthermore, as an inherent part of the investment in a debt instrument in Citigroup, in the event of a default, investors would also face a capital loss.

TABLE 1.2.3

Date	Maturity Conditions & Values	Compound Annual Return	If Conditions not met
03/02/09	If FTSE 100 index closes at or above 4,703.84 investment matures for 112.5p	12.50%	Proceed to Yr 2
01/02/10	If FTSE 100 index closes at or above 4,703.84 investment matures for 125.0p	11.80%	Proceed to Yr 3
01/02/11	If FTSE 100 index closes at or above 4,703.84 investment matures for 137.5p	11.19%	Proceed to Yr 4
01/02/12	If FTSE 100 index closes at or above 4,703.84 investment matures for 150.0p	10.67%	Proceed to Yr 5
31/02/13	If FTSE 100 index closes at or above 4,703.84 investment matures for 162.5p	10.20%	OR
	If FTSE 100 index closes at or above 2,939.90 investment matures for 100.0p	0%	1% loss of capital for 1% fall in market from outset

Performance analysis

The structured investment delivered the highest return over the period, albeit it was a bumpier ride than that for the FTSE 100 index as illustrated in Table 1.2.4. From its launch to the market lows, the structured investment fell by 27.4 per cent, which was less than the FTSE 100 index and Dexion Absolute but much more than BlackRock Absolute Alpha, which did a phenomenal job in preserving value over the period (generating a 0.20 per cent return) but failed to beat the performance of gilts. Overall, the BlackRock Absolute Alpha offered the best risk-adjusted returns with minimal volatility.

The fall in the value of the structured investment was a reflection of both the fall in the level of the stock market and the travails of Citigroup. While this investment never lost its capital protection against the fall in the stock market, the market did price in the risk that Citigroup might not be able to repay all of the underlying debt position. This was an extreme market and the structured investment was actually more volatile than owning the FTSE 100 index.

TABLE 1.2.4

Investment name	Investment type	Performance %	Launch* – market low**	Annualized historical vol at maturity	Sharpe ratio
Citigroup FTSE Auto-Call	Structured Investment	25.00	-27.40%	40.53	1.71
iShares FTSE UK Gilt All Stocks	UK Gilts Total Return	12.73	8.62%	9.17	–
BlackRock Absolute Alpha	Absolute Return	9.07	0.20%	4.26	1.80
FTSE 100 Index	FTSE 100 Total Return	-1.93	-36.22%	34.17	-0.38
Dexion Absolute	Fund of Hedge Funds	-11.01	-32.30%	34.58	-0.78

SOURCE Catley Lakeman Securities. From 31.08.08* – 01.02.10 **09/03/09

Three-year experience – issued at 100p on 23 January 2008 at 5,609.30 on the FTSE 100 index

The Morgan Stanley FTSE 100 Auto-call offered the chance to earn 15.9p pa on the first occasion that the FTSE 100 index closed higher than 5,609.30 on the anniversary of its launch, and has capital protection provided that the FTSE is higher than 3,646.05 at maturity (see Table 1.2.5).

Again, there is real equity risk should the index close at or below 3,646.05 at maturity on 23 January 2012. Furthermore, as an inherent part of the investment is debt instrument in Morgan Stanley, in the event of a default, investors would also face a capital loss.

At the time of writing, this investment has yet to mature and, in hindsight, its purchase can be viewed as a crass piece of market timing. Those who purchased this investment (including the author) could have entered the FTSE 100 index some 2,000 points lower over the subsequent 12 months and this fall and the following recovery should have provided a rich environment for skill-based investment.

TABLE 1.2.5

Date	Maturity conditions and values	Compound annual return	If conditions not met
23/01/09	If FTSE 100 index closes at or above 5,609.30 investment matures for 115.9p	15.90%	Proceed to Yr 2
23/01/10	If FTSE 100 index closes at or above 5,609.30 investment matures for 131.8p	14.80%	Proceed to Yr 3
23/01/11	If FTSE 100 index closes at or above 5,609.30 investment matures for 147.7p	13.90%	Proceed to Yr 4
23/01/12	If FTSE 100 index closes at or above 5,609.30 investment matures for 163.6p	13.10%	OR
	If FTSE 100 index closes at or above 3,646.05 investment matures for 100.0p	0%	1% loss of capital for 1% fall in market from outset

TABLE 1.2.6

Investment name	Investment type	Performance %	30-day volatility	Sharpe ratio
Morgan Stanley Bonus Note	Structured Investment	45.34	23.73	1.98
iShares FTSE UK Gilt All Stocks	UK Gilts Total Return	16.36	7.51	–
FTSE 100 Index	FTSE 100 Total Return	13.70	17.12	0.84
BlackRock Absolute Alpha	Absolute Return	11.29	2.35	2.69
Dexion Absolute	Absolute Return	-15.97	10.10	-1.20

SOURCE Catley Lakeman Securities. 23.01.08 – 17.12.10

Performance analysis

As Table 1.2.6 demonstrates, the structured investment delivered the highest return with the second-highest Sharpe ratio. The combination of the volatility in the value of bank debt as well as equity markets resulted in this investment being more volatile than the FTSE 100 index.

Dexion Absolute delivered negative returns and offered investors the worst risk-adjusted returns over the period as measured by the Sharpe ratio. BlackRock Absolute Alpha delivered the best risk-adjusted performance, capturing nearly all the returns available from the FTSE 100 index, while failing to match the returns from UK gilts.

Conclusion

The last three years have provided a challenging and potentially rich environment for active investment managers, especially for those in a position to exploit falling markets.

Dexion Absolute, our proxy for the fund of hedge funds sector, has had a torrid time, delivering negative returns with between 60 and 100 per cent of the volatility of the FTSE 100 index. Over the five years ending 30 November 2010, the HFRI Fund of Hedge Funds index has performed better than the Dexion Absolute share price, delivering an annualized return of 4.58 per cent pa. However, this is less than the return from the FTSE All Gilt index, which delivered an annualized 5.16 per cent pa, a poor reward for risks involved.

BlackRock Absolute Alpha delivered the most consistent performance and, unlike Dexion Absolute, this fund is an Open Ended Investment Company (OEIC) and therefore always trades at net asset value (NAV). The fund exhibited very low volatility and offered some of the most efficient returns for this volatility as indicated by the Sharpe ratios. While the managers of this fund have an excellent track record, the fund contains many inherent risks, as the tactics used include owning shares as well as shorting them (selling shares the fund doesn't own if there is a strong conviction that a stock price will fall) and using cash, as the managers can tactically choose to invest up to 100 per cent of the portfolio in cash or cash-like instruments. These tactics are bound together by the investment process and fund manager skill.

My concern is that BlackRock Absolute Alpha has only just outperformed gilts, albeit with much lower volatility. According to Bloomberg, from 13 April 2006 to 23 December 2010 the fund delivered an annualized return of 5.49 per cent pa, marginally ahead of the 5.32 per cent pa from the FTSE All Gilt index. The issue for investors to consider is whether the small additional return has been sufficient compensation for the additional risks of simply owning gilts. If investors cannot accept the risks involved in owning gilts, how should they feel about the inherent risks in this fund? It is also surprising just how much investors are prepared to pay, it would appear, not for returns but for volatility management, as the fund carries an entry charge of up to 5 per cent (circa one year's return) and an annual management charge of 1 per cent pa *plus* a 20 per cent performance fee for returns in excess of three-month Libor – currently 0.754 per cent subject to a high watermark (it can only be charged on new highs).

The structured investments delivered some of the highest returns, mechanically, and without 'skill' risk. However, the credit crunch provided unexpected volatility in bank debt, which directly fed through to these investments. The one-year experience illustrates what can be achieved – equity-like returns with low volatility – and is the general expectation for these investments. However, the banking crisis changed this dynamic as the structured investments often became more volatile than the FTSE 100 index and those backed by Lehman Brothers or certain Icelandic banks delivered large losses.

It is the holy grail of the funds industry to seek equity-like returns without risk, as sales of such products will be high. It is disappointing to see how few of these investments have even matched the returns available from gilts. While gilts may face difficult days ahead, in my view these funds should at least have the potential to outperform high-quality sovereign or company debt. I remain to be persuaded about the merits of absolute return – the sector is new and given the 'unknown unknowns' involved in equity markets I remain sceptical, especially in light of current returns.

My conclusion, based on practical experience, has been illustrated through this article. In seeking to achieve returns of 8 to 10 per cent pa I have found it easier and more consistent to replace exposure to fund of hedge funds and absolute return funds with structured investments. I prefer to make a clear distinction between volatility, returns and the potential for permanent loss of capital. In order to control the volatility 'cost' of this approach, investors can perhaps retain more funds in fixed income and/or cash investments.

Promises, promises

SIMON GIBSON, ATKINSON BOLTON CONSULTING LTD

The principles of asset management – my word, this could be a turgid affair. Here then is my first promise: it won't be! I shall refer throughout not to asset management but to wealth management, and it is an important distinction. Wealth management is the integration of financial planning and asset management (see Frank's dilemma in Figure 1.3.1), and all too often one or the other are forgotten. This integration is important – it is extremely rare to find an individual who doesn't need that integration to be part of their financial lives. **So what is all this about promises?**

FIGURE 1.3.1 The financial planning and asset management dilemma

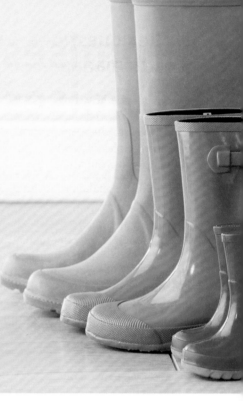

- Friendly
- Communicative
- Professional

A personal touch...

There is no 'one size fits all' solution when it comes to advising on financial matters or the management of wealth.

We meet different people every day from all walks of life. Building individual relationships with these clients and providing a highly personalised approach means that we can develop long term partnerships.

Our number one priority is providing the quality of service our clients have come to expect. All our actions in this respect make a positive difference and this attitude is reflected throughout our team. Their commitment ensures the very best for our clients at all times.

- Financial Planning
- Wealth Management
- Self Invested Personal Pensions
- Retirement Management & Planning
- Life Assurance & Protection
- Tax Planning
- Investment Planning
- Employee Benefits

Thoroughbred Wealth Management – creating and preserving wealth.

Our Thoroughbred Wealth Management team engender the trust of our clients, understanding their needs and ultimately creating and implementing financial solutions that will give direction, providing solid foundations for the future.

Visualising the future you desire can be both exciting and challenging. Your financial solutions may require management of investments, tax mitigation, retirement and inheritance planning and will provide you with the comfort of knowing you and your loved ones are protected now and in the future. Perfecting this and ensuring it evolves as your circumstances and objectives change is at the heart of everything we do.

For more information contact:
Tel: **0845 458 1223** Fax: **0845 458 1224**
Email: **info@atkinsonbolton.co.uk**
www.atkinsonbolton.co.uk

Atkinson Bolton Consulting is Authorised and Regulated by the Financial Services Authority

ATKINSON BOLTON
Consulting Ltd

Celebrating our 10th Anniversary *2001–2011*

Six key questions ... followed by seven stages of wealth management

You may have heard of Kipling's six honest serving men – who, what, when, why, where and how. These provide the basis for six questions about promises that follow. I will also introduce my seven stages of wealth management, ending with a summary of the principles of wealth management which, by then, you may have gathered are not what you would have expected.

- Who do we make promises to?
- What do we promise them?
- Do we tell them when the promise will be fulfilled?
- Why do some (many?) of our promises fail?
- Where can we go for help when it comes to promises that are financially based?
- How can we be sure of delivery?

The word promise can be an assurance to do a particular thing, or to guarantee that it happens, or it can mean the quality of potential excellence. It is also used to give good grounds for expecting a pleasant situation or occurrence, or as an announcement.

We make promises to our friends and family, to young people and the elderly, to loved ones and acquaintances, to mortgage providers and colleagues, to shareholders and stakeholders.

We promise them a wide variety of things: love, security, protection, financial gain, care, affection, repayment, respect, a helping hand, a thought, a prayer, to do our best and even a legacy – sometimes all of these, sometimes just one. We also promise people our time!

As to when a promise will be fulfilled, it can be instantly or it can take a lifetime – quite often it has an unknown (and unexpected) delivery date. Our promises fail for many reasons too – from simple forgetfulness to a lack of anything from time (we all have the same amount of that, though) to money. Does Figure 1.3.2 illustrate what you do?

For help in making and/or keeping our financial promises, there are not too many natural places to go; the pub (a social environment) has always been one – how often do you hear 'social experts' pontificating on what will happen to the value of their (or even your) house, car, pension? All you need to do is buy, sell, renovate, take risk, de-risk ... and that leads to the final question from Kipling's men: how can you be sure of delivery?

A promise is only worth anything, really, on delivery. By making a promise we might make ourselves feel better, and invariably we provide some comfort to the person we are making the promise to, but *being sure* of delivery is key.

The need for help with our promises is recognized at an early age ... as is the unwritten but undeniable value of a promise, even to a three-year-old!

FIGURE 1.3.2 Promises can fail from simple forgetfulness...

I promise to be good – so Father Christmas comes.

I promise not to bite my fingernails – so that I get more pocket money.

I promise to read to you tomorrow night. (This is *never* forgotten; at least, not by the recipient of the promise.)

It is very unlikely that most or many reading this will have children or grandchildren who are financially literate. I don't wish to appear rude – my experience advising wealthy individuals backs this up. However, we should all be promising to help to put that right. Teaching children the value of money is key to our prosperity. In my experience, people are best convinced by reasons they discover on their own.

As adults, and only then, our children will know that there are only two problems for them and their loved ones when it comes to money – living too long or dying too soon. At Atkinson Bolton Consulting, we promise to help … and here comes my next promise: whatever age you are, there is something helpful in at least one of the seven stages of wealth management that follow. If you are at the younger end, this could provide a useful framework for your financial future. For the more 'experienced' reader, preserving rather than creating wealth is likely to be most important.

Seven stages of wealth management

Stage one: learning the value of money

This checklist is aimed at anyone under 18.

Learn the value of money at an early age. If you can and do, you will appreciate it for the rest of your life – from pocket money received to Christmas gifts in an envelope, allocate your money in the first years of your life to one of the four pots:

- 'Today' money: 30 per cent goes in here, and is for spending, enjoying, being frivolous or sensible with, but the choice is yours.
- Saving for something special – this will resonate with parents or grandparents reading this stage – 30 per cent is put away towards an important, but not yet urgent, personal purchase or investment.
- Long-term savings. My daughter has been using this system since she was three and now, eight years later, she believes that the sorts of things she will need this money for are a car or the deposit for a house – 30 per cent goes here (Figure 1.3.3 is an unlikely example).
- Charity/ good causes. The final 10 per cent is put away for the good of others, be it to spend at the church fete, to donate to a favoured cause or charity, or to put in the collecting tin of the right person at the right time.

FIGURE 1.3.3 Discipline at an early age is key

Discipline at an early age, when it comes to future wealth management, is key, and if you are already beyond this stage, perhaps you can promise to educate a young person about this. Albert Einstein said 'Imagination is more important than knowledge,' to which I would add 'Enthusiasm is essential.'

Stage two: creating and preserving wealth (1)

This refers to financial and/or human wealth, from first job through to the certainty of our own beliefs – our mid-20s!

If the fact that we will all live too long or die too soon is incontrovertible, this is the stage where our own personal dogma suggests that only the latter is a problem – I promise!

In early life, when we first go to work and start to build a framework, physical or human, around us (home, family), we need to keep Kipling's six men in mind, perhaps more than at any other time in our lives:

- The 'who' is our family, spouse, children, but maybe a lender.
- 'What' covers financial security/stability and may refer just to our own needs.
- Maybe 'when' is more difficult to contemplate, but it must include consideration of our death/illness/disability – all potentially too soon.
- 'Why' is either love or commitment – and I am not suggesting that we all love our lender!
- As to 'where' we can go when we need advice, a chartered financial planner is a good place to start – they subscribe to a code of ethics, have both technical and 'real life' experience and can provide the essential elements to complete your personal framework.
- 'How' is a separate chapter on its own, though using the leverage/discipline of monthly sums will help you to keep your discipline (and your promises).

Check what promises your employer makes to you when it comes to your finances. I don't mean your salary; more the 'peripheral' (but often very valuable) benefits – intangibles such as life assurance, sick pay entitlement, maternity/paternity leave and pension. If you are self-employed, have a stern chat with yourself on this subject.

Stage three: it depends...

This takes us from that bright, carefree time all the way to early middle age, our 40s.

Imagine yourself as Frank in Figure 1.3.4.

You will now have assets/wealth to manage, although they may not be what we are traditionally led to believe 'wealth' means. Yes, there may be a house, ISAs, heirlooms, jewellery, etc, but you have spent around a third to a half of your life now building human capital. How would you/your loved ones cope in an emergency? It may be a financial one pure and simple, or it may be a health/well-being-related issue that results in the former. Some or all of the following will be essential:

FIGURE 1.3.4 Stage three: it depends …

- Are your life assurance and other protection in place and adequate?
- Are your investments, be they regular savings or lump sums (perhaps from an inheritance or a bonus) invested, taking into account your own acceptance of or aversion to risk, and are the timescales obvious to whoever is providing the advice?
- If you have not been in this position before, make sure that investments are diversified, as protection against the unknown unknowns!
- Tax is likely to be a bigger issue for you than when you were younger: obtain tax relief and/or exemptions where you can.
- Make sure you are not overpaying for services, from your mortgage costs to professionals, but also remember the need for value.
- The wealth manager who promises you something that is good, quick and cheap will only ever be able to deliver on two of those three (promises) at a time!
- Make a will; part of the promise to your loved ones, friends or even a charity that you are taking seriously is your recognition of the need for planning what is, after all, inevitable.

Stage four: retirement

At age 40 to 50, this becomes something to focus on personally – not just something that old people do.

By now you may have started to think more about living too long rather than dying too soon, though others, when they think of you, will still be concentrating on the latter. Ensure that your promises to those you love and who are younger are realistic, and that your promises to those who are older are practical. If your own affairs are in order, perhaps you can spend some time thinking about the generation below and/or above. After all, they will (both) soon be making you think about having more or less money/time. For stage four, my checklist assumes that stage three has been read, and offers some 'alternative' steps to be considered as regards your wealth management:

- Not about the amount, more about the options – if you are serious about retirement flexibility, make sure you carry out an audit of your retirement plans. Will they allow you to do what you want to do?

- Are you planning for or simply reacting to 'events'? If you have children, have you thought about wedding costs? Your dream of having a 'less practical' car is not far off as the children have grown up/left home, but are the financial resources in place?

- Also on dreams, have you thought about having a gap year? I haven't found the rule book that says this is the domain only of the under-25s.

- Have a family discussion (heart to heart) about the future – there is never a right or wrong time, so why not now?

Stage five: creating and preserving wealth (2)

Possibly the last time we do both? This is the period from having lived through a half-century to retirement at age...

Picture yourself now like Frank in Figure 1.3.5.

Decisions, decisions, decisions (and promises, promises). You may now be financially well-off. You may have worked for more than half of your life (perhaps as much as 70 per cent of your age) and you may still need to protect loved ones or ensure repayment of debt in the event of your death. If you are in business, make sure your commitments there are: a) known and b) prepared for. Equally, you could be approaching the time in your life when you have the most disposable income (and capital for the first time in your life). Asset management and financial planning meet head-on at this stage – wealth management actually becomes something you seek out and regularly consider:

FIGURE 1.3.5 Stage five: creating and preserving wealth (2)

- If you haven't done so previously, urgently consider what your income needs are in retirement, as you move from 'pay-cheque' to 'play-check'.
- Consider getting a lifetime cash-flow forecast, to help you to see, in graphic (and frank) terms whether, as regards your money, there is a danger that you will live too long.
- Look back at what you have promised yourself along the way and, if it isn't too late (and it isn't!), make yourself some new promises – maybe more for you than ever before. Your family and work colleagues will not thank you for dying unhappy or unfulfilled.
- Read stage six and see what's ahead – that alone will help you to plan for this stage and for the 'golden period' ahead.

Stage six: now we can do all the things we haven't had the time or money to do

This stage runs from the day we retire to the end of our 'golden' years.

What have you always wanted to do that you have not had the right combination of time, money (or location) to be able to do previously? I always suggest to clients that this should be one of their first questions when they start thinking about/ preparing for their imminent retirement. Also, consider how, financially, you want to live the rest of your life. Of course, you should have been planning for this via your personal financial framework years ago but, let's face facts, now that your earning capacity has ceased (or at least is likely to be waning), you have what you have, and need to make the most of it, without outliving your assets:

- Your investment strategy was never more important, but don't be fooled into thinking that just because you have retired you should change it – you may wish to, but the timescales of your investment requirements are much more important than your age!

- Consider when you will be able/minded to spend the most money – the first 10 to 15 years of retirement or the following 10? My experience suggests the former, so budgeting, which, if you have followed these checklists for 60 years or so was important as a teenager, is just as important now.

- Take advice – even if you have managed your own affairs thus far, is that really what you want to be doing now you don't have to work? For some, the idea of having enough time to devote to managing their own finances is exciting but, for most, it is not.

- Make sure your will is up to date.

- Enjoy your money and your 'spare time' – though I expect you will find you have no idea where the time to work came from now you are retired!

Hopefully, you will be like Frank in Figure 1.3.5.

Stage seven: being prepared and accepting that we haven't died too soon

This period is about outliving the statistics, but hopefully not the money.

There is a danger that this stage is about being morbid, only about death, funerals and eulogies, nursing homes, loss of mobility, loss of lifelong friends. Well, if that's what you think, please promise to make it otherwise. I have many clients aged over 80 who are as sharp of thought and word as many half that age. If you are in stage seven, please share what you know, what you have learned, what you have seen and what you have experienced. I for one have so much more I need to know.

And so to the last section of the checklists – one line only:

- Promise that you will reflect, enjoy your time and your money, be passionate about helping young people to learn the value of money and be generous with your greatest asset – you.

FIGURE 1.3.6 Stage seven: being prepared and accepting that we haven't died too soon

Seven principles of wealth management, one each from the seven stages above

1 Teach children and young people the value of money, and to have financial discipline.

2 Start making financial promises, to your family and friends, to yourself and to those that are helping you build your financial framework – and enquire of others what their promises to you consist of.

3 Remember, if someone promises you something that is good, quick and cheap, you should only expect them to be able to deliver on any two of those promises at one time.

4 Think about financial dreams – old ones fulfilled or yet to be realized, or new ones, like a gap year at 47.

5 Plan for your golden years before they arrive, or they will only appear when it is cloudy.

6 Enjoy your money, while ensuring that it is working just as hard as it needs to for you.

7 You will never know how valuable your greatest asset became, because it dies with you, so share what you can, invest (not necessarily financially) in the future and decide what being wealthy means to you.

Thanks for reading – it was easy to write. I have the best job in the world!

What is a Venture Capital Trust (VCT)?

DAN TUBB, BESTINVEST

VCTs were introduced to encourage individuals to invest in smaller UK companies whose shares and securities are not listed on the main UK stock exchange. Such companies tend to be higher risk than larger 'blue chips', so the government offers tax breaks as an incentive to attract investors.

VCTs are listed on the London Stock Exchange, which lays down rigorous standards on the qualifications and experience of the managers. Money raised from individual investors is pooled by the VCT to acquire a number of different investments, with the aim of spreading risk across the company's portfolio.

In order to qualify for tax relief, the VCT manager must invest at least 70 per cent of new proceeds in 'qualifying holdings' within three years (that is, shares or securities that meet the conditions set by the scheme). The underlying investments tend to consist of shares or securities (including loans of five years or more) in unquoted companies and shares traded on the Alternative Investment Market (AIM) and PLUS Markets. Qualifying companies must have 'gross assets' of less than £7 million prior to investment and less than £8 million immediately after investment, have fewer than 50 employees, have raised no more than £2 million from venture capital schemes over the previous year and their shares must not be listed on a 'recognized stock exchange'.

Each VCT can invest up to £1 million in a qualifying company subject to each individual investment representing no more than 15 per cent of the VCT's assets. The balance of new proceeds can remain invested in other 'non-qualifying' holdings.

Some of the companies will be special purpose vehicles set up to implement a certain strategy, for example, investing in a particular type of asset.

Why VCTs now?

With rates of income tax for the highest earners increasing to 50 per cent in the 2010–11 tax year and tough new limits on pension contributions, we believe that many more investors will find VCTs an attractive option, not least because the income from VCTs is not subject to tax.

Wealth Planning
Portfolio Management
Financial Advice

Looking for help with your financial matters?

We're here to help you identify your priorities and set out a plan to achieve them.

Our bespoke solutions ensure you get the best, tailored, impartial advice with an unrivalled choice of investment opportunities. Call us or go to our website for more information.

020 7189 9999
bestinvest.co.uk

bestinvest

Investment options are likely to include funds - please remember that the value of an investmen can go down as well as up. Bestinvest (Brokers) Limited and Bestinvest (Consultants) Limited are authorised and regulated by the Financial Services Authority.

1304-106

Meanwhile, we've seen an improvement in the range and potential quality of investments available to VCTs. The credit crunch has reduced the supply of loan finance to smaller companies, and where loans are available they are often on very expensive terms. As a result, VCTs are seeing a stronger flow of potential new deals and are able to negotiate better investment terms.

Who should consider investing in VCTs?

We would recommend that VCTs are only considered by experienced investors who:

- are liable to higher rates of income tax;
- are willing and able to hold their investment over the longer term;
- and are comfortable with taking on a high level of risk.

Before you invest in a VCT, we strongly recommend that you carefully read each VCT's prospectus, especially the section on risk factors. This is particularly important for those who are considering investing in a VCT for the first time.

If you do decide to invest, be careful to make sure that your overall commitment to VCTs is modest in relation to your overall investment portfolio and that you spread your risk across several VCTs.

Not all VCTs are the same

It is important to realize that many different VCT investment strategies are available.

Some have been designed to emphasize capital preservation through lower-risk investments and rely mainly on the tax reliefs available to generate returns for investors. These VCTs will typically seek to enable investors to exit their investment once the five-year minimum qualifying period has been achieved. These VCTs are typically described as 'asset backed' or 'limited life'.

Other VCTs invest largely in business ventures that are expected to deliver growth in the value of your investment, in addition to the benefit of tax reliefs. These have the potential to generate higher returns, but the downside risks are also greater and there may be greater uncertainty over when you might be able to exit your investment.

What types of investment do VCTs hold?

VCT investments can be divided into four categories. Most trusts will specialize in one of these, but some deliberately have a balanced strategy. The performance characteristics of each group have distinctive features.

Private equity

This represents traditional venture capital activities and accounts for more than half of all VCT investment. Private equity investment requires many different procedures compared with buying quoted shares. For example, since there is no immediate ability to sell the shares, the VCT manager needs to be extremely confident in the purchase decision. This requires extensive investigation (called 'due diligence'), which can take several months, with the whole transaction process often taking six to nine months. Once the investment has been made, the subsequent monitoring of the company can be very time consuming; hence it's not uncommon for groups to make only three or four investments each year. Most private equity returns tend to come in the later years of the underlying companies' development, so it's important to hold for the long term. Success rates also vary widely, so investors should seek as much diversification as possible, without lowering the quality standards of the manager.

Alternative Investment Market

Investing in AIM companies should give VCT managers greater flexibility. Research covering these companies is more widely available than for private equity; there is a daily share price and the ability (at least in theory) to sell the shares. However, the AIM admission rules do not require any minimum track record, so even start-up companies can join. Risk can therefore be on par with private equity or even greater in some instances. There are many AIM VCTs available and in the past there has been considerable overlap in some of their portfolios. This diminishes the potential diversification benefits of spreading your investment across several AIM VCTs.

Asset-backed VCTs

This approach will usually be adopted to maximize security and generate income. VCT rules allow up to 90 per cent of an individual investment to be structured as loans and the overall qualifying portfolio can have up to 80 per cent.

Although the obvious asset-backed investments such as hotels, nursing homes and property development have been specifically excluded from VCTs, there are still several sectors which can offer the investor the benefit of a fixed asset security, such as public houses, garden centres, golf courses or plants and equipment. Asset-backed VCTs should be able to sustain a more consistent level of dividends and are commonly used as limited-life VCTs.

Specialist

Some VCTs concentrate on a specific sector, such as technology, healthcare or renewables. These trusts are usually riskier. Their ultimate performance will usually be reliant on whether just one or two of the individual investments prove successful.

Pros and cons of VCTs

VCTs are a potentially useful addition to some investors' portfolios given the availability of tax reliefs. Investing in VCTs may increase your portfolio's exposure to smaller UK companies, so you should keep an eye on your overall portfolio's balance of assets to ensure it remains appropriate to your objectives.

We would generally recommend that investors diversify risk by selecting several VCTs across the various types available. Additionally, as these investments are considered high risk, you should ensure that your total VCT holding remains in line with your investment objective.

Pros

Tax credit

This is available at 30 per cent on up to £200,000 invested in a tax year. It is available on new issues of VCT shares (which must then be held for at least five years). You must have paid the amount of tax that is being rebated, whether that is lower, basic or higher rate tax. If shares are sold within five years, you lose the tax rebate.

Ongoing tax relief

No income tax is payable on any dividends received. In fact, they do not even need to be declared on tax returns. This tax relief is available on purchases of new and existing shares. There is a notional tax credit attached but this cannot be reclaimed. The tax relief is particularly attractive for higher rate tax payers. A 5p tax-free dividend would be an equivalent return of 8.3 per cent for a higher rate payer (40 per cent tax) or 10 per cent for a top rate payer (50 per cent tax).

Exit tax relief

There is no capital gains tax liability, even if the VCT shares are subsequently sold at a profit; however, losses from VCT shares cannot be used to offset future capital gains.

Cons

Higher charges

VCTs are more expensive than most other types of investment. The initial charge is typically 5 per cent (but this can be substantially reduced by investing through Bestinvest) and the ongoing annual costs are typically 2.5 per cent to 3.5 per cent.

Greater risk

Risk varies between different VCTs, usually depending on their investment policy. Most of a VCT's assets will be invested in small UK trading companies. These do not have to be start-up ventures but you should regard the overall risk level as being higher than that of a unit trust investing in 'blue chip' companies.

Poor liquidity and share price discounts

Although VCT shares are listed on the London Stock Exchange (LSE), the volume of shares traded tends to be low. The spread between buying and selling prices can be wide, and most VCTs trade at a discount to their underlying net asset value, and you may have difficulty in realizing your shares at the value you expect. Discounts vary considerably from trust to trust. Those VCTs that Bestinvest favours tend to have defined buyback policies.

Charges and discounts available

Charges for VCTs are high, with total annual fees running in the order of 3.5 per cent per year. Initial charges are also high at about 5.0 per cent (although Bestinvest will discount these by as much as 4.0 per cent). In addition to initial and annual charges, managers often apply performance fees and in some cases 'sweet equity' deals for the individual managers, where they may co-invest their own money on the same or perhaps even better terms than the VCT itself. Managers may also charge the underlying companies for certain services they may provide.

How and when to invest

New issues vs C-shares vs top-up

One of the first decisions an investor will face will be whether to invest in a new issue, a C-share or a top-up.

New issues

This is a new VCT seeking a listing on the LSE.

New issues will have fresh capital and no legacy investments, but will be subject to 'cash drag' (that is, funds may remain uninvested for a period and only earn low rates of interest), which could be a concern in current conditions.

C-shares

These are VCTs that are already listed on the LSE and can raise money to be invested in a separate share class.

This money may or may not immediately merge with the ordinary share pool. A C-share will benefit from economies of scale, and will share the cost of administrative services/director fees with the ordinary share portfolio. Like new issues, C-shares will have fresh capital and no legacy investments, but will also be subject to cash drag, which could be a concern in current conditions.

Top-ups

Top-ups are VCTs that are already listed on the LSE, and are seeking to raise money to be invested alongside the existing pool of ordinary shares.

Top-ups will dilute the existing shareholders, meaning that investors may be able to access a more mature, dividend-producing portfolio of investments. However, investors may be subject to a fall in net asset value (NAV) if the current portfolio is revalued downwards in the future. VCT rules have changed much over the years, and money raised in earlier tax years is subject to less onerous restrictions regarding the investee companies.

Often managers raising money through top-ups are using this money solely for the provision of buybacks, payment of dividends and for non-qualifying/liquidity investments. Keeping the new money separate in this way allows money raised under previous regimes to be invested under less restrictive conditions.

Specifically, the reduction in the net assets test in 2007 and the introduction of a maximum of 50 employees test has meant that certain service businesses are now excluded for investment with new money raised.

VCT capacity

It is unlikely that all VCTs will raise enough funds to meet their capacity. In some situations, the VCT may cancel the issue and return funds to investors.

Alternatively, the manager may go ahead with insufficient funds to achieve a sensible level of diversification, which could increase risk.

However, it is also possible that VCTs will fill their capacity and therefore it may be advisable to secure your allocation early.

How do I sell my investment?

Limited-life VCTs

Limited-life VCTs aim to repay capital back to investors shortly after the minimum five-year holding period. This is made possible by tailored structuring of the underlying investments. These VCTs tend to have a very narrow investment focus and may contain concentrated exposures to certain counterparties.

Historically, the majority of the return has come from the upfront income tax relief. Typically, the majority of these investments will be made in loan stock structured with a term that coincides with the conclusion of the minimum five-year holding period. A refinancing will then occur, providing the potential for the VCT to exit.

Equity holdings are often exited through a sale to a trade buyer. Investors in limited-life VCTs can then elect to wind up the VCT.

We believe that certain limited-life VCTs face the high risk of a change in tax legislation.

The proposed VCT rule changes due to be implemented for money raised from the 2010–11 tax year onwards could adversely affect the ability to structure VCTs capable of returning shareholders monies.

This means there may be a limited opportunity to invest in this type of VCT.

Evergreen VCTs

In contrast, evergreen VCTs are established to provide a pool of permanent capital for the purpose of investing in smaller companies. In the absence of a mandate to return capital to investors within a specified time frame, evergreen VCTs are not forced to exit investments under suboptimal conditions.

Many of the evergreen VCTs periodically offer a buyback facility. This will be at a discount to NAV (that is, less than the underlying value of the investments held by the VCT) but will often represent the most efficient exit option. If a VCT has no plans to wind up or offer an exit, the only way to realize your investment is to sell the shares on the stock market. (If you need to sell, Bestinvest can provide this service).

You should be aware that only one market maker may be offering to buy the shares, which inevitably will result in a wide bid/offer spread. Investors into earlier VCTs who have deferred a capital gain could potentially be liable for that gain once again when selling the VCT shares.

Further information on VCTs is available on the HMRC website (www.hmrc.gov.uk/guidance/vct) and from the British Venture Capital Association (www.bvca.co.uk).

Claiming tax relief

After approximately four weeks following the allotment of the shares, you will receive your share and tax certificates directly from the VCT company. This tax certificate must be sent to HMRC to claim your income tax relief. Those investors paying income tax under PAYE can choose to have their tax code adjusted immediately and so pay less tax or can apply for an immediate tax repayment if they are investing at the end of the tax year.

Next steps

For further information, including an up-to-date list of current launches and Bestinvest's full research, please visit our website (bestinvest.co.uk/vct).

How can we help?

Bestinvest offers investors one of the most experienced independent sources of research on VCTs. To date, we have researched every VCT launched since they began in 1995. We are also able to reduce the cost of investing by offering some of the largest discounts on standard investment terms available in the market.

If you have any questions regarding the content of this guide, require further details on any of the investments described or would like to discuss the suitability of a particular investment, please call us and talk to one of our investment experts.

You can see an up-to-date list of the current VCT offers available to investors, together with our discounts and our research at bestinvest.co.uk/vct.

How to invest

Please call one of our investment professionals on 020 7189 9970. They can arrange to send you a prospectus and application forms.

You can also download prospectuses and application forms for each fund from our website: bestinvest.co.uk/vct. Your cheque should be made payable to the VCT. (Application forms should be returned by post to Bestinvest in order to benefit from Bestinvest's discounts.)

The sharpest minds need the finest advice. **Kogan Page** creates success.

www.koganpage.com

You are reading one of the thousands of books published by **Kogan Page**. As Europe's leading independent business book publishers **Kogan Page** has always sought to provide up-to-the-minute books that offer practical guidance at affordable prices.

KoganPage

Gold:
the investors' insurance policy

JEREMY BECKWITH, KLEINWORT BENSON

Gold in 2010

The price of gold rose by 30 per cent in 2010, its 10th consecutive calendar year increase in value, which has seen it rise from about $250 an ounce in 2000 to over $1,400 at the end of 2010 (Gordon Brown as Chancellor sold 400 tons of the UK's gold reserves between 1999 and 2002).

In 2010, the price rose fairly steadily over the year, benefiting in the first half of the year from the sovereign debt crisis within the eurozone, as it became clear that the Greek government's finances were no longer sustainable and the country required a bailout.

Without the rescue package from the rest of the eurozone, Greece would have been forced to default on its outstanding government debt. This is actually quite a common phenomenon since Greece became independent in the 19th century but the other members of the eurozone were unhappy to allow one of their club members to go into default.

As Greece came under pressure in the markets via a dramatic widening of their bond spreads relative to Germany, so to a lesser extent did bonds in Ireland, Portugal, Spain and Belgium. Thus the very nature and survival of the euro began to be called into question. In this environment, many owners of euros, particularly in Germany, where memories of valueless paper currency still remain, sought other homes for their savings. Their immediate ports of call were the Swiss franc and gold.

The second half of the year saw the Federal Reserve worrying about the possibility of a double-dip recession in the United States and a possible fall into deflation. Its response, officially announced in early November but widely leaked and discussed in the months before, was a further injection of money into the financial system – a policy known as QE2 (the second round of Quantitative Easing). The first round occurred in April 2009, at the very worst of the market and banking crisis and was coordinated with the central banks of the UK and Japan, but this second round occurred when the crisis appeared to have passed and economic recovery, although not vigorous, was clearly occurring, and was only pushed through in the United

States. International investors who owned dollars became concerned that the value of the dollar in international markets would be significantly weakened by this unilateral move, and they too sought other avenues for holding their wealth. The dollar fell and other currencies around the world, and gold, all rose in value.

In 2010, it seemed, gold clearly became viewed by international investors as an alternative currency. Indeed, one of the most successful hedge funds in the 2008 crisis was that managed by John Paulson, who in 2009 introduced a gold-hedged share class for his fund, in which most of his own wealth was placed.

Gold and mankind

Throughout human history, gold has held an irresistible allure for both men and women. Men have competed and fought for it and women have adorned themselves with it. Humans have always found gold attractive and considered it precious, and it is also the element that best combines the three key requirements as an ideal medium of exchange or money:

1. It has no inherent value in terms of functional uses to which it can be put.
2. It cannot be created – despite the attempts of alchemists down the ages.
3. It cannot be destroyed. Gold differs from silver and base metals in that it is not soluble in nitric acid.

Fiat or paper currencies usually have only one of these criteria (the first), occasionally two but never all three. In addition to these three, gold has a very high value to weight/size ratio. Only about 160,000 tonnes of mined gold are believed to exist, and so a relatively small amount by size or weight can be readily transported by someone from one place to another and accepted there as something of value. From time immemorial, gold has been an insurance policy against being forced to flee from persecution and start a new life elsewhere.

Ways to own gold

In many poor countries, gold as wealth is owned in the form of jewellery and worn on the body to minimize the risk of loss. In richer countries, governments will sell official gold coins of particular weights to their citizens, though usually at a premium to the underlying value of the gold. These are the tangible and portable ways to own gold today, for those who fear for their homes and assets and even their lives.

Gold bullion

For those who are wealthier and more physically secure, but who are concerned about protecting their financial wealth and don't have trust in traded securities, gold bullion can be owned and held within the safe custody of a bank. This can be in one of two forms: an allocated account or an unallocated account. An allocated account means that your bullion has your name attached to it in the bank's vaults, while an unallocated account means that the bullion you own is part of a pool of bullion held by the bank in its vaults. Those investors holding gold as an insurance policy against a total collapse in the global banking system would probably want the extra security of an allocated account so that their gold is not confused with a large pool of gold held in the bank's name, which might get used repaying a bankrupt bank's creditors.

Shares of gold-mining companies

For many investors until recent years, the easiest way to access gold has been to own the shares of gold-mining companies. Historically this has been a leveraged way to get exposure to the gold price, since the value of a share reflects the profitability of a company, not its revenue. So, for example, a gold-mining company may be producing gold at a cost of $900 per ounce. At a gold price of $1,400, the company is making $500 per ounce in profit, but if the gold price were to fall by 25 per cent to $1,050, then its profits would fall to $150 per ounce or by 70 per cent. Similarly, a 25 per cent rise in the gold price would see its profits rise to $850 per ounce, an increase of 70 per cent. Further, if the gold price fell to $700 per ounce, then the company might go bankrupt and be worthless. Thus shares in gold-mining companies can be extremely volatile.

Derivatives

The rise of derivatives markets in the last 25 years has meant that banks have been able to offer clients structured products that give effective exposure to changes in the price of gold. It is important to understand that these products are liabilities of the issuer, and so the credit risk of the issuer needs to be considered. In general, though, because the future price of gold is nearly always higher than the spot price of gold (since gold is not income producing as an investment), the terms of structured products that are based on a positive view of the gold price are not particularly attractive to investors. For investors with a more negative view on the development of the gold price they can be much more attractive. For many investors, though, gold is held as an insurance policy against a breakdown in the banking system, and so relying on a bank to be able to repay a structured product in that environment may not be a sound idea.

Exchange-traded funds

In the last five years, a new form of gold ownership has really taken hold among the world's investors, and that is exchange-traded funds (ETFs) that just own gold bullion. Investors can buy or sell units in these funds on traded markets, and units can be created or redeemed by the fund at will, so that the amount of gold owned by the fund for each unit in existence is always the same. The price of the units will thus reflect the constant per unit amount of gold (usually one ounce) less any costs of the structure.

There are significant economies of scale with the management and administration of such funds, so that the costs of owning gold via these funds are low. In addition, by being exchange traded, small investors have much more liquidity and ability to trade. More recently, some swap-based ETFs have appeared where the funds do not own the bullion themselves but instead enter into a swap agreement with a bank to give them exposure to changes in the gold price. Once again, counterparty risk is an important consideration here.

Exchange-traded funds are now very large owners of gold, with the largest, SPDR Gold Shares, now owning 1,120 tonnes, making it the sixth-largest individual owner of gold in the world, ahead of China.

When does gold perform well?

For much of history, currencies have had firmly fixed values relative to gold – so the price was set by governments who were then forced to regulate their economies with regard to the amount of gold they held in their reserves, since investors could opt to sell their currency notes for gold. In the 1970s, President Nixon famously took the dollar off the gold standard linked at $35 per ounce since the 1930s. Gold was allowed to trade freely and the gold price rose to $800 by 1980. This may have reflected a degree of catch-up after a long period set at an official price, but it was also concurrent with the dramatic rise in the oil price as OPEC became an effective oil cartel, and inflation became a significant feature in Western economies. Gold's nature of proving to be a long-term store of value was reinforced by its performance in the 1970s. In the 1980s and 1990s, however, it entered a long bear market, falling from $800 to $250 over those two decades as inflation fell back to much lower levels.

However, the strong bull market in this century has not been marked by inflation in the world; in fact, it has been more marked by a lack of inflation given the strength of global growth. The common link between the 1970s and the 2000s and the common contrast with the 1980s and the 1990s lies in the level of *real* interest rates. In the 1970s, although nominal interest rates were high, in fact they were always chasing behind the rate of inflation, and the level of real interest rates was often negative.

In the early 1980s, US policymakers under Paul Volcker determined to get on top of inflation and pushed interest rates up significantly above the rate of inflation. The very high level of real interest rates persisted through the 1980s and 1990s. Even though interest rates fell to much lower levels, they were always well above the rate of inflation. It was only in the US downturn in the early part of this century when Alan Greenspan reduced nominal US interest rates to 1 per cent that the real rate of interest turned negative again.

In the recession following the credit crisis, Ben Bernanke reduced interest rates to 0.25 per cent and has publicly stated his intention to keep them very low for a long period of time. Thus the real interest rate is still very low (in fact, negative), and this has kept gold performing well. Another way of understanding this is that when the rate of interest is less than the rate of inflation, then holding onto the paper currency means that the investor is losing value, so he seeks other outlets that are more likely to protect the real value of his savings.

At the current time, it appears very unlikely that Western central banks will be seeking to push interest rates up above the rate of inflation.

The rise of China and India – long-term effects on demand for gold

Throughout the 20th century, US and European central banks have held the largest part of their foreign reserves in the form of gold rather than paper currencies as a signal to international investors that their economies and currencies were strong and safe to invest in. The rise of the Chinese economy in the last two decades has, however, seen their rapidly growing foreign exchange reserves essentially reinvested into US dollar Treasury bills. So China now has one the largest level of reserves but actually one of the smallest proportions held in gold. This may help explain their unhappiness when the United States pursues policies such as QE2 which threaten to lower the value of the dollar in the foreign exchange markets.

In China, gold is a symbol of prosperity and good fortune – yet with all China's newfound prosperity, its reserves of gold are one-eighth those of the United States and one-third those of Germany, a country with only 6 per cent of China's population. Today gold represents less than 2 per cent of total reserves, whereas in 1980, when admittedly its reserves were much smaller, gold represented 95 per cent of reserves.

At the individual level too, gold has always been important. China is a high-savings economy, and historically individuals have held gold as a key part of their savings. But for over 50 years until 2002, the Chinese were not permitted to own gold personally, and only in the last few years have markets opened in China that allow ordinary people to actually buy gold.

It seems highly probable that demand for gold from both the state and individuals in China will be very strong for years to come.

India, the second most populous country, and another economy growing very fast, has long been recognized as having the largest consumption of gold in the world. The gold industry in India employs 500,000 people and is worth $20 billion every year. Gold is the major savings vehicle for lower- and middle-class households, so continued rapid growth in their incomes is also likely to lead to good growth in demand for gold.

Gold as part of an investment portfolio

The trends in demand for gold appear very positive for the next few years – real interest rates in the West are likely to remain low or negative as high unemployment is likely to deter governments from tightening monetary policy to any great extent. In addition, the outlook for future demand from China and India as they grow rapidly is very strong. The supply outlook is fairly steady; annual new production has remained at about 1.5 per cent of total gold available for some time, and is expected to remain there. This is approximately the same rate of growth as the global population, so there is not enough gold for everyone to own more by physical weight. Any desire for gold to form a bigger part of everyone's portfolio can only be accomplished by the price of gold going up.

There are 5 billion ounces of gold in the world today and 7 billion people, which equates to five-sevenths of an ounce per person, which is worth approximately $1,000. Given gold's universal attractions throughout human history, that should be the minimum that everyone should want to own.

The current economic problems in the West following the credit crisis have highlighted the weaknesses of the Western banking system and our dependence on the major banks continuing to be in existence. This is forcing Western governments to take on the losses and bad debts of many banks, but is damaging the governments' own creditworthiness. Ultimately, the least painful solution to this array of problems is inflation and low real interest rates – gold has historically offered a very potent insurance policy against this outcome.

Private equity and venture capital:

an investment model for private investors

ALLAN WALLACE, OCTOPUS

Private equity and venture capital clearly offer high potential rewards but there can also be considerable risks. An individual investor typically faces several challenges. Identifying the best opportunities is far from easy. The first challenge is finding outstanding opportunities with excellent management teams with the combination of youth, energy, experience and commitment. The Octopus investment model enables investors to resolve these issues.

Investors can access the private equity and venture capital world in a variety of ways. At Octopus, we have two main ways for investors to get involved in the sector: either as active or as passive investors, as illustrated in Figure 1.6.1. As active individuals, selected investors might be invited to join the Octopus Venture Partners, and as passive investors, retail customers can invest in a Venture Capital Trust (VCT) or Enterprise Investment Scheme (EIS) solutions as a way of gaining exposure and diversification in their investment portfolios.

The Venture Partner route: an active investor

The approach we have adopted at Octopus involves the identification of opportunities and testing the ideas via a unique business model involving Venture Partners who have been there and done it themselves. With 110 individual partners, 66 per cent of whom have managed their own businesses, Octopus reduces the risk while seeking returns in excess of 10 times the money invested.

According to Alexander Macpherson, head of the venture team at Octopus, Venture Partners are 'like-minded people, seeking similar investments, co-investing to their mutual benefit – and at lower cost and risk than they can achieve on their own'.

FIGURE 1.6.1 Alternative ways to invest in the private equity and venture capital sector

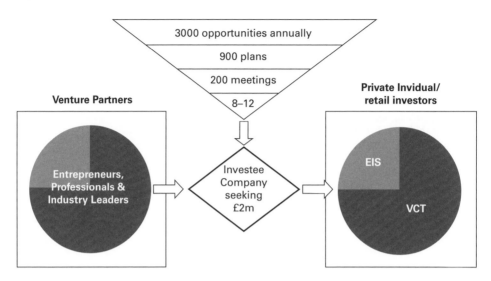

The Venture Partners assist in deal flow selection, assessment and mentoring management teams in the investee businesses. In addition, if they cannot help, they usually know someone who can. As a result of this unique model, Octopus has become one of the UK's best-performing private investor groups, with a realized return of 39 per cent and a failure rate on its businesses of less than 20 per cent after three years against an industry average of around 50 per cent. More importantly, the failures represent less than 10 per cent of invested capital over 10 years.

Some of Octopus's successes include LOVEFiLM, ITM Power, EquatorNet.com, Plum Baby and SiteConfidence. The current portfolio includes many outstanding businesses, such as Zoopla.com, Graze.com, Calastone, True Knowledge and PrismaStar.

Octopus's Venture Partners are typically entrepreneurs, senior executives and wealthy private investors, who can provide expertise as well as capital. The variety and extent of the knowledge capital these investors bring to the businesses they invest in are a resource far beyond the reach of most other small businesses and are an important contributory factor to Octopus's success.

A typical year will see Octopus screen some 3,000 opportunities, typically sourced from Octopus's own Venture Partners, business angels and venture capitalists. Of these, over 150 management teams are met. Key areas of focus include: the market need for the product or service; the business's strategy; its growth potential; and its projections. Particular attention is paid to the strengths of the management team and its ability to exploit the opportunity's potential. The selection process eventually distils the number of opportunities to approximately 12 per annum, and these are then formally presented to the Venture Partners.

Once an investment is agreed in principle, Octopus coordinates the commercial, financial and legal due diligence. This is shared with the Venture Partners prior to a meeting with the management team who present to the Partners who, in turn, question the management team, teasing out the risks as well as the opportunities. All participating Partners sign up to a shareholders agreement, and capital is subscribed by a syndicate of individuals, under the name of Octopus Nominees, rather than as one investment, thus enabling investors to benefit from EIS and other tax advantages. Each Partner makes their own decision whether or not to invest. There is no maximum or minimum.

Economic and market conditions and the performance of the businesses themselves determine exit timing, but most investments typically have a timescale of around five years. Octopus has to date invested in over 32 companies.

Private equity investment was previously the preserve of venture capital and private equity funds. The emergence of professionally managed business angel groups such as the Octopus Venture Partners has, at last, enabled private investors to participate profitably in this potentially very rewarding sector.

'Early-stage venture capital is not for widows and orphans,' says Macpherson, 'but we do our best to work with our investors in finding good opportunities, maximizing their potential and minimizing the risks. For an individual with a reasonable amount of capital, it can be appropriate for a moderate proportion to be in this asset class, ideally with a good spread to mitigate risk.'

The retail investor route: a passive investor

Private equity has changed a great deal since the term was first coined in the 1980s to denote investment in private rather than publicly quoted companies. The investment approach of teams has changed, along with the type of investor and investment vehicles they use. Private equity is now an accessible asset class for retail investors.

VCTs, along with investment trusts, offer a way into this area for investors. As highly tax-efficient investment vehicles, they're particularly attractive because any growth from investment is tax free. VCT tax benefits include upfront income tax relief of 30 per cent, along with the potential for tax-free dividends and tax-free capital gains. Advisers looking to manage clients' portfolios in a holistic manner can also bear in mind that VCTs have more to offer investors than just tax relief: they can be used as a complementary solution within pension planning.

The move towards tax products can be seen as part of a wider shift away from the traditional approach to retirement planning. In the wake of the financial crisis, investors may no longer want long-term investment in equities to be the sole focus of investors' pension plans. Instead, investors can use tax products to build a retirement nest egg in a tax-efficient manner, one that is not related to stock market performance and offers an element of diversification. In this way, tax products are coming to be viewed as part of an integrated approach to effective long-term financial planning.

So, the next question is whether now is the right time to be investing in this asset class. Many smaller companies were hard hit by economic upheavals and the subsequent refusal of banks to lend, which continues to this day. This has created a mismatch between supply and demand for funding, which in turn has led many company valuations to fall. What this means for investors is that VCT fund managers can buy into companies at attractive valuations, picking up bargains that have the potential to provide long-term returns as the market recovers. Finally, VCTs are structured so that they can invest gradually over a three-year period. This means clients can be assured that fund managers are able to take the time to seek out the very best deals.

The increased need for tax-efficient investments, combined with potential returns from investment in VCTs, has proved a powerful combination. This area is no longer dominated by the wealthy and institutional investors. The last tax year saw a surge of investment into VCTs by retail investors. In fact, 2009–10 was one of the most successful fundraising years in their 10-year history, with inflows of more than £340 million (source: Association of Investment Companies). And there's plenty of room for more investors to get involved. Highly skilled venture capital teams, who draw on both their own experience and others' entrepreneurial expertise, are the ones adding value to investments, and in doing so are driving value for investors.

Good businesses that can serve their customers' needs VC houses such as Octopus with the cash and wherewithal to invest and investors prepared to take a long-term view will be able to make the most of opportunities this year. Both investment managers and businesses can know this and help investors understand it. In this way, the venture capital industry will be continuing to build not just companies but confidence as well, both essential to a flourishing future UK economy.

It is these investors and these teams who represent the new face of private equity.

PART TWO
Good practice in asset management

Operational due diligence:

2.1

a necessity in hedge fund review

**NICOLE D'ANGELO AND MARK DAVIDSON,
CITI PRIVATE BANK**

What is operational due diligence? In its most basic form, operational due diligence can be viewed as a fundamental analysis of an investment manager's operational capabilities and the ability for their infrastructure to support execution of their investment thesis.

A hedge fund investment is more than an investment in a fund or trading strategy; it is also an investment in a manager, their operation, their people and their processes. As hedge fund investing has proliferated over the course of the last few years operational due diligence has been gaining prominence as an integral aspect of investment decision making. However, it was the events surrounding high-profile Ponzi schemes such as those of Bernard Madoff, Marc Drier and Tom Petters that have recently brought operational due diligence to the fore. Although not directly related to alternative investing, operational risks manifested themselves in unexpected ways throughout the crisis of 2008. With the near-failure of Bear Stearns in early 2008, followed by the failure of Lehman Brothers and the bailout of AIG, counterparty risk management became a material (and systemic) issue for virtually all financial institutions (hedge funds included). While the reasons why Lehman failed are diverse and somewhat muddled, it is generally agreed that the balance sheet values that Lehman (an ostensibly mark-to-market institution) ascribed to a significant portion of its assets were grossly overstated and not representative of fair market value. While Lehman (and other financial institutions) had material funding issues throughout the crisis, there is no doubt that Lehman's lax valuation processes contributed to its ultimate failure.

These more visible examples of operational failures only begin to scratch the surface of the intricacies and nuances that compose a hedge fund manager's operational infrastructure. In this article we discuss three key aspects of operational due diligence:

- the case for a strong operational due diligence function;
- hallmarks of effective operational due diligence;

- key operational considerations.

In 2009 in the United States, the *Report of the Investors' Committee to the President's Working Group on Financial Markets* stated that hedge fund investing will require 'deep, meaningful due diligence in relation to investment strategy and operations both at the outset of an investment and on an ongoing basis'. The operational due diligence function is a key aspect of satisfying these basic investor needs.

Due diligence practices and procedures have evolved over the last 10 years, informed throughout by events occuring in the financial markets, in particular most recently the worldwide financial crises and the discovery of large-scale frauds such as the Madoff and Stanford Ponzi schemes. Behaviour that previously would not have raised concerns in the context of a due diligence exercise would now do so when considered with these frauds in mind. Any person or institution setting out to design or revisit due diligence processes does so in light of the 'lessons learned' from such events.

The case for a strong operational due diligence function

The most compelling argument for a strong and effective operational due diligence process is the number and magnitude of operational related failures. A 2003 study by consultant Capco suggests that over half of hedge funds that failed did so due to operational shortcomings. More recent studies of operational failures suggest that hundreds more hedge funds have failed due to improper operations. Moreover, operational concerns extend well beyond the high-profile frauds that have made headlines. Evidence also exists that the incidence of hedge fund failures cannot be segregated to one type of manager or strategy. In fact, perhaps counter-intuitively, we see that hedge fund failures frequently arise from the simpler strategies, as illustrated in Figure 2.1.1.

FIGURE 2.1.1 % of Defaults* by Instrument Complexity

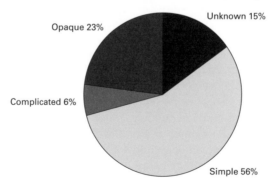

Unknown 15%
Opaque 23%
Complicated 6%
Simple 56%

SOURCE EDHEC Risk and Asset Management Research Center, © 2007 EDHEC, Quantification of Hedge Fund Default Risk, January 2007. *In the context of this study 'default' generally refers to a hedge fund's inability to return capital to investors or lenders. Definitions: Simple: Equities, Listed Derivatives; Complicated: OTC Contracts, Fixed Income Derivatives, Credit Derivatives; Opaque: Liquid and/or Complex Instruments to Price.

TABLE 2.1.1

What do you consider to be the main criteria for considering a third-party provider of alternative investments?	
Performance	72%
Quality of compliance and risk management process	49%
Transparency	46%
Quality of reporting	33%
Product innovation	27%
Independence from large financial services institutions	18%
Size	14%
What do you consider to be the main criteria for deselecting a provider?	
Quality of compliance and risk management process	41%
Transparency	41%
Performance	40%
Quality of reporting	39%
Size	24%
Independence from large financial services institutions	14%
Product innovation	6%

SOURCE PricewaterhouseCoopers/EIU survey, January 2008

What we now find is that clients have come to expect effective risk controls throughout all levels of an investment. As we see in Table 2.1.1 it is the prospects of good risk-adjusted returns that overwhelmingly entice investors to select alternative investments. However, performance (or lack thereof) is not the most compelling reason for investors to shun alternative investments.

Institutional investors, foundations, endowments, private clients, high net worth individuals and others paying for advice on alternative investments have come to expect that their advisers are providing them with the 'deep, meaningful' due diligence referenced by the Investors' Committee (see above). The responsibility of identifying the facets that should comprise deep and meaningful due diligence resides with the adviser. Clearly the analysis of a manager's investment capabilities is critical. However, the effective development of a robust and meaningful operational due diligence programme and its integration into the investment process are similarly critical.

Hallmarks of effective operational due diligence

An effective operational due diligence programme will typically have certain hallmarks to its process. Specifically, a programme should provide for the initial assessment of a manager as well as some form of periodic monitoring in order to address any changes that may occur over time. Additionally, in conjunction with the initial assessment and any periodic assessments, managers and funds typically produce substantive documentation that can provide meaningful insight into their operation. Furthermore, an effective due diligence programme should have the flexibility to respond to market events and evaluate those events in the context of a manager's operations. Of course, in order to be effective, these processes must be complemented with experienced and seasoned professionals who can continually execute the programme summarized in Figure 2.1.2 in a consistent manner.

Experienced professionals

The judgement as to a hedge fund manager's operational effectiveness is typically a qualitative and subjective assessment. While a 'tick-the-box' approach may yield a high-level understanding of a manager's operations, it is unlikely to yield a thorough and meaningful assessment. Instead, the utilization of experienced and knowledgeable operational due diligence personnel is critical to the effective deployment of an operational due diligence programme. With the broad proliferation of strategies and asset types (and differing controls related to each), a dedicated and experienced team with broad experience among various asset types and control functions is necessary to develop a meaningful qualitative assessment of a manager.

Certain industry participants apply a rote tick-the-box approach while others will merely include the operational assessment within the scope of the investment analysts' responsibilities. We would suggest that the industry participants with the most effective and robust operational due diligence programmes are those who dedicate distinct qualified resources to the assessment and evaluation of a hedge fund manager's operations.

Initial review

An initial onsite meeting with a manager is crucial to gaining a detailed understanding of their operations and building a rapport with management. Close interaction between the operational due diligence team and the investment team is also necessary

FIGURE 2.1.2

Experienced Professionals	
Initial Review	Desk Review
Periodic Review	Ongoing Evaluation

as a new fund moves through the research process. Many aspects of a particular fund's strategy and business will be included in the investment analyst's work and an open dialogue between the investment and due diligence teams facilitates the investment process. A comprehensive initial review is typically composed of multiple facets: requisition and analysis of data and documentation (see also 'Desk review', below); onsite meeting; service provider contact; final analysis; and documentation. As a fund progresses through the investment process and reaches a point whereby an investment into the fund seems imminent, the operational due diligence team will begin the process of collecting relevant documentation and gaining a basic understanding of the manager's strategy and operation. The operational due diligence team will subsequently organize an in-person meeting with the relevant operations, legal/compliance and technology professionals. After meeting with relevant representatives of the manager, the operational due diligence team will liaise with relevant service providers (eg administrator, auditor, prime broker, etc) as necessary in order to better understand and verify the roles that each play in the operational processes of the fund. In certain circumstances, in the event that material operational deficiencies are identified, the operational due diligence team will document the relevant findings and recommend that the fund not be approved for investment. In the event that no material concerns are identified, the operational due diligence team will indicate that no material adverse findings were identified and comment on any noteworthy operational considerations, approve the fund for investment (from an operational perspective) and document the relevant facets of the manager's operation for future reference.

Desk review

A necessary aspect of hedge fund operations and structure is documentation. Offering documents, regulatory documents (eg Form ADV), organizational charts, audit reports and due diligence questionnaires all serve to provide additional background and information related to a manager's operations. Both prior to an initial manager review, as well as on an ongoing basis, various documents need to be continually reviewed. For example, updated organizational charts or due diligence questionnaires can identify staff turnover, annual audits can uncover a wealth of financial information and offering documents can provide valuable insights into fund structure, fees and expenses. As noted above, while it is unlikely that any one document will reveal a material operational issue, it may be the case that a detailed review of various documents can weave a tale about a manager's operating processes.

Periodic review

After a manager is approved for investment, it is important to remain abreast of changes that may occur within the manager's business over time. Certainly a consistent review of associated manager/fund documentation is necessary; however, a periodic, post-funding operational review is crucial to remaining assured of effective manager operations. Particularly over the course of the last two years, numerous managers experienced significant declines in assets under management that were met with commensurate workforce reductions. Furthermore, due to the substantive illiquidity in certain asset classes and structural liquidity mismatches experienced by many industry participants, numerous funds chose to impose gating mechanisms, side-pockets or other techniques to restrict investors' liquidity. Periodic ongoing reviews became critical during this period in order to remain abreast of fund changes and, in certain circumstances, take proactive steps to combat manager behaviour that was arguably not in the best interests of shareholders.

Ongoing evaluation

An ongoing evaluation differs from a periodic review in that the ongoing evaluation occurs all the time and with no predefined period. While certain aspects of a manager's operation may change over time and be addressed as part of the periodic review, other external events may have a more immediate impact on a manager's operations (eg the failure of Lehman, the passage of legislation requiring SEC registration, etc). In the case of such occurrences it is important to begin an immediate dialogue with the manager(s) to understand how the external event is being addressed.

Key operational considerations

While the considerations noted in this section are some of the more critical considerations, the discussion is by no means exhaustive. The best assurances that a manager's operations are sound come from the effective implementation of a comprehensive operational due diligence process executed by seasoned, experienced professionals.

Valuation

The hedge fund industry today is composed of total assets in excess of $1 trillion and well over 5,000 funds (by some accounts nearer 10,000). Numerous asset classes and securities are traded by these funds, each with varying degrees of liquidity and price transparency. At the highest level, a manager's valuation process and the independence associated with that process are critical. However, as funds invest in less liquid and less transparent assets, the quality of the value becomes increasingly critical (not just the process). For example, it is unlikely that two parties will reasonably disagree on the value of a common share of General Electric. However, it is reasonable (and in fact frequent) that two parties (or even different third-party pricing agents) may have materially different perspectives on the value of less liquid assets such as structured products, private loans (sometimes even including bank debt), less liquid corporate debt instruments and private equity (just to name a few).

One of the most prominent examples of differences of opinion relating to valuation is the recently highly publicized dispute that occurred in late 2007 and 2008 between Goldman Sachs and AIG. In this instance, Goldman Sachs ascribed materially lower values than AIG to swaps between the two parties It is not always reasonable to assume that pricing, because it is received from a third party, is 'the right price'. In normal market conditions it is important to understand how a manager values their book, what inputs are utilized and who (if anyone) independently verifies the inputs. However, in times of market stress, while it is always important to be assured of an independent and consistent process, it becomes crucial to understand the inputs that comprise a valuation (ie discount rates, broker quotations, credit assumptions, collateral appraisals, etc), and not only the manager's process. As we see in Figure 2.1.3, there are clearly varying opinions as to the quality and/or ability of third-party valuation agents to effectively value certain assets. It is therefore incumbent upon the investor (ie via the operational due diligence programme) to ensure that they understand not just the valuation process, but the quality of the valuation itself.

Existence

While it may seem obvious – and became glaringly evident through Madoff's and other Ponzi schemes – an important aspect of effective operational due diligence is assurance that the assets of a fund do, in fact, exist. Such assurances can be obtained in a variety of manners.

FIGURE 2.1.3 Ability of third-party valuation agent to value portfolio of illiquid investments

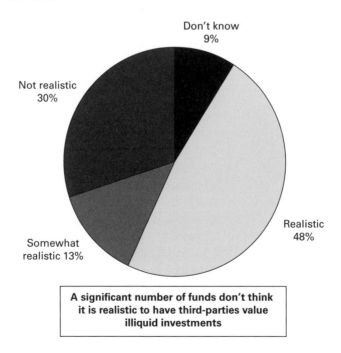

Don't know 9%

Not realistic 30%

Realistic 48%

Somewhat realistic 13%

A significant number of funds don't think it is realistic to have third-parties value illiquid investments

SOURCE Ernst & Young, ©2009 EYGM Limited, www.ey.com

First, audited financial statements. As a function of any effective audit, it is incumbent upon the auditor to verify asset existence at the balance sheet date. Unfortunately, an audit typically occurs only once per year.

Secondly, the Madoff fraud has highlighted the need for independent custody of assets and periodic independent reconciliation between the books and records of the fund and the independent custodian. Prime brokers and custodians have become more willing to interact with investors by verifying equity balances to provide investors with assurances that assets exist. Private assets (private equity, private debt, etc), however, are typically not held in registered form nor is there a counterparty to independently verify the other side of a trade. In these circumstances, the operational due diligence analysts would seek additional verification dependent upon the nature of the asset (perhaps a review of select loan documents in the instance of private debt).

Thirdly, effective controls surrounding individuals authorized to move/transfer assets (cash) on behalf of the fund.

To put it in perspective, by outward appearance Madoff had none of these controls in place. The auditor was, more or less, a sham, and no meaningful verification of existence was performed during the audit; assets were supposedly held by Madoff's affiliated broker/dealer, not an unaffiliated, independent third party; no independent third party was in place and all books and records were maintained by Madoff. These were all glaring operational deficiencies that should have been identified by effective operational due diligence practices. As we see in Figure 2.1.4, six of 11 large operational failures are directly related to misappropriation/existence.

FIGURE 2.1.4   The Rogue's Gallery: examples of significant hedge fund operational failures

Case	Estimated Financial Impact ($)	Year Discovered	Primary cause
Bernard L. Madoff Investment Securities	64,000,000,000	2008	Existence of Assets – Ponzi Scheme
Petters	3,500,000,000	2008	Existence of Assets – Ponzi Scheme
Bear Stearns	1,800,000,000	2007	Marketing Misrepresentation
Weavering Capital	637,000,000	2009	Conflct of Interest
Westridge Capital Management	554,000,000	2009	Theft and Misappropriation
Lancer Management Group	500,000,000	2003	Legal/Regulatory Violation
Beacon Hill Asset Management	472,000,000	2002	Misvaluation of Fund Assets
Bayou	450,000,000	2005	Theft and Misappropriation
Drier	400,000,000	2009	Theft and Misappropriation
Manhattan Capital Management	393,000,000	2000	Concealment of Trading Losses
Agape World Inc.	370,000,000	2009	Theft and Misappropriation

SOURCE Castle Hall Alternatives. From Manhattan to Madoff. The Causes and Lessons of Hedge Fund Operational Failure. www.castlehallalternatives.com

Compliance

In light of the recent crisis, it seems relatively agreed that 'The Street' and the financial system generally will be coming under increased regulatory scrutiny. Notwithstanding, in the last few months alone we have witnessed Pequot, one of the pioneers of the hedge fund industry, shut down largely due to accusations of insider trading and an SEC investigation; Galleon, a multi-billion dollar hedge fund, became embroiled in an insider trading scandal that ultimately led to the liquidation of Galleon funds and the indictment of its principal; and most recently, both criminal and SEC charges have been levied against Goldman Sachs for alleged regulatory (and criminal) violations.

While it is very difficult to guard against, or analyse for the possibility of, compliance violations, an investor can seek certain assurances that a particular manager takes compliance seriously and applies a general 'tone of compliance' within the organization. Ideally, the manager will have a dedicated compliance function staffed by knowledgeable and competent compliance specialists. Additionally, it is preferable to see that managers have proactively registered as investment advisers with the SEC. While SEC registration is not currently mandatory for hedge fund managers, it appears that Congress may enact legislation that will require hedge fund managers to register with the SEC.

Service providers

The evaluation of service providers (typically include auditor, prime broker(s)/ custodians, administrator, valuation agents) is critical to ensuring the proper operation of the fund. While there may be reasonable and justifiable reasons why a manager chooses a smaller, lower-quality service provider, those reasons must be well understood prior to investing in a fund that utilizes such providers. Particularly in such instances, an operational due diligence analyst would seek to evaluate the control functions performed by the various service providers, understand which service providers purports to undertake which function and obtain assurances that the relevant control functions are being executed in a manner consistent with effective performance of such controls.

Counterparty management

Prior to the crisis there was an inherent understanding that counterparty risk was important. However, until the peak of the crisis it was not clear that all market participants had fully prepared for counterparty failures nor fully appreciated the impact that a failure of their prime broker could have on their funds. Obtaining an understanding of a manager's counterparty management process is critical in effectively evaluating their operation. Furthermore, understanding a manager's contingencies in the event of an imminent failure of a counterparty is also critical. For instance, does a fund have multiple prime brokerage relationships; should balances/ positions need to be moved away from a perceived weak counterparty? Does a fund have bilateral or unilateral margining agreements in place? How aggressive is a manager at requesting excess margin (when possible)? As illustrated in Figures 2.1.5 and 2.1.6, counterparty risk is certainly appreciated today and the need for multiple prime broker options also appears to be increasing.

FIGURE 2.1.5 Importance of counterparty risk

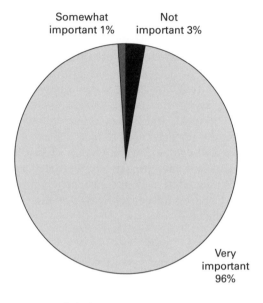

SOURCE Ernst & Young ©2009 EYGM Limited, www.ey.com

FIGURE 2.1.6 Counterparty risk concerns drive hedge funds to add prime brokers

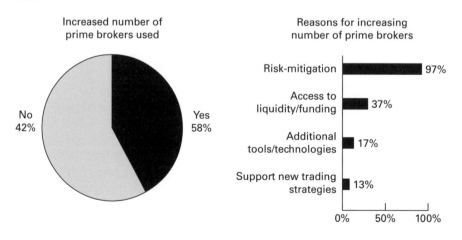

SOURCE 2010 Hedge Fund Operational Challenges Research.
Note: Based on responses from 26 hedge funds in N.A., 17 in Europe, and 9 in Asia.

Competence of management

Last, but certainly not least, perhaps the most critical aspect of an effective hedge fund operation is staffing it with competent and experienced professionals. While the judgement of competence is certainly a qualitative one, it is one that cannot be taken lightly. Any hedge fund manager can deliver impressive marketing materials and organizational, systems and process charts depicting a robust operating environment. However, only after an investor has taken the time to meet with the relevant professionals, evaluate their operation and assess their qualifications and experience can an informed judgement as to management's competence be drawn.

Conclusion

As we see in Figure 2.1.7, the operational due diligence landscape has changed for managers, administrators, and for investors with capital at risk.

The effective implementation and execution of an operational due diligence programme is critical to the broader effectiveness and long-term success of an alternative investment platform.

The myriad issues that can arise through investments in alternative funds have only been addressed at a high level in this article. We hope it has become evident that evaluating alternative fund managers is a nuanced task that requires a combination of qualitative assessment and procedural rigour implemented by qualified experienced professionals working hand in hand with the investment teams.

FIGURE 2.1.7

What impact, if any, has the market crisis and/or the news of recent financial scandals had on your operational due diligence process?

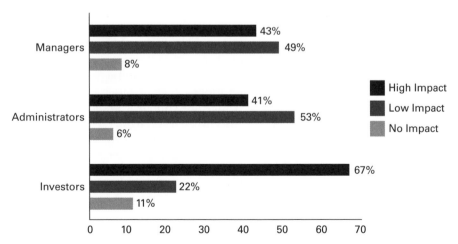

SOURCE ©KPMG International Cooperative, The Future of the Alternative Investment Industry

Disclaimers

All expressions of opinion are subject to change without notice and are not intended to be a guarantee of future events. This document is for information only. Opinions expressed herein may differ from the opinions expressed by other businesses of Citigroup Inc, are not intended to be a forecast of future events or a guarantee of future results or investment advice and are subject to change based on market and other conditions. Past performance is not a guarantee of future results.

Investments in alternative assets (eg hedge funds, private equity) are speculative, not suitable for all clients, and intended for experienced and sophisticated investors who are willing to bear the high economic risks of the investment, which can include: loss of all or a substantial portion of the capital invested due to leveraging, short-selling or other speculative investment practices; lack of liquidity in that there may be no secondary market for the Portfolio and none expected to develop; volatility of returns; restrictions on transferring shares/interests in the Portfolio; absence of information regarding valuations and pricing; lack of diversification and concentration of risk due to a single manager delays in tax reporting; less regulation and higher fees than mutual funds; and manager risk.

Investments in alternative investment products are generally limited to investors that qualify as 'Accredited Investors' under the Securities Act of 1933, as amended, and/or 'Qualified Purchasers' under the Investment Company Act of 1940, as amended, depending on the terms of the alternative investment product. Accordingly, prior to making any investment in an alternative investment product, an investor will need to satisfy the relevant suitability qualifications related to that product. The information contained herein is directed exclusively to those investors that are 'Accredited Investors' and/or 'Qualified Purchasers.'

Although information in this document has been obtained from sources believed to be reliable, Citigroup Inc and its affiliates do not guarantee its accuracy or completeness and accept no liability for any direct or consequential losses arising from its use. Throughout this document where charts indicate that a third party (parties) is the source, please note that the source references the raw data received from such parties.

Citi Private Bank and Citi Personal Wealth Management are businesses of Citigroup Inc ('Citigroup'). Citi Private Bank and Citi Personal Wealth Management provide its clients access to a broad array of products and services available through bank and non-bank affiliates of Citigroup. Not all products and services are provided by all affiliates or are available at all locations. In the United States, brokerage products and services are provided by Citigroup Global Markets Inc ('CGMI'), Member SIPC. CGMI and Citibank, NA are affiliated companies under the common control of Citigroup. Outside the United States, brokerage services are provided by other Citigroup affiliates.

Citi and Citi with Arc Design are trademarks and service marks of Citigroup and its affiliates and are used and registered throughout the world.

In the UK, certain services are available through Citibank, NA ('Citibank') and Citibank International plc, 33 Canada Square, Canary Wharf, London E14 5LB, which is authorized and regulated by the Financial Services Authority for the conduct of investment business in the UK and is a subsidiary of Citigroup Inc, USA.

© Copyright 2011, Citigroup Inc

Lending to unlock liquidity

MICHAEL DARRIBA,
DEUTSCHE BANK PRIVATE WEALTH MANAGEMENT UK

It is universally accepted that a manifest reduction in readily available credit has been one of the key after-effects of the liquidity crisis. What is perhaps far less appreciated is how this situation has affected the wealthy.

Wealth, after all, does not eliminate the need to borrow – quite the contrary. High net worth individuals usually have high net expenditure, and a defining characteristic of high net expenditure is that it often fluctuates heavily – leading to cash-flow issues at inopportune times.

In light of this, not least in an age when many financial institutions are still operating with minimal lending activities as they bid to repair their balance sheets, the ability of a small number of wealth managers to offer specialist credit facilities is becoming a major distinguishing factor within the industry. It is therefore imperative to disregard the flawed notion that the wealthy should not need to borrow – strange though it may seem to some, this is a misconception – and to pay closer attention to the numerous benefits that high net worth clients can derive from access to a credit facility.

Liquidity benefit

In a climate of rock-bottom interest rates we should not be surprised that investors keen to protect their wealth from predatory inflation are willing to consider longer-term and potentially less liquid investments. In such instances the wealth manager's task is not merely to help minimize the enhanced risk but to surmount the challenges presented by the liquidity cost.

An investor whose wealth is tied up in more rewarding but less liquid assets is susceptible to unanticipated financial shocks, however quotidian in nature those shocks might at first seem. The arrival of a large tax bill or even a demand for the children's tuition fees can be sufficient to leave such individuals with little choice other than to fund the expense through the liquidation of part of their portfolios or the sale of property. The worst-case scenario is that they find themselves compelled to sell assets at an unfavourable juncture when it might be prudent to wait for a more auspicious market.

Deutsche Bank
Private Wealth Management

Our strength. Your success.

The more challenging market conditions, the
more important your choice of partner.
At Deutsche Bank Private Wealth Management,
our commitment to our clients' success is
constant, no matter what is on the horizon.
When trust may seem a rare commodity, you
can rely on our determination, global vision and
resources to help you succeed and optimise
opportunity in today's rapidly changing world.

To discover how Deutsche Bank Private Wealth
Management can help you, please call visit

www.dbpwm.co.uk

Passion to Perform

Investments are subject to investment risk, including market fluctuations, regulatory change, counterparty risk,
possible delays in repayment and loss of income and principal invested. The value of investment can fall as
well as rise and you might not get back the amount originally invested at any point in time. Deutsche Bank
Private Wealth Management is a trading name of Tilney Investment Management. Registered in England
No. 2010520. Tilney Investment Management is a member of the London Stock Exchange and is authorised and
regulated by the Financial Services Authority. FSA Register Number 124255. Tilney Investment Management is a
member of the Deutsche Bank Group.

That investors want to maximize returns is a given: they do not want to dispose of what they consider long-term investments before these have had a chance to perform. It is in such circumstances that access to a flexible cash loan facility becomes an attractive proposition.

The very knowledge that such a facility is available can influence investment decisions. It allows clients to invest money that might otherwise be held in reserve in a cash account, generating scant return, with the comfort and peace of mind that the resource is there in the future if cash is required quickly. This can be particularly useful in the event that a promising prospective investment that might otherwise have to be shunned – a business venture, for example, or the availability of a long-coveted and now heavily discounted property – presents itself. Opportunities, like bills, can arise unexpectedly: the ability to access cash with speed enables rapid and shrewd investment.

Leverage opportunities

It is important to note that credit facilities are not only of interest to investors with undetermined future cash needs; they can also play a vital role in successful leverage strategies. Although it is not an approach for the faint-hearted, investors with an appetite for enhanced risk may consider a loan to leverage their exposure to a specific investment.

At this point I must be abundantly clear about the inherent risks. Specifically, for this option to be viable, the potential net return on the investment *must* be higher than the cost of the loan facility. There is little sense in taking out a loan at an interest rate of, say, 3 per cent to increase investment in an asset unless it offers significantly more than a 3 per cent rate of return. Investors will have differing views as to what constitutes 'significant' in this scenario; and all must consider the possibility that the investment may underperform, in which eventuality even a marginal return can metamorphose into a capital loss. Where a leveraged investment itself loses money, the leverage exacerbates the loss.

There is a strong culture of leveraged investing in Asia and the United States, where it is reasonably commonplace for lending to be used in this way. Leveraging in the European market is not especially frequent and tends to be confined to highly sophisticated investors – at this stage at least. This, of course, may change.

Diversification advantages

Few would argue that diversification lies at the heart of good wealth management. Events since 2008 have served only to reinforce the conviction that a sensible spread of assets is fundamental to effective investment, and the merits of a meaningful insurance layer to protect against unpleasant surprises is rightly enjoying increased recognition. Somewhat less understood is the role a credit facility can play in funding a diversification strategy within a portfolio.

This is a philosophy that should appeal to those investors who have an attachment to (or who through personal circumstances are required to hold) a particular stock or stocks. They may grasp the advantages of encompassing other assets classes but might not have the liquidity to fund diversification. Using a loan to acquire other assets allows them to retain favoured stock positions while enjoying the potential gains of more diversified risk.

Although the costs of the loan should still be considered against the overall return of the 'rebalanced' portfolio, in general terms investors who employ leverage in this way should be protected against market downturns. As opposed to the case of leveraging exposure to a single investment, it is unlikely that all assets would fall in value if the market were to drop.

This strategy requires sagacious portfolio construction, ideally drawing on the expertise of a qualified and skilled wealth manager. It is not a low-risk proposition. Again, if investments fall in value the loss is exacerbated by the added exposure created by the loan as well as the loan costs. The risk profile has to be correct.

Collateral

Once the liquidity benefits of a lending facility have been understood, the next concern is security.

The most commonly available type of lending is secured against a portfolio of shares and bonds. This is a more cost-effective or flexible form of borrowing. There is usually no arrangement fee, interest rates are comparatively low (because the loan is secured against the portfolio of marketable securities) and the loan can be repaid and redrawn as required.

This is the 'plain vanilla' of lending, and we should not overlook its comparatively simple allure. There are more exotic flavours, however, that cater for the tastes of the most sophisticated clients.

The fine art of borrowing

The demand for art lending, for instance, is growing. Many high net worth investors – and especially many ultra-high net worth investors – have a sizeable percentage of wealth locked into art collections. Adorning the walls of their owners' homes, fine works may constitute investments in their own right – and might even give aesthetic pleasure as well – but by using them as collateral it is possible to release cash to use for various other investments.

Generally speaking, depending on the work in question, investors can borrow from 20 to 50 per cent of a piece's market value. Banks will normally want to take custody of the pledged collection, but in certain circumstances clients may be allowed to keep their treasured possessions *in situ*.

Deutsche Bank's own collection of contemporary art has grown to 55,000 pieces in more than 900 of our buildings worldwide, reflecting our expertise in this nascent field. A dedicated art team such as ours not only serves to assist ultra-high net worth clients in acquiring art as an investment; it helps develop the skills and relationships necessary to appreciate art fully and, crucially, to value it appropriately. Expertise also tells us that structured loans offered against art should be based on the strength of the client: income, the ability to repay and capital accumulated over the years.

Recently we have also observed a marked rise in the number of clients looking to borrow against residential and even commercial property. The latter in particular, driven largely by the prospective yields and the hope of participating in capital growth, has interested many more clients than it did only a few years ago. Deutsche Bank has arranged loan facilities on properties in multiple jurisdictions – including, to name a few, the UK, France, Germany, Monaco, Spain and Greece.

What all this tells us is that clients and wealth managers alike ignore eclecticism at their peril. Art, residential property, even offshore property – all can play a part. Much as those who seek effective diversification of their assets must cast their nets ever wider, so those keen to maximize the benefits of borrowing and lending must increasingly think beyond the accepted norms. In this and other regards it is fair to suggest that the modern-day credit facility has truly become an art in itself.

Pooled resources

We should acknowledge, too, the powerful argument for bringing wealth management and lending requirements together under one roof. Straightforward convenience may well be the first plus that occurs to investment-minded individuals with hectic lives when they contemplate the concept of dealing with a single institution, but such an arrangement should represent far more than mere time saving.

A bank that commands an immediate overview of a client's investable assets, balance sheet and liquidity can move quickly to tailor a lending facility that takes into account credit worthiness, investment risk profile and strategy for growing wealth; and, because it is looking after assets as well as lending, such a bank can offer more favourable loan terms. Regular dialogue between investor and wealth manager should also help identify probable liquidity needs before they arise and provide solutions at the earliest opportunity. The two case studies that follow are examples of such a relationship.

Case studies

Riviera high life

Most high net worth individuals seeking a credit facility simply desire the ability to access liquidity. They wish to invest their money in less liquid assets that will deliver higher returns than cash, but they need to know that should the need arise (for instance, if an enticing investment opportunity comes their way – or, less appealingly, an unexpectedly large bill) they can obtain funds speedily and efficiently.

There are other reasons for wanting credit. In one case a high net worth individual was seeking a loan facility secured against a number of luxury properties he owned.

A Deutsche Bank Private Wealth Management client and experienced property developer, he realized he had been over-exposed to the property market. The financial crisis provided the wake-up call he needed to rebalance his affairs by diversifying his assets into more liquid investments.

It was agreed Deutsche Bank would provide a loan facility secured against the properties to repay the existing debt and provide cash for other investments recommended by Deutsche Bank.

What started as an initial loan of €10 million secured against one property has now developed to an €80 million facility secured against a selection of the best-quality homes he owns in the area.

Artful investing

It is common for lending to be against marketable securities, but more complex deals can be arranged. In one case, the London-based family office of a wealthy Middle Eastern client came to Deutsche Bank Private Wealth Management seeking a £10 million loan against a collection of paintings, furniture and antique silver. The purpose of the loan was to create liquidity to aid private equity acquisitions in the UK.

With the assistance of Art Advisory – Deutsche Bank's specialist art advisory service – the collection was independently assessed and valued. A loan was then tailored to the specific requirements of the client, taking into account important factors such as international tax, multiple jurisdictions, location and storage of the assets and expenses.

Although the transaction was very complicated, due in particular to wealth management and tax considerations, the five-year loan facility was agreed and drawn down within just one month of receipt of all the necessary details.

Conclusion

The continued tightening of credit in the wake of the liquidity crisis has created a challenge for wealthy individuals who want their capital to work harder but require liquidity. The organizations best placed to meet that challenge are those that weathered the financial storm without needing a direct injection of public funds and which are able to offer bespoke lending as well as wealth management.

Such institutions can help investors unlock liquidity, opening up the opportunity for better and, in some cases, more sophisticated investing. It is our own experience that the liquidity benefit of a lending facility is a notable attraction to high net worth individuals, and for this reason we expect to extend the service to many more clients in 2011.

Disclaimer

Investments are subject to investment risk, including market fluctuations, regulatory change, counterparty risk, possible delays in repayment and loss of income and principal invested. The value of investment can fall as well as rise and you might not get back the amount invested at any point in time.

Reversion in the FX markets: an old wives' tale?

2.3

**PHILIP WATSON AND MICHAEL SCHMEJA,
CITI PRIVATE BANK**

Introduction

In this chapter we explore the risks that investors assume, either intentionally or unintentionally, through their foreign exchange exposure. We argue that advisers and investors should pay greater attention to managing foreign exchange risk. We support this argument by looking at past currency returns and their impact on portfolio returns.

We explore currency risk at its most basic – translation risk. We highlight the choice for multi-currency investors as to whether to hedge or not and examine the implications of this choice on potential returns. In particular, we challenge the widely held assertion that currency pairs revert to their historical levels in the long term. We believe this leads to a false sense of certainty and ill-advised consequences for investor hedging behaviour.

What is foreign exchange risk?

The credit crisis served as a reminder of the many risks that investors assume when investing across financial asset markets. It would be beyond the scope of this chapter to cover these comprehensively. Focusing on foreign exchange risk, we instead explore a few of the more widely applicable risks, concentrating firstly on translation risk – how local currency returns on portfolio holdings are impacted by their translation to an investor's reference currency ('reference' implies home or accounting currency and we will use this term throughout the chapter).

Translation risk applies to any unhedged investor who, after investing in any currency[1] other than their own reference currency, introduces foreign exchange risk into their portfolio. For example, the final return that an unhedged[2] GBP- (pounds sterling) referenced client receives when selling their holding of Hong Kong listed

Aluminum Corporation of China Limited stock will be directly impacted by both the stock price as well as GBP/HKD (Hong Kong dollar) changes over the holding period. A fairly obvious statement, perhaps – but are investors as persuaded of the merits of introducing GBP/HKD risk into their portfolios as they are of the stock itself?

How can investors manage the risk?

Investors can manage their foreign exchange risk in different ways, accepting the risk of translation losses or by engaging in a strategy that serves to reduce or eliminate currency translation risk over a defined period. This usually involves defining an exact or acceptable range of translation rates at a specified point in the future.

For example, an investor may sacrifice all of any upside resulting from an appreciation in the non-reference currency in order to set a defined translation rate into their reference currency at a future date. At the same time, an investor hoping to participate in some but not all of the potential upside may accept a certain amount of downside translation risk. In an abbreviated sense, numerous strategies exist for clients that can be tailored to meet their exact needs.

Is currency management necessary?

An obvious yet frequently overlooked question!

Starting from a historical perspective, there are ample periods of time where the management of currency would have been a shrewd move. Let's take a simple example: a USD- (US dollar) referenced currency investor investing into a Eurostoxx 50 exchange traded fund (ETF) received on 3 January 2005 and selling at the end of the year on an unhedged basis would have experienced a return of 6.0 per cent (all returns are gross of fees). Meanwhile, a EUR- (€) referenced investor would have received a return of 20.5 per cent in EUR. All this is the result of an equity rally (20.5 per cent in EUR terms) combined with a EUR weakening over the year from 1.35 to 1.18 (12 per cent depreciation of EUR).

In Figure 2.3.1 we show the net return to two investors, both investing in Eurostoxx 50 on 3 January 2005 and selling their position on 30 December 2005. One investor is EUR-referenced and receives their return in EUR, the second is a USD-referenced investor unhedged who translates their return to USD at the prevailing exchange rate. The example excludes any fees.

Looking across currencies, the consequences for unhedged investors naturally vary but can be significant. In Table 2.3.1, we show how much investors invested in Hedge Funds of Funds (HFRIFOF) in USD would have received in their respective reference currency by investing at the start of each year and subsequently selling at the end of the year. The same exercise is repeated for 10 years.

FIGURE 2.3.1 Translated return of Eurostoxx 50 for EUR and USD Investors (unhedged)

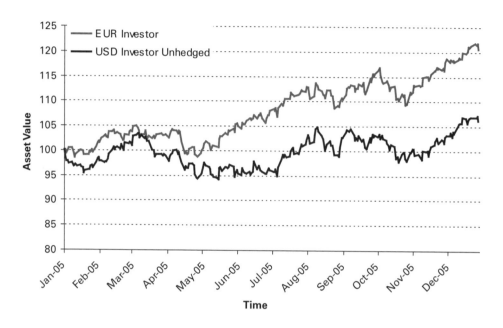

TABLE 2.3.1 HFRIFOF returns 2001–2010, USD, EUR unhedged, GBP unhedged

HRFI Funds of Funds Index Returns	USD	EUR	GBP
2001	2.8%	**8.8%**	5.7%
2002	1.0%	**-14.3%**	**-0.8%**
2003	11.6%	**-6.9%**	**0.7%**
2004	6.9%	**-0.9%**	**-0.6%**
2005	7.5%	**23.1%**	**19.8%**
2006	10.4%	**-0.9%**	**-3.0%**
2007	10.3%	**-0.3%**	8.8%
2008	-21.4%	-17.9%	**6.7%**
2009	11.5%	8.8%	**0.9%**
2010	5.7%	**13.1%**	5.7%

For simplification, we assume the HFRIFOF index to be representative of funds of funds returns. Highlighted numbers are those where the deviation to the USD return are greater than 5 per cent (which occurred in 75 per cent of the outcomes).

So far we have constructed a fairly simple assessment of currency risk – simple both for its assumption of a defined holding period and for the certainty of the results that arise when electing a historical time period! Without either an exact holding period or a reliable crystal ball with which to predict the future, investors should consider what the impact of adding non-reference currency exposure to their multi-asset-class portfolios will be on an *ongoing basis*. This in a more technical sense is defined as *volatility* risk – ever-present fluctuations in currency returns that underpin the translation risk. Herein lie many risks for investors that are at once variable by frequency, magnitude and certainty.

The lack of predictability in currency returns is a main source of risk. Fluctuations in currency pairs, also termed volatility, are a complex fusion of factors. Currency volatility – especially for those currencies that are non-managed – stem from an array of factors including the market participant's perception of future growth, inflation and, leading from this, interest rate differentials. Further influences such as non-profit-oriented central bank intervention, technical positioning of market participants, political risk factors and natural disasters, for example, are also contributors of price movements.

Given this, currency models that forecast fair value – frequently on more fundamental data – can be hopelessly wrong, at least in a near-term sense. On 15 September 2010 the Bank of Japan intervened to choke off unwanted yen strength. The yen had climbed to a 15-year high the previous day against the USD on the DPJ Kan vote win. The result of the intervention on 15 September was an intraday movement of over 3 per cent in USD/YEN. Conceivable therefore that an unhedged USD investor selling a yen holding of Y1 billion into USD (approx $12 million) ahead of the intervention would have received nearly $400,000 dollars more on translation than a day later.[3]

Measuring currency risk

Looking at some charts of currency volatility in a historical context invites a few important conclusions. Figure 2.3.2 shows the rolling 10-year average volatility of a basket of 13 currencies and one trade-weighted composite index assumed to have been held since 1971.[4] The volatility measure is based upon monthly returns.[5]

The first point is that aggregate 10-year risk in the markets has remained in a range of 8.5 per cent to 10.5 per cent over the whole 40-year period despite some obvious swings; for example, investors in the 10-year period preceding the late 1990s experienced some of the lowest foreign exchange volatility.

Strikingly, it is also evident that investors in recent times have suffered some of the highest foreign exchange volatility risk of the past 40 years.

Data used are monthly FX rates from January 1971 to December 2010. Volatility is the average of annualized 10-year rolling window volatilities of the 13 currencies and one composite used in our analysis.

FIGURE 2.3.2 Average volatility of currencies

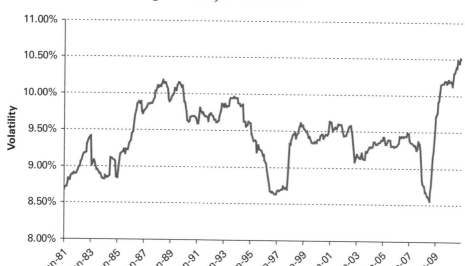

So how risky is foreign exchange compared with other asset classes? Extending this analysis further to compare currency volatility with other asset classes, it is worth highlighting that the volatility experienced by currency investors is substantially higher than the equivalent risk measure for Treasuries, corporate bonds and hedge funds. This is demonstrated clearly in Figure 2.3.3, where currency risk is depicted as a percentage of another asset class risk (currency/equities, for example). The effect of this analysis on asset managers is frequently cited as a reason why asset managers will hedge lower-risk asset classes.

Currency risk is the average volatility of the 14 currencies in Figure 2.3.2. Equity risk is defined as the volatility risk of the S&P 500; Treasury bond risk is defined as the volatility risk of Citi World Government Bond Index (USD); corporate bond risk is defined as the volatility risk of Citi World Broad Investment-Grade Bond Index (USD); and hedge funds risk is defined as volatility risk of HFRIFOF Index (USD). Both the volatility of the currencies and asset class indices are calculated using a 10-year rolling window of monthly returns.

Compared with world equities, risk is lower, at around 60 per cent (based upon an assumed annualized volatility of 16.5 per cent for MSCI World). We believe that this may understate the risk of currency volatility for equity investors. We draw this conclusion by observing currency risk during extreme periods of equity market risk. Figure 2.3.2 shows that the highest periods of foreign exchange risk often coincide with periods of extreme volatility in the stock markets. Falls in stock markets in 1987, 1998 and 2008 were also accompanied by spikes in foreign exchange currency risk. Unhedged equity investors usually suffer elevated currency risk at just the wrong time – when equity risk is at its most prevalent! This was certainly the case in recent times when unhedged investors in equities would have suffered some of the highest foreign exchange risk of the past 40 years.

FIGURE 2.3.3 Percentage of currency to asset class volatility

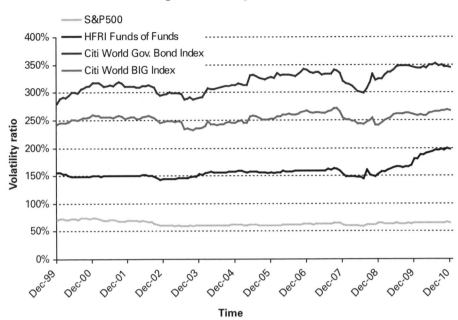

This analysis doesn't refer to the effect of correlations on overall portfolio volatility as well as any potential diversification benefit. This is beyond the scope of this analysis; suffice to say that there will be an impact.

The first part of this chapter was intended to expose the extent of foreign exchange risk but also how it has changed over time. As an aggregate analysis, currencies were neither trade nor volume weighted, nor adjusted for asset management trends. This was deliberate given that, from each investor's perspective, there is a unique currency risk associated with their portfolio that can be managed. It is also important to note that an analysis that takes the average will potentially understate the risks experienced by an investor with fewer currencies in their portfolio, overlooking short-term and often spiky variations in currency price levels.

Ultimately, we could easily replace the term volatility with timing risk. One is the cause, the other the effect. This extra uncertainty has implications, particularly for investors with undefined time horizons. Unintended but required conversion at specific points in time can be hugely impacted by timing risk, as we have noted.

So, taken altogether, this would imply that currency management is necessary.

Then why do so few investors hedge or manage the risk?

The only reasonable conclusion to be made is that unhedged investors are introducing risk into their portfolios. What isn't known is how much of this is intentionally or unintentionally accepted. An 'unknown known', possibly!

There are, after all, instances where investors very rationally opt for unhedged strategies. A USD-referenced investor taking exposure to gold in the fear of USD fiat money debasement is purposely unhedged. A GBP-referenced investor investing in Singaporean equities but believing that GBP will structurally weaken over the holding term may intentionally accept the translation risk. These, we would argue, are knowledge-based decisions, potentially correlation or tactically based. While some may disagree, all of the above would be viewed as rationalized decisions.

Dismantling the old wives' tale

But there is one assertion – an FX folklore, perhaps – that is so frequently heard among investors that its implications for foreign exchange management cannot be ignored. This is the claim that most currency pairs revert back to a starting point.

'Currency translation risk washes out,' is the view, usually supplemented by a time period such as 'in the long term'. Elaborating on this, some define long term as 10 years.

This is rarely, if ever, supported by empirical evidence. The claim is usually made as boldly as those in the UK who make the claim that the weather experienced at weekends is on average worse than the weather during the working week! (Has anyone analysed this?)

The implication is that hedging strategies may be unwarranted or even costly. Conversations around hedging are immediately derailed, rendered worthless. And though the formulation of this argument may appear awkward initially, the authors would like to point out that arguments made for currency reversion are not wholly unfounded, and can be supported by reference to specific economic theory and rationale. However, a discussion of this is beyond the scope of this chapter.

Instead of challenging the theory, we prefer to assess whether there is substance to the claim and later to concentrate on the behaviours that stem from this belief – notably an appeasement of investors' concerns about currency risk.

In the following passage, we analyse the assertion that currency pairs revert to prior levels (which we shall call a 'reversion'). Analysis is used to test and identify reversion patterns, studying the behaviour of multiple currency pairs. In a historical context, our analysis aims to show how often currencies revert to their prior levels and when this is likely to occur.

How frequently reversion occurs

To understand the results means to understand the framework for the analysis. The analysis uses monthly data for 20 currency pairs over the 1971 to 2010 period.[6] We test reversion by looking at rolling 10-year periods from January 1971 to December 2010 – a total of 360 10-year periods.

The analysis aims to reduce period-specific factors by introducing random interval selection. To do this, we randomly choose 100 set starting points which we then apply for all currency pairs (effectively examining just over a quarter of total possible periods). Then, for each of the randomly chosen 10-year periods, we count the number of months where a reversion occurred. We assume a reversion occurs when the exchange rate crosses the starting level, ie:

$$FX_{t-1} > FX_{start} \text{ and } FX_t < FX_{start}$$
$$\text{or } FX_{t-1} < FX_{start} \text{ and } FX_t > FX_{start}$$

– where FX_t is the month-end exchange rate of month t, and FX_{start} is the exchange rate at the starting point. We then compute the average number of reversions for the 100 periods per currency. Then we represent this as an average across all the currencies.

The authors wish to point out that by using monthly data, it is conceivable that a reversion may occur on several occasions within a month. Furthermore, the analysis results may be reduced for intra-month periods where reversion occurred but where this was a temporary phenomenon only – not enduring until the month end.

Lastly, we run the same analysis looking at both nominal and real exchange rates where the latter are adjusted for differences in inflation levels from the starting point.

We begin with the results on a nominal currency basis. Figure 2.3.4 shows how often, on average, the currency pairs revert back to their starting level in each 10-year rolling period. All results are expressed as a percentage of total 120 months (10 years × 12 months).

The results are truly staggering. Most currencies revert back to their starting level only *3 to 4 per cent* of months during each 10-year period. This equates to a reversion occurring during just four or five months of the total 10-year period. The solid line is the average of all the 20 currency pairs, which is 3.9 per cent of months (just under five out of 120 months).

FIGURE 2.3.4 Average % of reversions to starting level over each 10-year period: nominal exchange rate

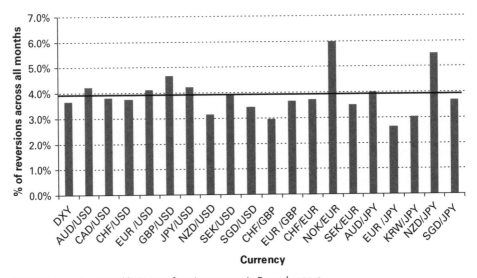

NOTE Data used are monthly FX rates from January 1971 to December 2010

FIGURE 2.3.5 Average % of reversions to starting level over each 10-year period: real exchange rate

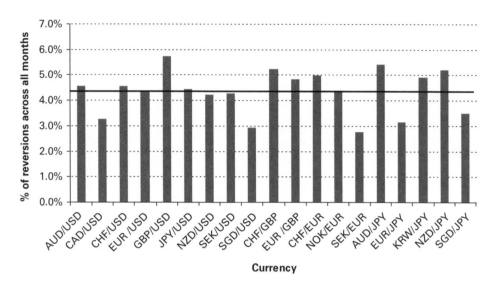

NOTE Data used are monthly FX rates from January 1971 to December 2010

The results for real exchange rates are similar. Figure 2.3.5 is the result of the same analysis but instead looks at how frequently reversion occurs based on real exchange rates. Most currencies revert back to their starting level only 4 per cent of months during each 10-year period; and viewed as an average of all currencies, that is only four to five months where a reversion occurs. The average number of touches for the currencies is around 4.4 per cent probability (which could also be expressed as less than five of 120 months) during each 10-year period. This is depicted by the solid horizontal line.

The first conclusion is that these analysis results contradict any claim that reversion events happen frequently. An unhedged investor hoping for multiple reversion points to crystallize potential gains on portfolio positions would have been disappointed.

And where reversion didn't occur?

Perhaps most problematically, the average percentage of 10-year rolling periods examined where reversion did not occur at all was 13 per cent. An average of 13 per cent of periods examined for these currencies experienced no reversion at all over the 10-year analysed periods.

To explore this in more depth, we show the results per currency following the same analysis methodology as previously, separating the results by nominal and real exchange rate.

Figure 2.3.6 shows how many rolling 10-year periods as a percentage of total experienced no reversion at all by currency taking nominal rates. The solid horizontal line is the average of the 20 currency pairs, which is 13 per cent.

Figure 2.3.7 shows how many rolling 10-year periods as a percentage of the total experienced no reversion at all by currency taking real rates. The solid horizontal line is the average of the 20 currency pairs, which is 8.5 per cent.

FIGURE 2.3.6 Percentage of 10-year periods when no reversion occurs: nominal exchange rate

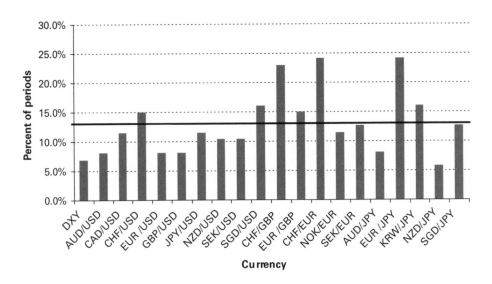

FIGURE 2.3.7 Percentage of periods when no reversion occurs: real exchange rate

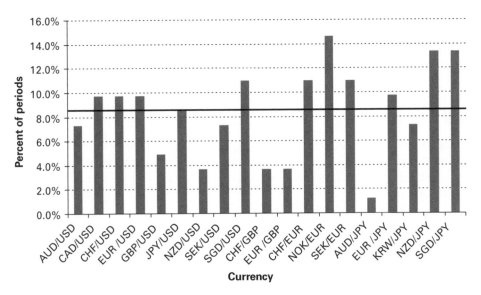

So, by way of conclusion, for the majority of the months in the investors' holding period, an unhedged investor experiences a translation risk.

When reversion is more likely

Now we want to see when the reversion occurs, testing the thesis that reversion occurs in the longer term. We aim to identify any patterns, perhaps a clustering of more frequently witnessed periods, in which reversion to the starting currency level occurs. Or to promote a modification to the assertion of currency pair reversion over a 10-year holding period – an argument that could be used to rationalize investors' hedging behaviour. In the event that the time period for reversion is proven to be unpredictable or even random, then the conclusion is that investors should pay attention to currency translation risk unless wishing to fully accept this uncertainty.

As before, the analysis is based on 10-year periods. For each of these periods, if the currency touches its starting level, we count the years between the starting date and the touch date. We accumulate these results per currency, per 10-year period. These results are aggregated across all time periods and currencies. We present the results in a histogram format – showing, as a percentage of total reversions, in which periods investors were most likely to experience a reversion. For fear of histogram fatigue, we have shown an aggregated histogram only; however, these are available per currency.

Figure 2.3.8 shows the percentage of reversions occurring in each year for nominal exchange rates.

Figure 2.3.9 shows the percentage of reversions occurring in each year for real rates.

FIGURE 2.3.8 Distribution of reversions: nominal exchange rates

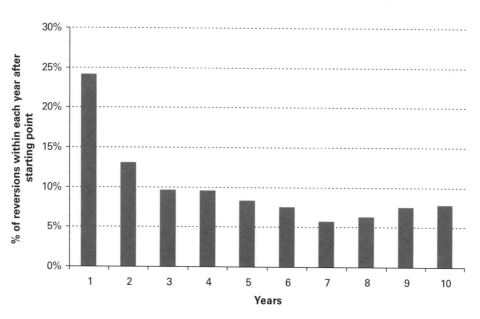

FIGURE 2.3.9 Distribution of reversions: real exchange rates

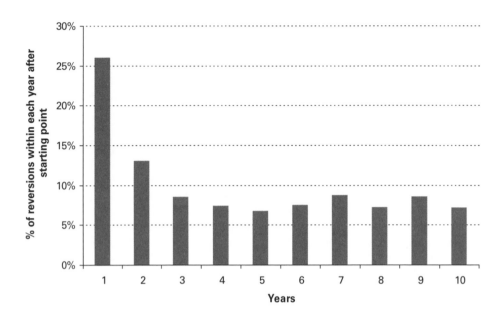

The results defy popular belief. As a percentage of total reversions, most reversions occur early on – substantially within the first three years. In fact, most of the reversions occur in the first year by a long stretch. This marks a stark contradiction to any longer term claim.

At this stage, it's also worth recalling that an average of 13 per cent of periods examined for these currencies experienced no reversion at all over the 10-year analysed periods which were excluded from the histogram results above.

When translation risk leads to negative returns

With the support of empirical evidence, this is an irritating finding measured against the claim that currency exchange rates revert.

A question that is perhaps more important for investors is how much translation risk leads to losses when converting back to reference currency. The question is begged as to whether the risk of leaving positions unhedged leads to a gain or loss upon translation. In order to do this, we have assumed that where no reversion occurs, conversion takes place at the end of the 10th-year holding anniversary. Currency loss is assumed from the sale of an unhedged currency position at the end of each 10-year period.

Figure 2.3.10 shows, as a percentage of all periods where no reversion occurred, the number of 10-year periods in which investors would have suffered a loss. The solid line is the average percentage of losses across the 20 currency pairs, which is 63 per cent.

FIGURE 2.3.10 Percentage of loss periods given no reversion: nominal exchange rate

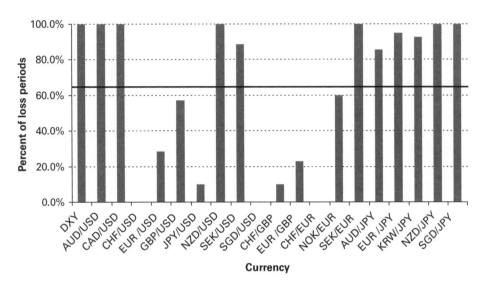

Figure 2.3.11 shows, as a percentage of all periods where no reversion occurred, the number of 10-year periods in which investors would have suffered a loss. The solid line is the average percentage of losses across the 20 currency pairs, which is 55 per cent.

FIGURE 2.3.11 Percentage of loss periods given no reversion: real exchange rate

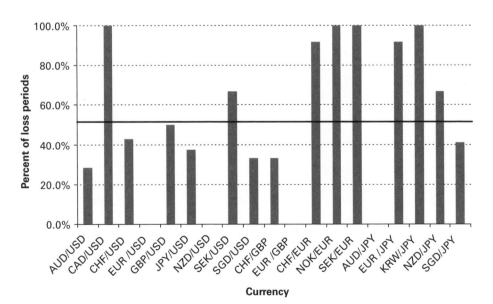

Our calculations show that investors across this group of currencies would have experienced a loss on translation in over 55 per cent of cases. Specifically, investors in AUD, CAD, KRW and NOK generally experienced losses while investors in CHF, JPY and SGD experienced mostly profits on translation. This mirrors broad currency performance, of course, but the key point remains that, historically speaking, currency risk was more likely to lead to translation loss than gain.

This again demonstrates that the behaviour of currencies is difficult to forecast and unhedged investors cannot guarantee that currencies will lead to profit at the end of the investment holding period.

Results

What we have shown is the extreme unpredictability of currencies. The first set of analysis results contradicted any claim that reversion events happened frequently within any holding period. The second set of analysis showed that reversion was more likely to occur in the near term rather than in the long term. Perhaps worse still, there were many occasions when currencies didn't revert at all; and when this occurred, losses on translation occurred in the majority of occasions.

All this would suggest that the FX folklore – the anticipated pattern of reversion – is at best uncertain and at worst improbable.

Conclusion

In this chapter we have explored currency risk at its most basic: translation risk. We have highlighted how the choice to hedge or not can have substantial implications on potential returns.

In particular, our analysis has shown that the widely held assertion that currency pairs revert to prior levels is overly simplistic if not plain wrong, leading to a false sense of certainty and ill-advised consequences for investor hedging behaviour. It has been our intention through this analysis to promote a superior, informed dialogue with investors on currency risk and its management.

Notes

1 Citi Private Bank can help support all investors' currency needs. These include hedging strategies, wealth preservation strategies and speculative needs. Citi Private Bank is a gateway to Citi's vast resources. Citi has a long and extensive history of providing foreign exchange services to clients. CitiFX, a division of Citi's Institutional Clients Group, offers a comprehensive foreign exchange and local market service to its diverse client base around the world. With a presence in 83 countries, CitiFX's 1,500+ professionals deliver an unparalleled breadth and depth of knowledge to clients, helping them to achieve their financial

objectives. CitiFX provides pricing in over 100 major and exotic currencies in plain vanilla and exotic products, as well as offering a comprehensive suite of investible products. By providing its clients with the broadest possible access to the global foreign exchange market, CitiFX helps them meet tomorrow's challenges today.

2 Readers should consult their banker for further information on Citi Foreign Exchange Management.

3 The authors would also like to thank the contributions of others within this article, including Lei Xu, Analyst, Investment Lab, EMEA.

4 Opinions expressed in this chapter are those of the authors and may differ from the opinions expressed by other businesses or affiliates of Citigroup, Inc. To adjust for this, Citi employs a sophisticated framework for analysing and adjusting recommended hedging policy that includes analysis of currency correlations in the context of the assets and liabilities held. This helps identify appropriate levels of hedge ratio.

5 The data used in this analysis was extracted from Bloomberg and Global Financial Data.

6 Over-the-counter derivative contracts, including foreign exchange transactions, are unsecured obligations of Citibank, NA. They are not bank deposits and are not insured by the Federal Deposit Insurance Corporation or any other governmental entity. They are also not guaranteed by Citibank NA or any of its affiliates and are subject to investment risks, including possible loss of the principal amount invested.

7 Country/regional risk: the possibility that adverse political events, financial problems or natural disasters in a country or region will cause investments in that country or region to lose value. The risks of investing in emerging or developing markets can be substantially greater than the risks of investing in developed markets.

8 Currency risk: one currency may decline in value versus another. The value of a multi-currency portfolio will fluctuate with exchange rates.

Notes

1 This is especially the case where a currency is non-pegged.

2 Unhedged implies that the investor is exposed to full currency translation risk, for better or for worse.

3 Example assumes movement from 83.05 to 85.75 between 14 and 15 September 2010. Exercise is gross of any fees.

4 The analysis embeds the following currencies, all against the US dollar: Australian dollar (AUD), Canadian dollar (CAD), Swiss franc (CHF), Danish krone (DKK), euro (EUR), British pound (GBP), Japanese yen (JPY), Korean won (KRW), Norwegian krone (NOK), New Zealand dollar (NZD), Swedish kronor (SEK), Singaporean dollar (SGD), Taiwanese dollar (TWD) and the DXY, which is a composite index of US dollar.

5 Volatility is calculated as annualized standard deviation.

6 The currency pairs used were AUD/USD, CAD/USD,CHF/USD, EUR /USD, GBP/USD, JPY/ USD, NZD/USD, SEK/USD, SGD/USD,CHF/GBP, EUR /GBP, CHF/EUR, NOK/EUR, SEK/ EUR, AUD/JPY, EUR /JPY, KRW/JPY, NZD/JPY, SGD/JPY and DXY, which is a composite index of US dollar.

PART THREE
Pensions and relieving the tax burden

are your assets in safe hands?

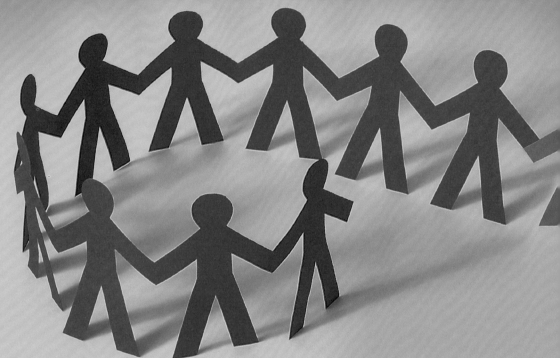

With regular changes being made to legislation, the legal aspects of financial planning can be complicated.

Davies Arnold Cooper LLP's private client team offers an expert and discreet service to individuals and their families to protect their assets, minimise tax payments and provide income security.

Contact
Ian Lane, partner

020 7293 4801
ilane@dac.co.uk

www.dac.co.uk/privateclient

DAVIES ARNOLD COOPER

Pensions:
a new revolution

**IAN LANE, DAVIES ARNOLD COOPER LLP,
AND ADRIAN MEE, MATTIOLI WOODS**

Pensions legislation in the UK has changed dramatically over the last five years. Prior to the announcement dealt with in this chapter, there were notable changes that took effect on so-called 'A Day', 6 April 2006, which were then amended further over the last few years. An observer might think that the 'A Day' changes were of great note but the new proposals contained in draft legislation published by HM Revenue and Customs on 14 October 2010 will change the fundamental basis of pension legislation in the UK.

The headline news is that the coalition government has taken the final steps to break away from the requirement that a pensioner must purchase an annuity at some point following retirement. This was always a great stumbling block to greater flexibility in pensions planning but was a jealously guarded area for the insurance industry. Many individuals resented the fact that, once the annuity was purchased, the pension fund they had saved over their entire life 'disappeared' forever into the insurance company's coffers. It was particularly galling for relatives of those who had bought an annuity and then died within a very short time leaving, at best, a widow's or widower's pension of half the original amount. The insurance companies always justified their stance on the basis of 'mutuality': that is to say, for all those annuitants who died early, just as many lived a long life in retirement and, as a result, the companies were able to maximize returns to them. I am not sure what comfort there was for those left behind without an income or with a greatly diminished one that those others were better provided for!

The changes proposed by the coalition government are generally to be welcomed as they would appear to usher in a more flexible approach to pensions provision in the UK. There is, I think, a recognition that the old system was no longer working and had been brought into stark contrast in this age of very low interest rates and limited investment growth rates.

As with all legislation, however, there will be winners and there will be losers. This article is intended to outline the provisions which are (at the time of writing) still in the draft stages. As seems to be popular these days, the proposals will be staggered and given effect over two tax years (2010–11 and 2011–12). I understand part of the reason for this is the need to reprogramme the Revenue's computers in relation to the changes on protected rights discussed below.

The changes to commence from 6 April 2011 are as follows:

Limits on pension contributions

An individual is entitled to contribute a maximum fixed statutory amount to their pension on an annual basis. This annual contribution allowance, which for the tax year ended 5 April 2011 is £255,000, will be reduced to £50,000. This is clearly a massive drop in the allowance which had been increased greatly under the previous Labour government. Thus the total contributions that it is possible to make into a pension will be considerably reduced. Of course, the reduction limits the tax relief available but from the government's perspective it reduces the tax loss to HM Treasury. For those with the ability to do so, it would seem the ideal opportunity to make large contributions to pension now before the allowance reduces so dramatically. However, there are what are known as 'anti-forestalling' measures to prevent excessive additions to pension in the current year.

Although the amount of the allowance has reduced dramatically, full tax relief will be available at marginal rates up to 50 per cent on that contribution. In addition, the government is going to introduce a three-year carry forward of unused allowances from previous years. Therefore, those who have not made contributions up to the equivalent of £50,000 per annum and who are able to do so will be able to carry forward the unused allowance and use it in later years. The intent of the legislation is to blend any contributions out across three tax years up to a maximum of £50,000 per annum. By way of example:

> During tax years 2008–9 and 2009–10, George makes pension contributions of £30,000 and £50,000. His contribution for the current year is £40,000.
> Over the three years the total contributions are £120,000. George has an unused allowance of £30,000 to carry forward to the tax year 2011–12.
> However, if George makes a contribution larger than £50,000 during one of the tax years in question, the amount of his carry-forward allowance is affected.
> If George had made no contributions in the earlier tax years he can use the carry forward allowance for all three tax years into 2011–12 and thus contribute £150,000.

Annuities

As headlined above, the requirement to purchase an annuity by the age of 75 (which was removed from 'A Day' for persons in 'alternatively secured pensions') will be removed in all cases from 6 April 2011. Some pension products already allow deferment for the purchase of annuity beyond the age of 75 but there will now be no compulsion to purchase an annuity; this will be enshrined in legislation. It cannot be stressed enough how revolutionary this proposal is for all individuals who will be making pension contributions and retiring in the years to come. In addition, it will now be possible to take sums of tax-free cash after the age of 75, another flexible innovation previously unavailable.

Income drawdown

The existing rules, in relation to income drawdown after retirement, for 'unsecured pensions' and alternatively secured pensions will be abolished. All such pensions will be converted into 'capped' drawdown pensions. This is similar to the existing unsecured pension, where income can be drawn down up to a capped amount under the current rules. The losers from this change are those with unsecured pensions who, at the moment, can draw up to a maximum income of 120 per cent (of equivalent annuity rates) from their pension fund. Capped drawdown is likely to represent a reduction for anyone on an unsecured pension because on a new capped drawdown pension, the maximum income will be only 100 per cent. Persons in alternatively secured pensions will be better off because they are currently limited to drawing an income of between 55 per cent and 90 per cent from their pension fund each year.

It is understood that the income limits for capped drawdown pensions mentioned above will be reviewed every three years and then annually after age 75.

The next revolutionary change is the introduction of a new type of drawdown called 'flexible drawdown'. This will allow the drawdown of all the funds in a pension, but subject to normal income tax rules. This option is, however, available only where an individual has a source of secure income (which can be other pensions and/or State benefits) and meets the annual 'minimum income requirement' of £20,000. The minimum income requirement will include the State pension itself and any other earned and unearned income.

This is a very radical departure, allowing the owner of the pension to draw down the entire pension fund during their lifetime, subject to the minimum income requirement, which may be met quite easily in a number of cases.

Inevitably, with one hand the government gives and with the other it takes back. The drawback of this arrangement is that the fund will be taxed as income and will therefore be subject to income tax at the individual's marginal rate which could be as high as 50 per cent depending again on that individual's circumstances. If that fund is spent as income during lifetime and thus does not form part of that individual's estate on death, then there is no further tax cost. However, if having incurred a high income tax charge to recover the funds from his pension, the individual dies with the fund in their own hands, their estate would be subject to inheritance tax at 40 per cent on their death. Assuming an income tax rate of 50 per cent (which will not apply in all cases) and a subsequent inheritance tax charge at 40 per cent, it is likely (taking allowances into account) that the total tax burden would be about 70 per cent of the funds so released.

Double taxation is not a welcome prospect for anyone but it is clearly the 'price' that the government intends to exact to allow this level of freedom with these funds, which would otherwise have been locked up in annuities or various forms of drawdown pension. So, although this appears to be a radical, flexible and welcome departure, there are taxation consequences which could make this a very expensive alternative.

Death benefit: lump sums

At present, on the death of a pension holder under 75 years of age, where that person is not drawing funds from their pension, any lump sum death benefit is payable to their beneficiaries free of tax, and if they are receiving payments from the funds the death benefit is subject to a 35 per cent income tax charge. Under the new rules any funds which are crystallized will now be subject to an income tax charge of 55 per cent of the death benefit lump sum.

If death occurs after 75, there will be a new option to pay out the fund as a lump sum, less the same income tax charge of 55 per cent. Under present rules that sum could be taxed as an 'unauthorized benefit' at an effective tax rate of up to 82 per cent, and therefore this is a welcome change, reducing the tax payable in those circumstances.

It must be borne in mind that this system will enable an individual to pass their pension fund to their family or beneficiaries as a lump sum, subject to tax at 55 per cent, and that no inheritance tax would be charged on that fund, which would be the case under current rules.

A minimum of 25 per cent of the pension fund can be drawn at retirement in either a one-off payment or can be partially drawn. This must be drawn before age 75; otherwise it is lost.

As death benefits prior to retirement can be paid tax free, the decision to take tax-free cash is important. Once taken, the tax charge to distribute the remaining capital will become 55 per cent. For this reason, partial tax-free cash may be drawn to provide an income for retirement at the same time as making the best death benefits position possible for beneficiaries.

Inheritance tax

Inheritance tax will continue to be payable where the pension holder has:

- nominated their estate to receive the pension fund (this is unusual and would generally be advised against); or
- they have control over the payment of the death benefits under the pension. This will not normally be the case, as in normal circumstances the trustees of the pension fund will have complete discretion over payment of pension benefits and therefore inheritance tax will not be payable.

There are anti-avoidance measures which are currently incurred where a member fails to draw benefits from their pension while in ill health. In those circumstances, as mentioned above, no inheritance tax is payable on the death benefit. Under the new proposals, these charges will be removed.

The above sets out the changes which it is intended be brought into force from 6 April 2011. As you will see, overall these represent a radical change in the way in which pensions are to be managed and taxed and may open up some inheritance tax planning possibilities in relation to pensions held beyond the age of 75.

Further changes to come into effect from 6 April 2012

Lifetime allowance

At present the 'lifetime allowance' (the maximum sum which can be held in your pension fund without excess tax charges) is £1.8 million. This allowance will reduce to £1.5 million. Anyone who has significant pension savings can register for 'fixed protection' and retain a lifetime allowance of £1.8 million but registration must take place before 6 April 2012; once registration has been made, no further contributions can be made to that fund. This provision does not include persons who previously registered for either 'enhanced' or 'primary' protection under the preceding legislation. Those persons will not be eligible to claim fixed protection under the new rules.

Protected rights

At present, a 'protected rights' fund must be separated away from other benefits on death. It cannot be commuted for a lump sum and can only be used to provide a spouse's pension on the pension holder's death.

From 6 April 2012, funds derived from contributions from the government on the opt-out from SERPS (subsequently S2P), which are known as protected rights funds, will be treated in the same way as the other funds in the pension. It will be permissible for them to be merged with other non-protected rights pension funds derived from normal employee/employer pension contributions. The limitations set out above which currently apply will be removed and any death benefit and lump sum payment from protected rights funds will not be subject to inheritance tax.

Planning and review

All the above information is based on our current understanding of the coalition government's proposals, which are included in the Finance Bill 2011 and will become law some time later in 2011. As is always the case, please seek professional advice before taking any action. However, in view of the radical nature of the shake-up of pensions provision, this is an area which should be reviewed by all those who are making pension provisions (and most especially those who are nearing retirement) as a matter of some urgency.

Big decisions follow you around.

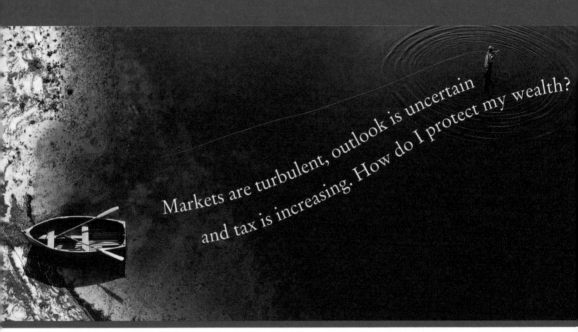

Markets are turbulent, outlook is uncertain and tax is increasing. How do I protect my wealth?

Our Private Client team understand that the big decisions you have to make are sometimes difficult, often intensely personal, always with you.

To explore this and other big decisions please call **Eric Williams** on **0121 232 5171** or visit our website.

Private Client Practitioner
top 25
most admired companies

www.grant-thornton.co.uk/privateclient

Audit • Tax • Advisor

© 2011 Grant Thornton UK LLP. All rights reserved.
'Grant Thornton' means Grant Thornton UK LLP, a limited liability partnership. Grant Thornton UK LLP is a member firm within Grant Thornton International Ltd ('Grant Thornton International'). Grant Thornton International and the member firms are not a worldwide partnership. Services are delivered by the member firms independentl

Surviving a high tax regime

**ERIC WILLIAMS,
GRANT THORNTON UK LLP**

F or the first time since 1988, the top rate of income tax in the UK is more than 40
per cent. While the introduction of the 50 per cent top rate by the last Labour
government was probably politically motivated, the huge structural deficit inherited
in 2010 by the coalition government has meant that it is also politically impossible in
the short term for the new government to reduce that rate. Indeed, George Osborne
has already indicated that the 50 per cent rate is likely to remain for the duration of
this parliament at least. Together with increased National Insurance rates for
employers (13.8 per cent from 6 April 2011) and the 1 per cent additional employee
National Insurance charge on salaries and bonuses without limit, this is representative
of a higher tax regime for the UK's wealth generators than they have experienced for
22 years. Managing personal wealth in this new high tax environment against the
added background of an unprecedented level of attack by HMRC on tax avoidance
has become a key agenda item for many high earners and investors.

So, what can be done by investors, directors and company owners in the face of
this increased tax threat to personal wealth?

Income tax or capital gains tax

For the 2011–12 tax year, the 50 per cent income tax rate kicks in at taxable income
over £150,000. Taxable income between £35,000 and £150,000 is taxed at 40 per
cent. The personal tax allowance is also completely lost where annual income is over
£112,950 and is phased out for incomes between £100,000 and £112,950, creating a
marginal rate of over 60 per cent for some individuals. In comparison, the first
£10,600 of capital gains are exempt and so not subject to any tax, with gains in
excess of this amount being subject to Capital Gains Tax (CGT) at rates between 10
per cent and 28 per cent. Therefore, structuring returns that are subject to CGT
instead of income tax is an obvious method of mitigating the impact of higher income
tax rates.

Employee share schemes

Employee share schemes are a means of both incentivizing employees and delivering returns subject to CGT. The disparity between the rates of CGT and income tax mean that equity reward schemes are a tax-efficient way of rewarding key employees, including private company owner directors.

An unapproved share scheme is straightforward, involving the issue of share options to an employee without HMRC approval. On the exercise of these options the employee will face an income tax charge on the difference between the price paid and the market value of the shares at the date of exercise. However, any subsequent growth in value will be subject to CGT and not income tax on an eventual sale.

There are also a number of other HMRC approved share schemes which, although not as flexible, offer a number of tax benefits and are often structured such that the whole of the increase in the market value of the shares from the grant of the option until sale is subject to CGT, so crystallizing a significant tax advantage for the employee.

In situations where it is either not desired or not possible to put in place share schemes (eg because it is not wished to dilute existing shareholders' interests), it is still possible to deliver a return to employees which will be subject to 28 per cent CGT rather than income tax, together with a tax deduction for the employer, by issuing securities to directors or employees which can acquire increased value subject to business performance. This allows a long-term incentive plan to be put in place which is tax efficient for both the employee and the employer, while aligning employee or director reward with the commercial objectives of the company.

Owner directors

The top rate of corporation tax is currently 27 per cent and will fall to 24 per cent by 1 April 2014. Some company owner directors take the view that it is better to retain profits within their company to take advantage of lower corporate tax rates, deferring extraction until such time as the funds are required personally. Extraction of accumulated profits by way of dividend perhaps in the next parliament, if tax rates come down again at some point, or by way of a sale, equity release or liquidation of the company, giving rise to a CGT charge, would ultimately result in a much lower overall tax cost than paying 50 per cent plus National Insurance Contributions (NICs) now.

It is important to note that retaining investments within a company could impact on the availability of CGT and inheritance tax reliefs, so advice should be sought if this is something being considered.

The use of loans

The old Companies Act prohibition on borrowing by directors from their company no longer applies; so owner directors could also consider borrowing from their company, subject to approval through an appropriate resolution. Accumulated profits could then be released in a more tax-efficient way, facilitating a repayment of any such loans at a later date. The maximum tax charge on such loans would be a one-off charge of 25 per cent payable by any close company (where the loan is to a shareholder or person or trust associated with a shareholder) plus a relatively modest personal tax charge based on the official rate of interest (currently 4 per cent), meaning the effective income tax rate on the use of these funds for a 50 per cent taxpayer is only 2 per cent per annum on rates as at May 2011. Also, when the loan is repaid or written off, the 25 per cent one-off charge is repaid to the company by HMRC.

These tax charges are clearly lower than the immediate charges at 50 per cent or 40 per cent plus NICs on salaries or bonuses, and the tax deferral achieved through this loan mechanism can be made permanent where the loan is repaid out of future income or capital gain, or is written off, in which case a tax charge arises on the individual at the dividend rate. This rate is currently 36.11 per cent for a 50 per cent taxpayer, but would fall in the event of a future reduction in the top rate of tax.

Employee benefit trusts and employer-financed retirement benefit schemes

Loans from employee benefit trusts (EBTs) or employer-financed retirement benefits schemes (EFRBSs) have sometimes been used as a mechanism for mitigating the tax charges which would arise if such amounts were instead paid as salaries or bonuses by companies.

However, new legislation effective from 9 December 2010 and formally announced in the budget on 23 March 2011, in relation to 'disguised remuneration', triggers an income tax charge when funds are transferred by an employer to the trustees of an EBT, EFRBS or a similar trust or when such trustees earmark or lend funds within the trust for an individual's benefit. 'Earmark' is not defined; so all sorts of transactions will potentially be caught by this legislation, even where the individual beneficiary may have no legal right to draw the funds and in fact may not benefit from them.

The severity and wide-reaching nature of this new legislation reflects the toughening of HMRC's stance on tax avoidance, and such planning is probably now only for those brave souls who are prepared to take on HMRC through the courts. Indeed, a loan from the company itself is now likely to be more tax efficient as noted above.

Taxation of investments

For investors, the exploitation of the disparity between the 28 per cent top rate of CGT and the higher income tax rates of 40 per cent and 50 per cent should also be a key tax planning objective.

Before even considering paying tax, investors should seek to maximize the use of tax exempt investment structures, making sure, for instance, that they are using their annual ISA allowance (£10,200 for the current year), of which half can be saved in cash. An ISA is ideal as a tax-exempt structure for holding a combination of equities and cash or, for those with a higher risk profile, wholly equities.

Utilizing your spouse's allowance

Married investors may want to consider transferring income-producing assets to a spouse to ensure that that their spouse's personal allowance and basic rate tax bands are being fully utilized. Undertaking this transfer could save the couple more than £10,000 for 40 per cent taxpayers based on the current tax rates, increasing further if the spouse making the transfer is a 50 per cent taxpayer. Sharing investments to double up on the annual CGT allowance (£10,100 for 2010–11) is also a good idea.

Pension contributions

Contributions to approved pension funds are an extremely tax-efficient way of investing. In addition to tax relief on the contribution, the fund will roll up free of all income tax and CGT.

However, from 6 April 2011, the annual allowance for pension contributions is reduced from £255,000 to £50,000 as part of yet more pension legislation which also reduces the lifetime pension fund allowance from £1.8 million to £1.5 million, albeit with protection provisions for those already over the new lower limit. This legislation is complex and specialist advice should always be sought before making contributions to an approved pensions scheme.

Tax-efficient investments

Recent changes to pensions legislation have reduced the amount an individual can invest in a pension and still receive full tax benefits. As a result, many people are reviewing their wider savings and investment strategies.

Some examples of tax-favoured investments that offer tax relief on the amount invested are Enterprise Investment Schemes (EISs), Venture Capital Trusts (VCTs) and Business Premises Renovation Allowances (BPRAs). Historically EISs and VCTs have been rightly viewed as high risk from an investment perspective, with capital losses often offsetting the income tax benefits. However, there are many types of underlying investments that can be made within EIS, VCT and BPRA funds, allowing advisers to pick investments which suit the investor's needs. As with all investments, advice should be sought from a specialist prior to investing in these tax-favoured products.

Investment structures

The true success of an investment portfolio is determined by returns after tax. While it is advisable to get the investment strategy right first, it is essential to then consider the most tax-efficient structure for the chosen investment strategy. Some of the options for structuring investments which seek to defer or mitigate tax charges are considered further below.

Unit trusts and open-ended investment companies

Unit trusts and open-ended investment companies (OEICs) are collective investment schemes that pool capital from a large number of investors and invest the money in one or more asset classes.

Such funds, assuming that they are UK resident, will be subject to UK corporation tax at 20 per cent on income received. However, no corporation tax is due on the gains made within the fund. Instead a gain arises when units in a unit trust (or shares in an OEIC) are sold by the investor with any gains subject to CGT. Consequently, if, as is common, the investment strategy is biased to capital growth both within the fund and in the investor's hands, this is an attractive way of generating tax-efficient returns through exposure to CGT instead of income tax. Offshore funds benefit from tax-free roll-up but the rules for these funds are complex and individuals should seek professional advice before investing in, or disposing of, any offshore fund investments.

Investment bonds

An investment bond is essentially a single-premium life policy with a UK resident or non-UK resident provider. Income and gains within a UK bond will be subject to corporation tax at 20 per cent. However, income and capital gains within an offshore bond are received tax free and the funds invested roll up free of all taxes, making offshore bonds more tax efficient over time. However, the income tax charge on encashment (see below) makes the CGT-based unit trust or OEIC alternatives much more tax efficient for 50 per cent or 40 per cent taxpayers, even after 'top-slicing relief', which reduces the level of tax due in some cases by averaging the gain over the period of the bond.

A policyholder can make withdrawals of up to 5 per cent of the amount invested in the bond each year without incurring an immediate income tax charge. This 5 per cent allowance is cumulative, so any unused part can be carried forward to future years, provided that the total withdrawals do not exceed 100 per cent of the original capital.

The 5 per cent allowance is not a tax-free allowance. When the bond is ultimately cashed in, all withdrawals are added to the final value of the bond in order to calculate the gain, which will be subject to income tax at the investor's marginal income tax rate. A gain on an onshore bond will come with a deemed income tax credit of 20 per cent reducing this liability, whereas there is no deemed tax credit attaching to gains on offshore bonds.

Structuring investments

The tax structuring of investments is a specialist area in its own right. It is no longer enough simply to decide upon asset classes, allocation and geographical spread and then leave matters to an investment manager. The tax playing field is not level and careful consideration needs to be given to the impact of different tax structures when selecting the most appropriate investment holding vehicles for a chosen investment activity.

Tax planning

The government and HMRC have deployed a range of tactics to discourage tax avoidance, but it is important to remember that, unlike tax evasion, tax planning or tax avoidance is not illegal. Taxpayers have a right to legally arrange their tax affairs in order to minimize their tax bill, just as HMRC has the right to challenge this where it believes the law has not been interpreted correctly.

The key is to ensure that appropriate tax advice is taken and that any planning arrangements put in place are robust and will stand up to close scrutiny from HMRC should they be challenged at a later date.

Taxation of UK resident non-domiciliaries

PATRICK HARNEY, FORSTERS LLP

The Finance Act 2008 introduced radical changes to the taxation of resident non-domiciled individuals. This chapter seeks to provide an overview of those changes and some practical tax planning advice for non-domiciliaries. Despite the changes introduced by the Finance Act 2008, the UK remains a fiscally attractive jurisdiction for well-advised non-domiciled individuals.

Overview

UK resident and domiciled individuals are subject to UK income tax and capital gains tax on their worldwide income and gains, and to UK inheritance tax on their worldwide assets. By contrast, UK residents who are not domiciled in the UK are able to enjoy a significantly more favourable tax treatment as follows:

1 Access to the 'remittance basis of taxation' on foreign income and gains (albeit subject to the payment of a £30,000 tax charge, in the case of long-term residents);

2 Non-application of some of the capital gains tax offshore anti-avoidance legislation;

3 Inheritance tax on UK assets only, coupled with the possibility of insulating all assets from inheritance tax even where the non-domiciled individual subsequently becomes UK domiciled or deemed domiciled.

What is the difference between residence and domicile?

Domicile must not be confused with nationality. In general terms, a person may be said to be domiciled in the place where they have made their permanent home.

STRONG TEAMS
OUTSTANDING INDIVIDUALS

At Forsters, we pride ourselves in handling our private clients' affairs with the utmost integrity, discretion and professionalism. Our Mayfair-based team, recognised as one of the top advisers in the UK, also offers superlative off-shore trust and international jurisdictional expertise.

Our advice on wills, tax and trust planning, estate administration and family matrimonial issues is second to none. We help UK and international clients structure and protect family wealth, business assets and private property.

Our lawyers passionately believe in working with their clients to create tailored solutions to maximise their interests and achieve the best possible outcomes.

All of which places us, we believe, in a class of our own.

For further information, please call Patrick Harney on:

020 7863 8333
www.forsters.co.uk

Forsters LLP • Solicitors • 31 Hill Street • Mayfair • London • W1J 5LS

Domicile, in English law, has a more technical meaning than is the case in most other jurisdictions, particularly continental jurisdictions where the concept is closer to that of habitual residence. A person is domiciled in a jurisdiction rather than in a country. Thus, in a federal system, such as for example Australia, a person is domiciled in a particular state.

A person will be regarded as a resident in the UK if:

1 they stay in the UK for more than 182 days in any tax year. This is the overriding rule; or

2 they visit the UK for an average of 91 days or more per year over a period of three or more consecutive tax years. In this case, for short-term visitors, residence status starts usually from the beginning of the fourth tax year. Residence may begin before that if the person intends to make such visits and actually does make them.

Unfortunately, the view of HMRC in their booklet HMRC6 (http://www.hmrc.gov.uk/cnr/hmrc6.pdf) is that spending less than 91 days on average over a three-year period in the UK does not of itself guarantee non-resident status. It states that other factors are also relevant, including an individual's connections to the UK such as family, property, business and social connections. In short, professional advice should be taken in order to ascertain the UK residence status of an individual.

What is the remittance basis of taxation?

The remittance basis of taxation is a special tax regime that applies to non-domiciled taxpayers who make an election in their tax return to be taxed on the remittance basis and pay the £30,000 remittance basis charge, if applicable. Where a non-domiciliary has elected to be a remittance basis user, they are subject to UK taxation on their UK income and gains and on their foreign income and gains to the extent that these are remitted (ie brought in) to the UK. An individual may decide each year whether or not to make a claim. If an individual decides not to elect for the remittance basis, by default, they will pay income tax and capital gains tax on an arising basis in the UK on their worldwide income and gains.

The £30,000 remittance basis charge: what is it and when must it be paid?

This is an annual tax charge of £30,000 for access to the remittance basis of taxation. It is in addition to any UK tax due on either UK income and gains or overseas income and gains remitted to the UK. The remittance basis charge must be paid by an adult non-domiciliary who has been UK resident for seven out of the previous nine UK tax years and who wishes to be a remittance basis user in a given UK tax year.

Generally, top rate (50 per cent) taxpayers will need to have overseas income in excess of £60,000 per annum to justify paying the £30,000 charge. As the claim to be a remittance basis user will be made on an annual basis, it will be important to plan when a non-domiciliary should make the claim and pay the £30,000 and when they should not. In years when the non-domiciled taxpayer has significant foreign income or gains, the claim should be made but their affairs could be managed to ensure that in some years, foreign income and gains are limited to avoid the need to pay the charge.

Figure 3.3.1 contains a chart (prepared by HMRC) which sets out whether the taxpayer needs to pay the remittance basis charge.

FIGURE 3.3.1 Do I need to pay the remittance basis charge (RBC)?

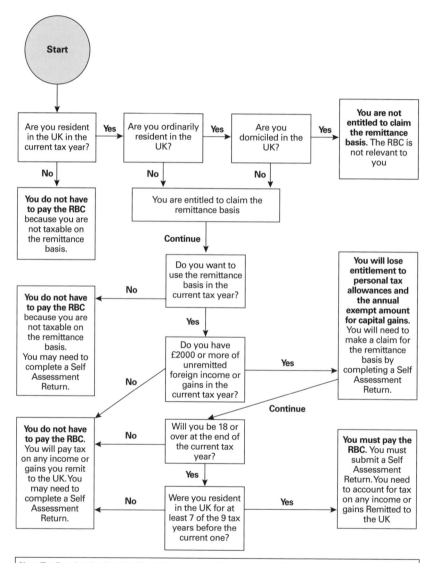

Note: The flowchart is a broad guide to help you decide if you need to pay the Remittance Basis Charge. You have a choice each year whether to claim the remittance basis. If, in a particular year, it would be more beneficial for you to pay tax on your worldwide income and gains than to pay the RBC, you may chose not to claim the remittance basis.

The remittance basis charge needs to be paid when the non-domiciliary is filing their UK tax return (ie by 31 January following the end of the tax year for which the return is being made). At that time the remittance basis user will normally have to make a payment of £45,000 (£30,000 plus £15,000 as a payment on account for the following tax year, assuming they are UK resident in that tax year and nominating income rather than capital gains to pay the charge).

The mechanics of the remittance basis charge require the remittance basis user to nominate a portion of their income or gains that is deemed to bear the remittance basis charge. The remittance basis charge then effectively represents income tax, capital gains tax or a combination of the two (depending on the nature of the nominated funds). If the nominated foreign income or gains on which the remittance basis charge has been paid is subsequently brought into the UK, the remittance basis user will not be taxed again on that income. However, should the nominated foreign income and gains be remitted, ordering rules apply, which provide that, in any year, previously unremitted foreign income or gains will be considered to have been remitted before any of the nominated foreign income or gains on which the £30,000 charge has been paid. A planning point here may be to keep a separately identifiable portion of income, chosen to bear the £30,000 charge, in a separate account.

As the £30,000 charge will be classified as either income tax or capital gains tax, it is hoped that it should be treated as such for the purposes of any double taxation agreements to provide relief against any tax which might be levied in the individual's country of domicile on the source income.

The remittance of £30,000 from foreign income or gains to pay the remittance basis charge is not itself deemed to be a remittance provided it is paid directly to HMRC. However, if it is first transferred to a UK bank account and then paid to HMRC, a remittance will have occurred. Since this chapter was first written, the remittance basis charge has been increased by the 2011 Budget to £50,000 from 6 April 2011 for taxpayers who have been resident in the UK for 12 years or more.

Consequences of electing for the remittance basis

An individual who makes a claim for the remittance basis to apply in any year will not be entitled in that year to any personal allowances when computing their income tax liability; nor will they be entitled to the annual exempt amount for capital gains tax (£10,600 for 2011–12). This does not apply to individuals whose unremitted foreign income and gains are less than £2,000.

In practice, for those earning taxable income of more than £112,950 this is not an actual downside because they would have lost their personal allowance due to their level of income anyway. However, the loss of the annual exempt amount of £10,600 for capital gains tax is a downside of claiming the remittance basis. In practice however, the tax cost for taxpayers of losing the annual exemption is only £2,968, which is negligible in most circumstances.

A remittance basis user is liable to tax at up to 50 per cent on the remittance of foreign dividend income. This compares with the effective rate of 36.1 per cent on UK and non-UK dividend income payable by top-rate non-remittance basis users from 2011–12 onwards.

Meaning of 'remitted to the UK'

A remittance will be made if money or other property 'is brought to, or received or used in, the United Kingdom by or for the benefit of a relevant person' or 'a service is provided in the United Kingdom to or for the benefit of a relevant person'[1] and (in either case) the money or the other property or the consideration for the service is, or is derived from, the overseas income or gains.

In this context, a 'relevant person' is:

1 the individual taxpayer;

2 their spouse or civil partner;

3 minor children or grandchildren of any of the persons at (1) or (2) above;

4 a closely held company in which any of the persons listed at (1) to (3) above or (5) below is a participator; and

5 a trust on which any of the above persons is a beneficiary.

For the purposes of the legislation, a man and woman living together as if they were husband and wife are treated as spouses, and same-sex couples living together as if they were civil partners are treated as such. The definition of 'relevant person' is wide enough to cover an indirect payment to a 'relevant person'. For example, if a non-domiciliary makes a gift abroad of remittance basis income to their adult child, the gift itself is not a remittance as the child is an adult and it can therefore be brought into the UK by the child without a remittance being triggered. However, if the child uses the money to pay for their minor child's school fees, that could be regarded as a remittance by the non-domiciliary, as a 'relevant person' (a minor grandchild of the non-domiciliary) will have received a benefit in the UK.

To avoid such a situation occurring, a non-domiciliary should not use any remittance basis income or gains for funding any relevant person (or any trust for someone within that definition) if there is any likelihood that the funds or assets derived from them could be brought to or used in the UK at any time.

Temporary non-residence

Non-domiciliaries who have run out of funds capable of remittance to the UK without a tax liability may think of ceasing to be resident in the UK for a year, on the assumption that in the year of non-residence they can then remit enough money to keep going for a further period. However, where such a taxpayer has been resident in the UK for four out of the preceding seven years, and then ceases to be resident for less than five complete tax years, they will be taxed on remittances made in the years of absence, which arose while they were resident, in the year in which residence is resumed.

Income which actually arises during the years of non-residence will be capable of remittance in that (or a subsequent) year without a tax liability. However, capital gains realized in years of non-residence which are remitted will be taxable in the year of return to the UK unless the taxpayer has been non-resident for five complete tax years.

Thus if a non-domiciled taxpayer has a period of non-residence from the UK which is less than five complete tax years, the greatest care must be exercised before any remittances are made to the UK in the years of absence.

Exempt property

The legislation contains a list of exempt assets that will not constitute a remittance even if purchased abroad with remittance basis income or gains and brought into the UK. These include:

- property such as works of art, a collector's item or an antique, which is or are on public display at an approved establishment (ie a museum, gallery or other institution);
- clothing, footwear, jewellery and watches for personal use;
- assets costing less than £1,000;
- assets brought into the UK for repair and restoration; and
- assets brought into the UK for less than a nine-month period.

The legislation provides for a clawback of this relief where the exempt property is sold or otherwise converted into money while it is in the UK or otherwise ceases to be exempt property. For example if a UK resident non-domiciliary used remittance basis income or gains to buy a Rolex watch abroad, for personal use, and brings it into the UK, it is exempt from being regarded as a remittance. However, if they then sell the Rolex while it is in the UK, a remittance of the remittance basis income and gains used to purchase it occurs at that time.

Property owned on 11 March 2008

The legislation provides a form of grandfathering relief for property owned by the taxpayer on 11 March 2008, other than money, that was purchased abroad with remittance basis income or gains. Curiously, the legislation does not specifically provide for a clawback of this relief where the property is subsequently sold or converted into money while in the UK.

Non-domiciled settlors of overseas trusts

UK-domiciled and resident settlors of overseas trusts who have an interest in such trusts are taxed on the chargeable gains arising to the trustees. Such gains are treated as forming the highest part on the amount on which the settlor is chargeable to capital gains tax for the tax year. This does not apply to non-domiciliaries.

Non-domiciled beneficiaries of offshore trusts

Non-domiciled beneficiaries (including the settlor) who receive a capital distribution from an offshore trust will be subject to UK tax on capital payments received in the UK which are matched with trust gains. This charge to tax will be subject to the remittance basis where the non-UK-domiciled beneficiary is a remittance basis user. This will be the case whether the trust gains arose on UK or non-UK assets. However, capital payments received by resident non-domiciliaries which are kept out of the UK will not be taxed even if matched with UK gains.

Non-domiciled shareholders in overseas companies

Gains made by offshore closely held companies will be attributed to non-domiciled shareholders if the offshore holding is 10 per cent or more (including the shareholding of their associates). Such a shareholder claiming the remittance basis taxation will be taxed on the attributed gains of the offshore company to the extent that they are remitted into the UK.

US citizens

For non-domiciled individuals other than US citizens, the decision to pay the £30,000 (or £50,000) charge will be a simple economic choice – the question will be whether the global tax bill will be less if the benefit of the remittance basis of taxation in the UK is retained.

For non-domiciled individuals who are US persons, the question is not so simple. US persons are taxable on their worldwide income and gains, and so avoiding UK tax under the remittance basis is only beneficial to the extent that the UK effective rate of tax that would have been paid is higher than the US effective rate on that income. There is also the lingering question as to whether the payment of the £30,000 (or £50,000) will qualify as foreign tax credit on the US return. At the time of writing, the IRS has not yet reached a decision on this issue.

Planning for non-domiciliaries post April 2008

Despite changes introduced by the Finance Act 2008, there are still tax planning opportunities for non-domiciliaries. These include the following.

Bank account planning

In order to achieve the most favourable tax position in the UK for a non-domiciliary, segregation of funds so that it is clear which particular category of income or gain has been brought into the UK is absolutely key. It is very important to get this right from the outset. There is no second chance to do so. Broadly, what a non-domiciliary needs to do is to establish a clean capital account that consists of capital or income or gains generated prior to becoming UK resident and several different accounts to hold the different categories of income and capital gains arising after they become resident.

Pre-entry gain crystallizations

For non-domiciled individuals who are coming to the UK and intend to become UK resident, of paramount concern will be to ensure, so far as possible, that they crystallize any gains before coming to the UK. The proceeds of such a disposal should be deposited in a pre-entry bank account, which should not be tainted by post-entry income and gains.

Inheritance tax

So long as an individual remains non-domiciled, inheritance tax on any UK-situs assets can be easily avoided by holding those assets through an offshore holding company. This effectively converts a UK asset into a non-UK asset since one only looks at the shares of the holding company and ignores the underlying assets owned by the company itself. However, it is essential to obtain professional advice when embarking on this type of planning, especially where the asset involved is the individual's UK home.

Excluded property trusts

Where the settlor of the trust is a non-domiciled individual, and the trust assets are situated outside the UK, the settlement will be wholly excluded from the scope of inheritance tax even if the settlor subsequently becomes domiciled or deemed domiciled in the UK.

Furthermore, the trustees of an offshore excluded property trust can realize a gain without it being imputed to the resident non-domiciled settlor. This provides a good vehicle to defer capital gains, even on UK assets. However, care needs to be taken if the funds are eventually distributed to a resident non-domiciliary not claiming the remittance basis or a UK-domiciled resident, as the additional charge could cause the rate of CGT to increase to 44.8 per cent. Income is automatically attributed to the settlor of a settlor-interested trust, subject to the remittance basis of taxation.

Offshore bonds

In certain situations non-domiciliaries may find offshore bonds attractive as they enable them to roll up investments gross offshore and the non-domiciliary could receive 5 per cent of the original investment 'tax free' as a return of capital, which could be remitted to the UK free of tax. It should be noted that the funds with which the offshore bond are bought must not be offshore income or gains. If the non-domiciliary investing in the bond holds it until such time as they leave the UK and become non-UK resident, they should be able to realize the bond free of UK income tax or capital gains tax provided they remain outside the UK for the requisite period.

Spouse or civil partner

Where both parties to a marriage or civil partnership are non-domiciled, it may be possible to arrange their affairs to ensure that only one of the couple needs to be a remittance basis user and suffer the £30,000 (or £50,000) charge.

Conclusion

Despite the changes introduced by the Finance Act 2008, the UK is still a fiscally attractive jurisdiction for non-domiciled taxpayers. However, this is a complex area and professional advice should be sought.

Notes

1   Section 809L Finance Act 2008

UK tax points for non-UK domiciled HNWIs and UK nationals moving abroad

CLIVE MACKINTOSH,
PRICEWATERHOUSECOOPERS

We are operating in a world of increasing international mobility. The relative convenience of international travel offers you greater opportunities for working and living in more than one country, whether short term, perhaps on an international secondment, or as part of a longer-term lifestyle choice. At the same time, continuing technological improvements not only make a global marketplace accessible to customers and retailers but also make it increasingly easy to find and run your affairs 'virtually' via e-mail, webcasts or virtual conferencing. However, while there may be 'one world' in terms of opportunities, there are many jurisdictions for tax purposes, and failure to take account of the impact of actual or virtual activities in somewhere other than your home country may be costly.

This chapter looks at two particular types of individual: those who are not domiciled in the UK but get involved here and those at the other end of the scale who decide to move their interests out of the UK. Your liability to UK taxation will be determined by your residence, ordinary residence and domicile, as well as by the rules which apply to other countries with which you are involved. These issues require reference to case law, guidance and double tax agreements, all of which have been subject to continuing change over recent years. Inevitably, lack of space means that these notes cover only some points and then only at a high level, and you should take specific, detailed advice on your situation before taking any action.

Non-domiciliary in the UK

If you are a non-UK domiciliary resident in the UK, you are subject to specific rules on the treatment of your non-UK income and gains.

What is non-UK domicile?

Space does not allow for a detailed analysis here of the concept of domicile. However, you are likely to have a non-UK domicile if, broadly, you consider somewhere other than the UK to be your permanent home, even if you have lived in the UK for some years:

- Your 'domicile of origin' is acquired at birth, and this is your father's domicile unless your parents were unmarried, in which case it is your mother's domicile.

- Assuming that your domicile of origin is outside the UK, this will stay with you unless you actively acquire a new 'domicile of choice' by establishing a permanent home here. HM Revenue & Customs (HMRC) may seek to argue this if you have taken steps which illustrate an intention to make the UK your permanent home by, for example, severing ties with your home country and making a will in the UK.

- For inheritance tax purposes, there is an extended concept of 'deemed domicile' if you have been resident in the UK in 17 of the last 20 tax years, regardless of any intention to stay here permanently.

- You should not take your non-domicile status for granted. Although the onus of proof is on HMRC should they seek to argue that you have acquired a UK domicile, you need to ensure that your actions and intentions reflect your permanent home being elsewhere.

The remittance basis: what is a remittance?

Assuming that you are successful in maintaining your non-UK domicile, you have the tax advantage of being able to claim that your non-UK income and gains will not be subject to UK tax unless you remit them to the UK – this is known as the 'remittance basis'. Subject to some minor exceptions, this basis has to be claimed and such a claim will mean that you lose some UK allowances, and if you are a long-term UK resident you will be liable to pay an annual 'remittance basis charge'.

You can claim the remittance basis for the following sources:

- Employment income arising from duties which are performed wholly abroad for an employer who is not resident in the UK;
- Other relevant foreign income; and
- Gains arising on non-UK assets.

Taxation under the remittance basis means that your foreign income will be taxed in the UK only if it is brought back to, or enjoyed in, the UK by you or by any 'relevant person': broadly your spouse or civil partner; your or their minor children or grandchildren; a 'close' company in which any of you is a participator; the trustees of a settlement of which any of you is a beneficiary; or a body connected with such a settlement.

There are complex rules which mean that, in broad terms, any money or property used directly or indirectly by you or a relevant person will be classified as a remittance. Examples of common remittances include:

- Transferring cash, bank balances, cheques, promissory notes or any other form of money to the UK;
- Receiving payment in the UK;
- Repaying, outside the UK, interest or capital on a UK loan;
- Repaying, outside the UK, foreign loans that have been remitted to the UK;
- Paying, outside the UK, interest on a foreign loan received in the UK, other than foreign investment income used to pay the interest on a qualifying loan (broadly, a loan taken out before 12 March 2008 for the acquisition of UK residential property, the terms of which have not been varied since that date);
- Purchasing assets in the UK, even if settlement is made abroad;
- Using overseas credit cards in the UK, if the settlement is made using foreign income or gains;
- Meeting overseas bills with a credit card issued by a credit card company in the UK; and
- Settlement of any credit card accounts in the UK with foreign income or gains, whether the money is spent in the UK or abroad.

There are some exemptions for assets. These cover clothing, footwear, jewellery and watches for personal use; assets that cost less than £1,000; assets that are in the UK for 275 days or less; assets that are under repair or restoration; assets owned on 11 March 2008; and assets already in the UK at 5 April 2008 (until sold in the UK). There is an additional exemption for works of art or similar objects which have been acquired with any foreign income or gains (not just investment income) which are brought to the UK for public display.

Apart from making sure that you are familiar with these provisions, it is important to be aware that a number of methods which used to be commonly used by non-UK domiciliaries to remit income and gains free of UK tax no longer work; so seek advice before considering other transfers of income or property into the country.

The remittance basis: the remittance basis charge

If you claim the remittance basis and you are over 18 years of age with at least £2,000 of unremitted foreign income and gains, you will be liable to the remittance basis charge if you are a 'long-term resident', defined as someone who has been UK resident in seven out of the preceding nine tax years. The charge is currently £30,000 per annum and is effectively in addition to the tax liability arising on remittances in the same year. At the same time as being liable for the charge, you will generally lose your entitlement to income tax personal allowances and to the capital gains tax annual exempt amount.

At the time you make the remittance basis claim, you must nominate to which offshore income and gains the charge relates, and this nominated amount must give rise to additional tax of no more than £30,000. There is a specific order for matching remittances against overseas amounts which have been nominated and those which have not. The rules which apply once there has been a remittance of nominated income are extremely complex and punitive, so the remittance of any nominated amounts should be avoided if it all possible. One recommendation is to avoid it by arranging for a small amount of, say, bank income to arise each year which will be nominated and not remitted. It is important that any amounts nominated are segregated from other funds: if remittances are made from an account containing nominated income or gains it is impossible to prove the nominated monies have not been remitted.

Inheritance tax (IHT)

As long as you are not domiciled in the UK under either general principles or under the IHT deeming provisions, gifts of non-UK assets during your lifetime or at death will not be subject to IHT. This is on the basis that any property which is situated outside the UK and which is either owned beneficially by you or held in an offshore settlement which you created while you are non-UK domiciled is excluded from the UK IHT charge. There is no need for any claim to be made.

A crucial point is to be careful with the IHT deemed domicile rules. Where you have moved to the UK without changing your domicile of origin, you need to know when you could first be caught by the 17-out-of-20-years rule. Should you acquire deemed domicile status, then you may find that non-UK property which was previously outside the UK IHT charge becomes subject to IHT even though neither an income nor a capital gains tax charge arises. In particular, any non-UK property which you own beneficially will no longer be excluded property, and an excluded property settlement already set up will be 'tainted' if you transfer in any further property.

In conclusion

There are some straightforward planning opportunities which really stem from an understanding of the remittance rules and working within them to minimize any tax charges. It is always advisable to take specific advice to consider these opportunities as well as those more complex tax planning opportunities which do remain.

UK nationals moving abroad

If you are a UK national considering a move abroad, although tax is unlikely to be the primary motivator for you to consider moving away from the UK, you do need to be aware of the UK tax implications of making such a move. In the same way as an international resident coming to the UK does not necessarily become liable to the full range of UK tax, a UK national leaving the UK does not necessarily lose UK liability. Liability will depend on residence, ordinary residence and domicile, and HMRC will expect to see a high level of evidence before agreeing that you have lost these states. You should seek specific advice in advance of your departure.

The broad scope of UK taxation

Income

If you leave the UK but still remain resident here, you will be liable to UK income tax on your worldwide income. If you cease to be resident, you will only be liable to UK tax on your UK income, including income from UK property, a trade which you exercise in the UK or an employment where you perform duties in the UK.

National insurance contributions (NIC)

If you leave the UK on assignment, your NIC liabilities will vary depending on where you are going and the length of your assignment. If your assignment is within the European Community and for less than 24 months, you will generally remain within the UK NIC system. If you leave permanently or semi-permanently, you will generally cease to be liable to NIC on your departure. NIC is an area heavily dependent on specific circumstances, and you should seek specialist advice.

Capital gains

If you remain UK resident and domiciled, you will be liable to UK capital gains tax on gains arising on all assets, irrespective of their location. If you cease to be UK resident but remain UK domiciled, you will only be liable on gains on assets situated in the UK and used in a trade or profession carried on in the UK. Anti-avoidance rules will tax certain gains realized during a period of temporary non-residence if you return to the UK before five complete UK tax years have elapsed. These rules apply if you were resident and ordinarily resident for at least four out of the seven tax years immediately before your departure.

Inheritance tax

You will be liable to UK IHT on your worldwide assets if you die or on some lifetime gifts while you are domiciled or deemed domiciled in the UK. The concept of deemed domicile means that even if you successfully establish domicile elsewhere under general principles, you will still be deemed to be UK domiciled for IHT if you were actually UK domiciled within three years prior to your death or the lifetime gift.

Note that if you successfully establish a non-UK domicile and then subsequently reacquire UK residence, you will be subject to the rules set out in the first part of this chapter. However, in such circumstances, HMRC may challenge your assertion that you originally made a clean break with the UK.

Implication of these general rules for different types of move overseas

Generally, if you are intending to go abroad for short periods only, including business trips, this will not change your residence status. Even extensive trips abroad are unlikely to result in your becoming non-UK resident unless you also change your normal place of abode to an overseas location. If you do not break your UK residence, your liability to UK tax on worldwide income and gains will remain, although there are some specific deductions and credits which may be available.

One exception to this is that if you go abroad to take up full-time employment under a contract for a period including a complete tax year, HMRC will generally regard you as ceasing to be resident from the time of your departure. This is subject to the proviso that your visits to the UK do not exceed the limits set out in order to determine residence. In addition, the term 'full-time employment' is not comprehensively defined in law or HMRC guidance and it is not clear to what extent it is possible to have ongoing duties in the UK without your resident status being affected. The best advice is to have no ongoing UK duties.

If you spend sufficient time outside the UK to become non-UK resident, your income tax liability will, broadly, reduce to that arising on your UK source income. Income from an offshore employer which relates to duties performed in the UK will constitute UK source income for these purposes. Should you become UK resident within five tax years of your departure, you will be subject to capital gains on disposals during your time abroad of UK assets which you owned before leaving the UK.

If you are regularly spending periods abroad and in the UK, you may become tax resident in both countries. You should seek specific advice in these circumstances as there may be advantages in choosing one country of residence over another, where it is possible to do so. In addition, under the terms of many double tax agreements there may be a tiebreaker clause which determines residence.

Assuming that you wish to establish non-UK residence and ordinary residence, you should consider the following general points:

- You should complete form P85 (residence or employment abroad) and send this to your UK tax office. You will also need to complete the non-residence pages in a self-assessment tax return. You should also check the tax compliance procedures for the country to which you are moving.

- You can be treated as neither resident nor ordinarily resident if you provide evidence that you are leaving the UK permanently. Such evidence could include the sale of your UK home and the purchase of a new property abroad. You need to be able to demonstrate that you have actually left the UK, and HMRC will look for a distinct break in your lifestyle and is likely to challenge factors such as any continuing family, financial and business ties in the UK as being evidence of continuing UK residence.

- Ideally, do not return to the UK before the anniversary of 6 April, following the date of your departure, even for an airport stopover. That is, the best advice is to spend one complete tax year out of the UK. If this is not possible, keep return visits to an absolute minimum in this first year. After that, ensure that return visits in the first four years are kept to a minimum and are less than an average of 91 days per tax year. Keep contemporaneous records of the trips, including air tickets, and keep some days in reserve to cover unexpected emergencies.

- Gather evidence to support your intention to live abroad permanently. This could include arranging medical cover abroad; purchasing property; acquiring interests, directorships, driving licence; voting rights and investments abroad; and disposing of any UK equivalent.

In conclusion

As mentioned at the outset, it is likely that your reasons for moving abroad will be for lifestyle considerations rather than for tax alone, and being able to demonstrate those lifestyle choices will support your argument that you have left the UK. However, although tax may not drive your decision, you should not ignore it and you should take time and advice to consider the tax consequences in both the UK and abroad of your intended move.

Guernsey:
a favourable tax regime

JOHN PICKLES, MOORE STEPHENS

Background

You would be forgiven for thinking that the Guernsey tax regime is straightforward and requires little more expertise than that required to subtract a small number from a big number and multiply it by 20 per cent. How difficult can it be to navigate the minefield of income tax at 20 per cent when the island has:

- no capital taxes;
- no wealth taxes;
- no gift taxes;
- no inheritance taxes; and
- no direct sales tax?

From a tax perspective, Guernsey is attractive; there is no doubt about it. Throw social security contribution requirements into the equation that compare favourably with most jurisdictions and a current personal allowance of £9,050 and you have yourself a British home without the complexities of British tax – or do you? This chapter will attempt to provide an awareness of the Guernsey tax regime that is far more than just a flat rate of 20 per cent, but is still relatively straightforward, if you know what you're doing!

Overview

Guernsey is a long-established low-tax area. A dependency of the British Crown but with its own legislature, Guernsey has been a separate and distinct jurisdiction since the early 1200s. Situated between England and France, it does not form part of the UK, nor is it a member of the European Community.

While the Guernsey tax regime has developed over time and has seen significant changes, unquestionably the change that has taken place over the past three years has been the most fundamental.

The Guernsey corporate tax regime underwent extensive change in 2008 and the once-simple system of 20 per cent tax on company profits was replaced, with effect from 1 January 2008, with the so-called 'zero/10' regime. The standard rate of tax applicable to most Guernsey companies is now 0 per cent. There are exceptions for profits derived from Guernsey land and property ownership/development (20 per cent), profits derived from banking activities (10 per cent) and the profits from regulated utility companies (20 per cent).

Guernsey resident shareholders are now taxed on actual distributions and on deemed distributions from companies (based on shareholding) when triggered by certain events. Sadly, our old corporate tax regime was deemed 'unfair' due to the 'high tax' that Guernsey residents paid when compared with non-resident shareholders who suffered no tax consequences in Guernsey. Accordingly, the island was directed to abandon this and certain other practices within the previous regime, which the European Union Code of Conduct on Business Taxation had identified and branded 'harmful tax practices', and collect corporation tax at 0 per cent or 10 per cent (zero/10) rather than at the previous 20 per cent standard flat rate! However peculiar a responsive action, the model was considered to be acceptable and dealt with the concerns of the Code of Conduct Group.

It soon became apparent that a zero per cent tax model such as our own would not be compliant, nor sanctioned by the UK or EU. The consultation process continues and we abide by the legislation in force. Despite this, Guernsey remains as stable a jurisdiction as any for international business and tax planning.

Inevitably, the move from 20 per cent corporation tax to zero/10 corporation tax has reduced the island's revenues and created our very own 'black hole'. In turn, this has led to a variety of further significant legislative changes being introduced to assist with its 'filling' and to encourage high net worth individuals to the island.

Guernsey tax residence

While it is relatively straightforward for new residents to fall within the scope of Guernsey taxation, it is important to consider the ongoing exposure to taxes levied by other jurisdictions. In particular, property will often cause additional liabilities in other jurisdictions for the unwary but, with careful planning, overseas taxes may be reduced and in some circumstances avoided completely.

Broadly speaking, there are four categories of residence for Guernsey tax purposes. From 1 January 2006, tax residence in Guernsey is established purely on the basis of the number of days an individual spends in the island.

For Guernsey tax purposes, a 'day' is treated as being spent in Guernsey if an individual is in the island at midnight. As such, days of arrival are counted but days of departure ignored.

Non-resident

An individual who does not fall within the other three categories (again very broadly), and who spends less than 91 days of the year on the island is regarded as 'non-resident'.

An individual who is non-resident is generally only liable to Guernsey income tax on Guernsey source income, although many sources are disregarded for these purposes.

Resident only

An individual is regarded as 'resident only' in Guernsey for tax purposes in a calendar year if:

● 91 days or more are spent in Guernsey during the year; or
● 35 days or more are spent in Guernsey in that year and, during the four preceding years, 365 days or more in Guernsey.

Solely resident

An individual will be treated as 'solely resident' in Guernsey in a calendar year if:

● treated as 'resident only' (see above); and
● fewer than 91 days are spent in one other place during a calendar year. In other words, if an individual cannot be treated as resident (under Guernsey tax rules) in one other country during a year, they will be treated as 'solely resident' in Guernsey.

An individual who is solely resident in Guernsey is liable to Guernsey income tax on their total worldwide income wherever it arises.

Principally resident

An individual who is not solely resident in Guernsey will be treated as 'principally resident' in a calendar year if:

● at least 182 days are spent in Guernsey during the year; or
● at least 91 days are spent in Guernsey during the year and, during the four preceding calendar years, at least 730 days are spent in Guernsey; or
● permanent residence is taken up in the island. For this purpose, an individual will be treated as taking up permanent residence in a calendar year if treated as resident only in the year, as described above, and is solely resident or principally resident in the following calendar year.

An individual who is principally resident in Guernsey is liable to Guernsey income tax on their total worldwide income wherever it arises.

You will note that there is an obvious category of residence which falls between these two extreme of broadly what is deemed to be resident and non-resident – those individuals who are 'resident only'. Historically, resident-only individuals were taxable upon Guernsey source income plus remittances of overseas income. With effect from 1 January 2010, this basis ceased to apply and was replaced by the following:

- In the absence of an election (see below), a resident-only individual is required to submit a tax return disclosing their worldwide income and is chargeable to Guernsey tax on said worldwide income after deduction of all applicable personal tax allowances.

- Alternatively, an individual may elect to pay the 'standard charge', which for the time being is set at £25,000. If such election is made, the individual must submit a return of only Guernsey source income (excluding Guernsey bank deposit interest) , which they are taxed on. The individual thus waives entitlement to personal tax allowances and other reliefs. The standard charge may offset against the individual's tax liability on Guernsey source income and therefore represents a minimum tax liability that such individual would bear if an election were made.

It is worth noting the definition of 'resident only'. Under the previous legislation, an individual needed to spend more time in one other place compared to Guernsey in a year, and fewer than 182 days in Guernsey in the year to be treated as resident only. So a four-month stay in Guernsey in a calendar year would require slightly more than four months to be spent in one other jurisdiction to achieve resident-only tax status.

The new rules make it far easier to achieve resident-only tax status. Take an individual that spends 170 days (fewer than 182 days) in Guernsey and 99 days in Spain. They cannot be treated as 'solely resident' because, under Guernsey tax rules, they will be regarded as resident in Spain (even though they are not resident there for Spanish tax purposes), and cannot be treated as principally resident because they have not been in Guernsey for at least 182 days. Consequently, they will be treated as resident only and liable to Guernsey tax on Guernsey source income and remittances of foreign income to Guernsey.

A pitfall of the rules occurs where an individual who is currently principally resident attempts to achieve the beneficial resident-only status. If our individual has been in Guernsey for more than 730 days in the previous four years and is in Guernsey for more than 91 days in the first year of attempting to achieve resident-only status, they will continue to be treated as principally resident. As such, it may be several years before they can achieve resident-only status.

A further pitfall for our individual is that they can be treated as solely resident in Guernsey if they spend, say, 99 days in the island but do not spend at least 91 days in Spain. As such, they could be liable to Guernsey tax on their total worldwide income even though they spend only approximately one quarter of the year here.

Domicile

Domicile has different meanings in different jurisdictions, but in general a long-term permanent resident of Guernsey will be able to acquire a domicile of choice in

Guernsey. Such status may facilitate planning to shelter a Briton's worldwide assets from UK inheritance tax.

As previously mentioned, there is no estate duty, inheritance tax or wealth tax in the island. Having said that, anyone contemplating moving here should take note of the centuries-old Forced Heirship Rules which still apply to anyone domiciled in Guernsey. Domicile is a term which is often confused with residence but, arising from the Latin '*domus*', it refers to an individual's homeland as distinct from whether they simply happen to be living in another jurisdiction for the time being. Someone moving to Guernsey from outside the island may or may not retain their domicile of origin. For example, someone with a domicile in England and Wales who moves to Guernsey may never form a fixed intention to remain permanently in the island to the exclusion of 'home' back in the UK and accordingly would not adopt a domicile of choice in Guernsey. However, for those who do come here and are domiciled in Guernsey, the Forced Heirship Rules restrict their ability to leave assets freely by setting aside a fixed portion of their estate which must pass to their children. While it is widely expected that these rules will be changed, for the time being they are still on the statute book.

Interest relief on borrowings

Sadly, interest relief as we all knew and loved it has been scaled back considerably in recent years. It used to be the case that allowance (tax relief) was given in respect of interest paid on borrowed money, no matter what the purpose of the borrowing. With effect from 1 January 2008, interest relief is now broadly only available, subject to specific rules, in respect of borrowings for the following purposes:

- Principal private residence (PPR): relief is available in respect of interest paid on money borrowed for the acquisition, construction, reconstruction or repair of an individual's Guernsey PPR, subject to a limit on qualifying borrowing of £400,000. Interest relief will also be available in circumstances where the individual's PPR is held through a company.

- Let property: relief for interest paid on borrowings to acquire, renovate or repair let property is available by way of deduction against rental income received in the same year. Excess interest may only be carried forward in very limited circumstances.

- Miscellaneous: interest relief will be available in respect of borrowings for:
  - the purchase of an asset used wholly, exclusively and necessarily in the performance of an individual's employment duties;
  - the acquisition of part or all of a business (or shares in a company carrying on a business) in which the borrower is actively engaged; and
  - the purpose of lending to a company in which the borrower holds not less than 10 per cent of the issued share capital and in the business of which the borrower is actively engaged, provided said funds are utilized for the purposes of the company's business.

- Business loans: interest paid in respect of borrowings used for the purposes of a business will generally be available by way of deduction from assessable business profits.

Tax capping

In 2008, a cap of £250,000 on the income tax liabilities of wealthy Guernsey residents was introduced and the cap applied to income derived from overseas sources, Guernsey bank interest and exempt investment schemes (including overseas income and bank interest arising within an investment holding company).

From 1 January 2009, the tax cap was extended. The cap has reduced to tax of £100,000 for overseas income (ie tax on assessable overseas income of £500,000) but there is now a facility to cap an individual's liability upon Guernsey source income also. An individual wishing to include Guernsey source income in the cap is (upon election) limited to tax of £200,000 on their worldwide income. This will broadly be advantageous where the individual has worldwide income in excess of £1 million, of which at least £500,000 is derived from Guernsey sources.

It should be noted that the application of the cap can be complex where an individual has interests in companies and/or trusts, the income of which is taxable upon that individual on a distribution or deemed distribution basis. In particular, the future distribution of trading profits from a company may present difficulties. The circumstance may arise whereby the profits out of which a dividend is paid have been taxed in an earlier period due to them being deemed distributed. Thus, an individual may have a tax liability in the earlier period without actually receiving a distribution only to receive a dividend in a later period that has to some extent already been taxed upon them.

It is therefore important to determine to what extent the recipient's liability on that dividend should be capped, by reference to their personal tax position in earlier years.

Participator loans

'Participators' broadly refers to Guernsey resident shareholders and directors, officers and persons connected with them. Prior to 2008, it was possible to withdraw funds from Guernsey companies in the form of director or shareholder loans without any adverse tax consequences.

With the introduction of zero/10 corporate income tax at company level, it was necessary to prevent the withdrawal of profits by way of loans as a mechanism for avoiding any distribution and deemed distribution tax charges. Consequently, from 1 January 2008, loans to participators in companies became, in certain circumstances, chargeable to Guernsey tax of 20 per cent. Of particular note is that the rules catch loans made by trading companies. Companies are required to disclose loans to participators under a quarterly reporting regime and to account for the tax chargeable thereon.

Pensions

Guernsey has a well-established pension regime to complement the beneficial tax consequences of being resident in the island. Recent changes to the double taxation arrangement between Guernsey and the UK means that from 6 April 2010 individuals resident in Guernsey who are in receipt of a UK pension will be liable to pay tax only in Guernsey. It is important that the necessary election is made to apply for this relief to the UK tax authorities in order for the pension to be paid gross.

The island is also well placed to deal with the pension arrangements of both residents and non-residents. Since 'A Day' in the UK, the Qualifying Recognised Overseas Pension Scheme (QROPS) regime has introduced a solution for individuals no longer resident or planning to leave the UK to transfer their UK tax-relieved pension funds out of their existing UK scheme, eg SIPPs. With this privilege comes a five-year HMRC reporting period for distributions.

A Guernsey QROPS requires HMRC and States of Guernsey Income Tax Approval and utilizes the long-established and highly flexible Retirement Annuity Trust Scheme framework in the island's income tax laws. Such schemes are open to both residents and non-residents and can be bespoke or multi-member schemes.

Of particular note is the 'approval' received by a QROPS from HMRC. While HMRC provides a reference number on HMRC-headed paper and includes QROPS on a published list, it currently performs no due diligence on the scheme in addition to the statement of fact that the QROPS Trustee provides in its application. Publication on this list should not be seen as confirmation by HMRC that it has verified all the information supplied by the scheme in the application. Therefore, should a scheme not satisfy the conditions to be a QROPS, any transfer that has been made to that scheme could potentially give rise to an unauthorized payments charge liability for the member. Reliance is therefore placed on the Trustee of the scheme to comply with the conditions on which it has applied for QROPS status.

While the scope and pace at which Guernsey's tax regime is changing demand constant awareness, the regime continues to be very attractive.

So why not join us?

PART FOUR
Forestry investments and overseas real estate

KMS BALTICS

Insulate your money from the economic freeze

Invest in forestry and property – growth, capital appreciation, plus annual cash income

For more information please contact:

UK Office
KMS Baltics
Woodland Place
Belford NE70 7QA

Felix Karthaus BSc FICFor
T: +44 (0)1668 213693
E: felix.karthaus@kmsbaltics.com

UK forestry
– is proving to be recession-proof; steady cashflow and returns with excellent tax advantages

Baltic forestry
– good returns, cash-flow and capital appreciation

Baltic property
– Tallinn property is emerging from the crisis and offering yields of 7–8%

Romanian forestry
– the jewel of European native forests, steady cash-flow, superb amenity and hunting possibilities

Current management: 50,000 hectares of forest land, 5,000 hectares of agricultural land and 10,000 m² of commercial property.

www.kmsbaltics.com

KMS Baltics is a partnership of independent companies: Border Consultants (Forestry) Ltd, AS Fest- Forest, SIA Fest-Forest Latvija, RSL Festil-Forest and OÜ EST Kinnisvara

European forestry and property investments

FELIX KARTHAUS, KMS BALTICS

K MS Baltics is a tightly knit group of independent companies offering forestry investment in Estonia, Latvia, Romania and the UK, with farming and commercial property investment in Estonia.

Timber has been used by man for millennia for every aspect of life and trade, and its diversity continues to be exploited. Reported annual timber use in the world is some 3.4 billion cubic metres. Laid end to end, the cubic metres would circle the world 85 times. Unreported felling will undoubtedly increase this considerably. More than half of the timber is used as wood for fuel (1.8 billion cubic metres), mostly in Africa and Asia, but that is changing. Increasingly, the developed world uses wood with modern technology as one way of producing renewable energy. Britain currently imports 50 million cubic metres annually and it is estimated that, if all the proposed wood-fuel power plants are built, timber imports will have to increase by 150 per cent. The largest net importers of forest products in 2007 are identified in Figure 4.1.1.

At the same time, there are increasing international measures to protect forests and their habitats through legislation and incentives, putting pressure on the supply of timber.

Investing in forestry

Forestry offers benefits from timber sales, capital appreciation and development. In some countries, these are enhanced by tax advantages and subsidies. Woodlands also provide an ideal environment for recreation, sporting and amenity.

Forestry has come through the financial turmoil well. Forest property values have not been affected at all in Western Europe during this period. They tend to be owned as long-term investments, proving their stability during economic downturns, as illustrated in Figure 4.1.2 by the progression of average forest land prices in Sweden.

FIGURE 4.1.1 Largest net importers of forest products, 2007

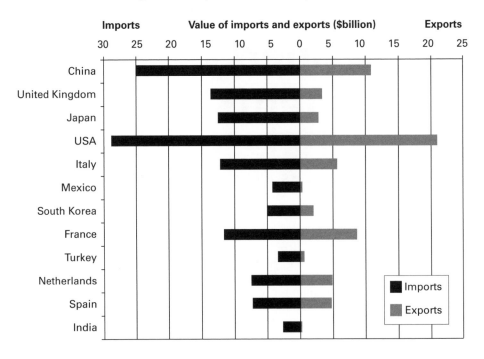

SOURCE FAO

FIGURE 4.1.2 Average forest land prices in Sweden 1999–2008

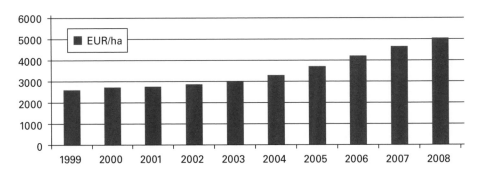

SOURCE www.skogsstyrelsen.se

In Eastern Europe, especially the Baltics, the experience was different. Forests had become expensive, but their new owners often had few financial reserves and had to sell when the economy crashed (see Figure 4.1.3 for average forest land prices in Estonia from 2000 to 2010).

FIGURE 4.1.3 Average forest land prices in Estonia 2000–2010 EUR/ha

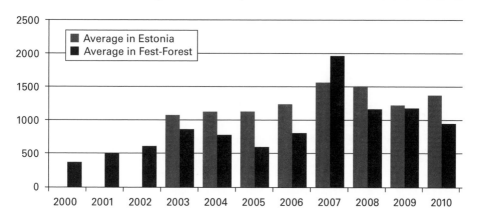

SOURCE MAAMET, EE and Fest-Forest

Timber prices suffered much more, because of a huge oversupply at the start of the recession, but prices and demand have recovered to their 2006 level and many forecasters believe prices are back on their long-term trend. This is in the middle of an unprecedented global financial crisis and a halt in new house building and wider construction. Figure 4.1.4 offers supporting evidence in respect of the trend in Estonian timber prices.

British and Swedish timber prices suffered much less, because their currencies weakened with the economic downturn.

Harvesting of timber is uniquely flexible: the time of felling can be chosen over several years, to optimize the market.

In the KMS group, we manage some 50,000 hectares, and we provide a complete service: forming the company, finding and purchasing forests, budgeting, bookkeeping, harvesting timber and regenerating the forest, as well as developing an exit strategy. In addition, we exploit the non-forest potential, such as agricultural land, quarries, house plots and wind farms. In Estonia, we also offer management of farmland and commercial property investment.

UK forestry: Border Consultants (Forestry) Ltd

Even without tax advantages, a woodland investment can typically return between 3 and 6 per cent.

The UK has 2.84 million hectares (12 per cent of the land mass) under trees, of which 2.02 million hectares are in the private sector and about 12 million cubic metres are harvested annually. The administration of forestry is a devolved issue, and thus the Welsh and Scottish governments have responsibility for the state woodlands. The UK government is responsible for the woodlands in England. There are continuous programmes of state forest sales in Scotland and England.

FIGURE 4.1.4 Estonian timber prices at roadside in state forest EUR/m³

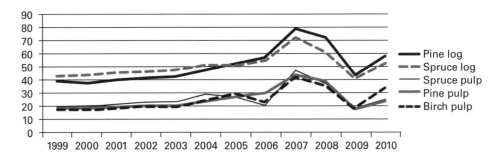

FIGURE 4.1.5 UK imports and exports of timber

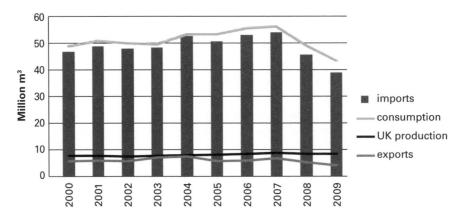

Both imports and exports dropped off since the peak of 2007

There is a wide variety of native tree species, such as oak, ash, beech, lime, poplar and birch, but only three conifers: yew, Scots pine and juniper. These native trees can produce excellent timber, but growth is slow, at least 80 to 120 years to reach maturity. However, British explorers introduced many useful species. One of these, Sitka spruce from the Western seaboard of North America, matures in 35 years and has good timber for sawmilling and wood fibre for paper and panel-board making. Commercial forestry in the UK is now dominated by Sitka spruce. There is a thriving timber-using industry; over the last 10 years £1 billion has been invested and demand is beginning to exceed the supply of timber available. Variations in UK imports and exports of timber are charted in Figure 4.1.5.

Britain produces only 17 per cent of the timber it consumes, but the recent weakness of sterling has meant that British sawmills have managed to increase their overall share of the market, as demonstrated in Figure 4.1.6, including exports to new markets. Moreover, the increase in timber production has translated into increased timber prices (see Figure 4.1.7).

FIGURE 4.1.6 Timber consumption by sawmills

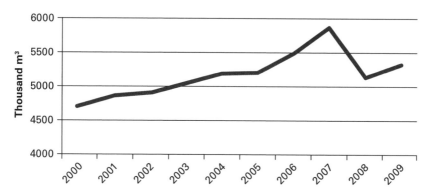

British sawmills increased production after an initial drop to replace imports

SOURCE Forestry Commission GB

FIGURE 4.1.7 Coniferous standing sales price index for the UK

(Fisher Index year ending September 2006 = 100, real terms)

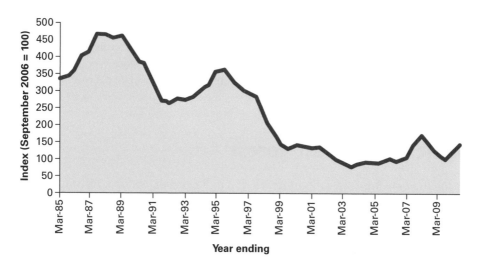

Year ending

Forestry is favourably treated by the tax system and also benefits from grants. At the turn of the last century only 4 per cent of Britain was covered by trees; these incentives were started after the First World War to create a strategic supply of timber.

Timber imports dropped sharply during the wars and Britain had to rely on its own forests for timber supplies, which were insufficient. For example, alternatives such as heather were used for papermaking. Woodland cover was increased from

4 per cent to nearly 12 per cent in less than a century: a remarkable pioneering achievement, from which the timber processing sector has developed.

Although the strategic need for timber as an objective for forest creation is no longer considered relevant, forestry has retained some special concessions in the tax system, and public benefits are encouraged through grants, which differ between the countries of the UK.

Three favourable taxation reliefs are available:

- Timber sales are free from income tax.

- Increases in timber value are free from capital gains tax.

- After two years' ownership, the value of forestry is excluded from inheritance tax.

Thus, woodland ownership is an excellent way to pass on wealth down the generations while creating a steady income. Hence the point made above: even without tax advantages, a woodland investment can typically return between 3 and 6 per cent.

There is a lively market in woodlands of all sizes. Annual sales amount to about £50 million. Many smaller woodlands are bought for amenity, but there are also sales of hundreds, or even thousands, of hectares.

Despite the credit crunch, woodlands have retained their value and competition remains strong, with sales often exceeding the asking price by 30 per cent.

Apart from timber, woodlands can provide deer stalking or pheasant shooting, or simply a superb environment for quiet relaxation. Often it is possible to let the sporting rights, providing additional income.

At the time of writing (January 2011), the government is consulting on future options for the management and ownership of the English state woodlands, with a strong emphasis on selling or leasing the commercial forests. The decision is expected in the summer.

Baltic forests: Fest-Forest

At today's timber prices, rates of return of 6 to 9 per cent can be achieved.

Estonian and Latvian forests are part of the natural Boreal forests, which circle the northern hemisphere in the higher latitudes. The main species, spruce, pine and birch, are usually regenerated from seed after felling. The quality of the spruce and pine is excellent, and used globally for house building. Birch is used in veneer for industrial plywood panels, as well as furniture and flooring.

The history of the Baltic countries has been turbulent. In the 13th century, they were invaded by crusading Prussians, or 'Baltic Germans'. Danes, Swedes and Russians all took ownership of the countries in turn and it was only in 1918 that the Baltics fought themselves free and they became independent.

Independence was short-lived as, in 1940, Russians, Germans and then again Russians invaded. Until 1991 the Baltics were part of the Soviet empire. Now they are a free, democratic state and part of the EU and NATO, however. The financial crisis ravaged their economies, but Estonia is now a eurozone member and Latvia hopes to follow in 2014. They swallowed the bitter economic medicine to recover, and they are emerging stronger, fitter and hungrier. Property prices were affected, but opportunities arise in both the forest and property market.

Forest values have recovered, but they remain a good investment. At today's timber prices, rates of return of 6 to 9 per cent can be achieved. In the Baltics, trees grow at about 3 per cent per year and the main factor in the rate of the return is the capital growth potential of crops that are not ready for felling. Typically, these are undervalued by around 40 per cent.

Because of the long history of serfdom, properties remained small: the average in KMS Baltics management is 20 hectares. Many are old farms, which lay empty following the expulsion of people to Siberia by Stalin and quickly seeded up with trees. We manage 1,352 properties and a good-sized portfolio may consist of 100 properties. This may appear complicated, but it has advantages. Insurance is not needed, as windblow or other damage will never threaten all the properties at the same time and the wide distribution makes many more markets available. Our management system is designed to cope with this distribution. Figure 4.1.8 tracks variations in Estonian Fest-Forest net standing timber prices; the recent drop in value is due to increased costs, mainly fuel.

Baltic timber processing is among the most modern in the world, as it is only 20 years old. Demand outstrips capacity by some 30 per cent and timber prices have been consistently strong, apart from a short period during the winter and spring of 2009.

FIGURE 4.1.8

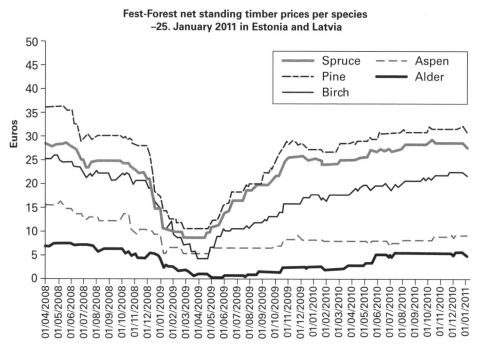

The recent drop in value is due to increased costs, mainly fuel

The terrain varies from flat to gently rolling hills, and working conditions are generally good, although on wetter ground, harvesting can be restricted to the winter, when the ground is frozen. The public road system gives good access to most forests. Road repairs have to be carried out occasionally, but new road construction is rare.

The spread of forests also increases the opportunities for adding value. Two-hectare, low-density housing plots can easily be created in the forests, increasing the land value by a factor of 5 to 10, depending on location. This will increase more, as the countries recover from recession. Every Balt wants to have a summer house. We have created more than 200 of these housing plots and sold 10 per cent during the recession. (visit www.maakoht.ee for details).

Land ownership is safe. All properties are recorded in the land register, as well as any mortgages or other liabilities. Any liabilities not in the land register cease following a sale. There is an annual land tax of about €5 per hectare. In Estonia there is no corporation tax, unless dividends are paid. In Latvia, a 15 per cent tax is levied on net profits from forestry operations.

Romanian forestry: Festil Forest

Returns from a forest investment can be from 2 to 10 per cent.

Romania is a large country (238,000 km²) with a population of 21.5 million. The 6.3 million hectares of forests are concentrated in the Carpathian mountains, with broadleaves on the lower slopes and spruce forests on the mountain tops. Only some 65 per cent are accessible and have been exploited. The remainder are still virgin woodlands, mostly on the steeper slopes of the mountains.

The main commercial species are beech, oak, Norway spruce and silver fir. Along the Danube, poplar is an important species, but as new plantation forestry rather than ancient native woodlands.

Romania used to be a very wealthy country before the Second World War: rich in oil and steel and with an affluent aristocracy, who were often large landowners with forests. During the communist era from 1945, all land was confiscated and managed by the state. After the revolution of 1989, the process of returning the woodlands to their previous owners was slow, accelerating only when Romania entered the EU in 2007. It remains an ongoing process.

Many woodlands have now been returned and some have been put up for sale. They range from a few dozen hectares to tens of thousands, with a few even exceeding 100,000 hectares. A minimum sensible size for an overseas investor is 300 hectares. Prices range from about €1,500 to €4,000 per hectare, drifting down since the financial crisis and now mostly around €2,500 per hectare. Returns from a forest investment can be from 2 to 10 per cent, according to the type and age of forest. A good assessment of the forest prior to purchasing is essential.

The woodlands are strictly regulated. A 10-year plan is prepared by independent, state-licensed surveyors. The plan has to be rigidly adhered to if any harvesting is done. Management can be undertaken only by licensed management companies with a minimum of 7,000 hectares (Festil Forest has such a management company).

The quality of the timber is superb and, since 1989, huge investment in timber processing has been made. Investment is not just in sawmills, but also in large panelboard mills and veneer mills, some of which use more than 1 million cubic metres per year. At the same time, there is a myriad of small sawmills, often using no more than 5,000 cubic metres per year. The larger modern mills are now processing 50 per cent of the annual timber production and are listed in Table 4.1.1.

The same dichotomy exists in timber extraction and other forest work. There are large firms with modern machinery, as well as many small contractors with horses or agricultural tractors.

This mixture of small mills and contractors has provided a buffer against the downturn in demand during the recession. However, there is much additional potential for development of markets and for exporting timber. India and China have become huge importers of timber, markets which have not yet been exploited.

Apart from timber, Romanian woodlands offer superb pride of ownership. The views, both inside the forests and over the landscape, can be stunning, with streams

TABLE 4.1.1

Company/type of mill	Capacity (million m^3)
Kronospan/MDF & particleboard	1.3
Schweighhofer (2007) sawmill & pellets	1.0
Schweighhofer (2009) sawmill	1.0
Egger (2009) MDF & particleboard	1.3
Romanel/sawmill	0.7
Celhart Donaris/pulp and paper	0.3
Regholz/sawmill	0.3
HLV/sawmill	0.3
MIS Grup/sawmill	0.3
Euroforest/sawmill	0.2
Somes Dej/pulp and paper	0.2
Finnforest Baco Production/blockboard	0.2
Petroforest/sawmill	0.2
Foremar	0.2
Forex	0.1
Robinia sawmill	0.1
Forestfalt/sawmill	0.1
Total	7.8

These modern mills now process 50% of the annual timber production.

and lakes adding to the attraction. Hunting is famed with boar, red deer and even bear and lynx available. A viable forest estate investment can include lodges, superb mountain scenery and a steady income through timber sales.

The right forestry investment, while Romania modernizes its administration and EU grants help to improve its labour force and infrastructure, could appreciate the return substantially, as has been demonstrated in the Baltics.

Short-rotation poplar production offers another investment opportunity. The ground-water level of soils around close to the Danube remains steady and close to the surface. Poplar planted on these soils can produce astonishingly high growth, with trees achieving a diameter of more than 40 centimetres in 12 years for high-quality veneer logs. The return can be in the region of 10 per cent. Alternatively, even shorter three-year rotations can be created for wood fuel. As the trees are planted on poor-quality agricultural land, the strict forest regulations do not apply.

Estonian property: EST Kinnisvara

Yields are typically around 7 to 8 per cent.

The property business grew from the profit that the forests produced, with clients investing in commercial and industrial real estate. We now manage some 10,000 square metres of floor space. Estonian property was badly hit during the crises (see Figure 4.1.9), but is now beginning to recover, offering opportunities which should benefit from the improvements in rents and values.

Estonia joined the euro in January 2011. Its management of the economy is quoted as being exemplary. With its low rate of borrowing and rebound of GDP, Estonia will soon return to wealth creation. Tallinn, the capital (population 400,000), is the main area for commercial investment. Before the crisis, vacancy was less than 5 per cent. In January 2011, it is running at 10 to 15 per cent overall, ranging from less than 10 per cent in the city centre to some 40 per cent in outlying areas.

FIGURE 4.1.9 The amount of new office space (m²) completed during 2005–2009 in Tallinn and forecast for 2010

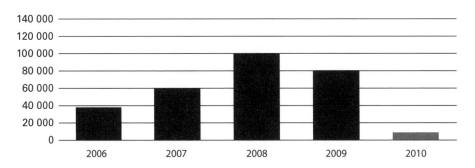

SOURCE BPE

FIGURE 4.1.10

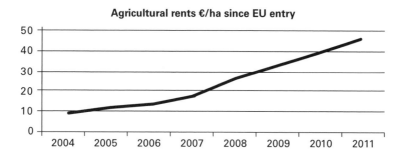

Agricultural rents €/ha since EU entry

Rental values dropped by 30 to 40 per cent from 2007, but are stable in January 2011. Yields are typically around 7 to 8 per cent.

EST Kinnisvara was ahead from the outset of the recovery, buying 747 square metres for a client in the centre of Tallinn with a sitting tenant and a yield of 7.8 per cent, which should improve dramatically as rental values rise.

Apart from Tallinn, the other two towns with investment potential are Tartu (population 100,000) and Pärnu (population 44,000). The latter is the seaside holiday town and the population doubles in the summer.

EST Kinnisvara also manages 3,000 hectares of agricultural land. EU subsidies and rents are climbing and farmland values have been following them (see Figure 4.1.10). The average is around €1,000 per hectare.

Conclusion

Forest and property can provide a long-term stable investment with an opportunity of capital growth in Eastern Europe and tax efficiency in the UK. The wide experience of KMS Baltics can provide an easy entry to these investments.

Buying overseas property in 2011

ADAM CHALLIS, HAMPTONS INTERNATIONAL

In focus: international property investment: a buyer's guide

The level of interest in overseas property investment is beginning to improve in 2011. Domestic savings rates are hardly worth consideration and there are recognized opportunities for strong investment returns elsewhere. Property offers an attractive alternative and in uncertain times can provide the reassurance of being an underlying physical asset, despite value fluctuations.

British buyers have had a long-held affinity for overseas travel, and property ownership has always been a part of that attraction. The global economic crisis and property market slowdown – collapse in some markets – forced many would-be overseas investors to pull back from new purchases. But, after three years of gloomy economic activity, many analysts view 2011 as the year to make strategic investments for the next economic cycle.

As can be seen in Figure 4.2.1, foreign direct investment (FDI) in property (both residential and commercial) has continued to grow over the past decade. Following the 2003 surge that pre-dated the entrance of accession countries into the European Union, there has been a steady rise in UK household FDI, growing by an average of 11.4 per cent per annum.

Multiple home ownership has become increasingly common, with real estate ranking alongside art, precious stones and exotic cars as legitimate alternative investments for more affluent individuals. Given the resilience of UK FDI investment flows through the economic downturn, it is difficult to see this trend abating in light of new opportunities and relative weakness in domestic property markets. But before considering the likely investment choices of UK buyers, it is worth reviewing the main methods of entry into foreign property ownership.

Outright ownership

Outright ownership, for most Europeans, still remains the most popular choice for second home ownership. It comes with real, tangible value and few, if any, restrictions

FIGURE 4.2.1 Foreign direct investment by UK households in overseas property

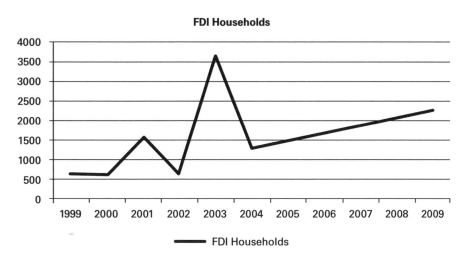

SOURCE Office for National Statistics

on usage. Any capital appreciation and depreciation are solely the owner's responsibility. Of course, the freedom to come and go at will also comes with the need for full-time upkeep.

For some, the downside of outright ownership is that in addition to maintenance costs, there is a sense of obligation to return to the same place for each holiday. This can be repetitive and offers little scope for variety. To counter this, many hotel resorts over the past decade have started selling private residences as well as reciprocal rights at partner resorts around the world. The owner is allocated certain weeks, similar to club membership, but retains ownership rights on at least one physical property.

Fractional ownership

Fractional ownership is a relatively new concept for Europeans, first developed in the United States in the 1980s and early 1990s. It has become an incredibly popular mode of vacation home ownership due to its affordability and flexibility. Fractional ownership has long been a popular method of yacht ownership and, with property, there is little difference. Essentially, a property can be owned by several individual investors (usually between four and ten per property) who each hold an equal share in the property, 25 per cent, 10 per cent, etc. Each owner will have usage rights to stay in the property over the course of each year and their preferred dates of usage are outlined and agreed by all respective owners to prevent a clash of dates.

This mode of home ownership means that the initial cost of purchase is much more manageable. For instance, if a property is worth £1 million in the open market and is sold using a fractional model, each owner will pay an equal price for their share. So for four buyers this would be 25 per cent or £250,000. Most vacation homes are only used for four to six weeks a year by their owners, which for a £1 million home may represent poor value for money. However, if that same £1 million home now only costs a quarter of that price and you still use it for four to six weeks each year, the value is much more attractive. In addition, all running costs can be split between the owners and, like any freehold title, there are full rights for transfer of ownership if a sale is required.

Membership clubs or residence clubs

Unlike fractional or outright ownership, this is an annual subscription membership that entitles you and your family to use a selection of homes, usually dotted around the world. These properties are held by the membership company, which will also manage the properties in most instances. As a member, you will never own the properties you stay in; however, for your annual subscription fee you can stay free of charge in any number of properties in the portfolio for a predetermined length of time. Similarly to fractional ownership, each member will receive an allocation of weeks per year to spend in the properties.

Most membership clubs also offer different levels of membership, with more expensive subscriptions buying greater privileges or usage rights. The homes themselves can be banded into categories; for instance, a Maldivian four-bedroom water bungalow would cost more 'points' or weeks to stay in than a two-bedroom apartment in the Algarve. Although this form of vacation 'ownership' is actually an entitlement (as there is no underlying property ownership), it offers immense flexibility and a huge selection of some of the best properties in their respective markets.

Resort residences or condominiums

Owning property on hotel resorts has become very popular with buyers in the middle- to upper-tier price ranges. This form of ownership offers all the comforts you would expect from leading four- and five-star hotels, while having your personal property on site. Owners usually have unlimited access to all hotel facilities with generous discounts for paid-for activities like spa treatments or diving tours. In addition, owners usually receive privileged discounts on their food and beverage bills and on-site stores.

Again, ownership comes with the potential benefit of full capital appreciation and, in most instances, owners have a choice to include their property in the hotel rental programme for periods when the property is not in use. Owners may have unlimited or a predetermined level of usage, usually between six and 12 weeks per annum.

Income earned from paying guests staying in the property is normally split between the owner and the hotel operator. The amount varies, but is generally between 40 per cent and 75 per cent of net income to the owner. Many large, well-known hotel operators offer this private ownership experience all over the world, including Four Seasons, Ritz Carlton and Fairmont Raffles. Luxury, comfort and convenience can be expensive, with high initial prices and annual service charges. However, for those who can afford it, the costs pale in comparison with receiving the quality they desire.

The relative benefits of the four main types of access to foreign property are summarized in Table 4.2.1.

Access points: choosing the right markets and property types

Depending on the budget and the type of foreign property ownership preferred, there is a seemingly infinite number of potential investment locations to choose from. However, not all ownership structures are prevalent in all locations, and many markets restrict or ban outright ownership of property by foreigners.

Most Western countries offer unrestricted foreign ownership of property (eg United States, Canada, United Kingdom, Spain), but there are a few out-of-bounds countries for the wider buying public. For instance, excluding nationals, only people of Indian origin (PIO) or non-resident Indians (NRIs) can own property in India. For the rest of the world, buying a property in India is highly difficult and risky, or nigh on impossible. Similarly, Mecca in Saudi Arabia has some of the most in-demand real estate in the world, but ownership is open only to Muslims and nationals of any of the Gulf

TABLE 4.2.1 Alternative structures for foreign property ownership

Type	Transferability	Income return	Capital return	Maintenance costs
Freehold ownership	Full rights	Yes/No	Yes	Significant
Fractional ownership	Some restrictions	Yes, minus costs	Yes, pro rata	Limited
Membership/ residence clubs	No rights	No	None	Limited
Resort residences	Some restrictions	Yes, minus costs	Yes	Significant

SOURCE Hamptons International

Cooperation Countries (GCC). Foreign interest for Chinese property is also surging at the moment, in line with the country's economic transformation. However, it remains restricted for direct foreign property ownership. Professional advice can help navigate the often confusing restrictions that exist on the foreign ownership of property.

In general, the four principal concepts already highlighted can be found right across international markets. Outright ownership is the most common method of acquiring foreign property. In contrast, fractional ownership is more frequent in the United States and Canada, where it has been around since the 1980s and is widely accepted and understood.

Hotel-managed residence properties can be found in most of the world's major metropolitan cities. In addition, these private residences are often included within new hotel developments in emerging markets as a method of funding the project. A common feature in the world's most coveted far-flung destinations, luxury hotel groups like Six Senses, Viceroy and Four Seasons all offer fully managed homes in tropical locations such as Thailand, the Caribbean and Seychelles. These branded and fully managed homes are playing an important role in offering excellent investment potential as well as a highly desirable lifestyle choice to the jet-setting fraternity.

Property investment may be either a short- or long-term prospect. Off-plan purchases can be a way to take advantage of significant discounts and investment growth, with the intention of 'flipping' the property at or even before completion. However, this form of property investment also comes with additional construction risk (eg failure of the developer to complete construction on time – or at all) and the potential sales risk of returning your unit to the open market at a time when many other units in the building may also be for sale.

Buyers should also consider the legal structure of their chosen markets in order to be confident that their investment is secure. Some jurisdictions have a taper relief on capital gains tax dependent on the amount of time the property is held. These rules, generally set up to limit the attractiveness of property to speculators, can have a significant impact on the investment return of the purchase.

Trends in foreign property investment for 2011

Economic uncertainty has stubbornly persisted in the UK and much of the developed world. Despite this, global output is currently forecast to remain well above 4 per cent this year, due to the continued strong performance of developing nations, including China and India in particular. This disparity between the relative prospects of developed and developing nations will encourage many property investors to consider locations further afield.

Exchange rates also continue to be a key factor that drives international property investment opportunities, as the pound sterling has eroded in value against many of the world's currencies since the beginning of the economic downturn in 2008.

The weakness of sterling adds extra impetus to identify locations where better value can be extracted. However, this window of opportunity may not last; according to Stephen Hughes, Director at www.currencies.co.uk, 'By the end of 2011, we may well see the pound/dollar exchange rate back to a level last seen towards the end

(September) of 2008.' It is also very difficult to predict the movement of sterling against the euro, with the protracted fiscal problems of PIGS countries (Portugal, Ireland, Greece and Spain) likely to drag on the euro for much of 2011.

House prices in many markets are off their long-run average value. As shown in calculations by *The Economist*, countries around the world are both above and below expectations. These figures may imply an opportunity in markets where a correction is expected; however, there may be fundamental reasons why prices have moved above or below the long-run average and may not return anytime soon. Table 4.2.2 identifies key markets where property is considered to be under- or overvalued.

In line with investment strategies for other property investment types post recession, it is expected that there will be a continuing shift away from riskier, secondary locations and properties. Western Europe is by far the dominant region for foreign ownership by UK buyers, due to short travel distances for use of the property and strong legal foundations for property ownership. However, the overdevelopment of holiday homes for some locations, notably Spain where it is estimated that upwards of 700,000 properties still remain vacant, has meant that not every 'traditional' holiday location will have the right investment characteristics.

The last business cycle saw British investors move ever eastward in Europe, attracted by cheap properties and the promise of rapidly growing house prices. Through the downturn, many of these markets saw significant price falls and a number of buyers lost heavily. This time around, we expect buyers to be more selective, with a greater proportion looking closely at the investment potential and long-term sustainability of the location.

An interest in the rental potential will consolidate demand towards proven locations. As a result there will be a significant differential in demand between properties with all of the right features (eg on the water, walking distance to town, easily accessible by road and air, etc) and anything which forces a compromise on buyers.

The off-plan buyer is also likely to be less keen than they once were. Off-plan purchases were typically an opportunity to chase strong capital growth, but the risk of failed completions or a limited resale market has reduced demand for properties in the early stages of a development. Some locations are still to show any signs of recovery from the overhanging supply of unfinished stock from the previous cycle.

In summary, overseas property investors will do well to remember the fundamentals of choosing the right location and selecting an appropriate property for that location. These general guidelines can then be aligned with personal investment criteria, such as ownership structure, income return vs capital growth and short-term vs long-term investment horizon. At that point it will be well worth doing extensive background research and speaking to a professional who knows the local market and can help secure the investment. If you can't find that investment right away, be patient; it will be out there somewhere.

TABLE 4.2.2 Over- and undervalued property markets

The Economist house price indicators % change	Latest	Q3 2009	1997– 2010*	Undervalued (–) or overvalued (+)**
		on a year earlier		
Singapore	23.1	−11.0	18.0	19.2
Hong Kong	20.6	3.2	−6.0	58.1
Australia	18.4	6.6	220.0	63.2
China	9.1	1.9	n/a	18.1
Sweden	8.9	1.4	173.0	41.5
Belgium	6.5	−2.9	157.0	21.6
France	6.0	−7.9	141.0	42.5
Germany	4.8	−4.4	n/a	−12.9
Switzerland	4.5	4.1	33.0	−6.4
Canada	4.5	−3.8	70.0	23.9
Netherlands	4.2	−6.8	92.0	23.6
United States (Case-Shiller ten-city-index)	4.1	−10.6	102.0	4.6
United States (Case-Shiller national index)	3.6	−8.6	65.0	−2.1
Denmark	3.4	−12.2	98.0	19.4
New Zealand	3.4	1.1	108.0	20.2
Britain	3.0	−3.0	181.0	32.0
South Africa	2.9	−0.2	421.0	na
Italy	−2.8	−3.8	94.0	10.5
Spain	−3.4	−8.3	157.0	47.6
Japan	−4.0	−4.0	−37.0	−34.6
United States (FHFA)	−4.9	−4.0	70.0	10.6
Ireland	−17.0	−13.8	129.0	13.2

SOURCES ABSA; ESIR; Hypoport; Japan Real Estate Institute Nationwide; Nomisma; NVM; FHFA; Quotable Value; Stadim; Swiss National Bank; Standard & Poor's; Thomson Reuters; government offices; The Economist.

* Or most recent available figure

** Against long-run average of price-to-rents ratio, latest available rents data

Learning in the woods

DIANNE LAING, SCOTTISH NATIVE WOODS

About us

Scottish Native Woods incorporated as a charity in 1994, following some years as a campaigning organization, and has been working tirelessly to promote the conservation of native woodlands in Scotland ever since. We are based in Aberfeldy and are dedicated to the restoration and expansion of Scotland's native woodlands. We work to improve access to these beautiful woods to encourage healthy lifestyles and tourism. Unfortunately, care of our environment is not always instinctive and we aim to impact on this through our many education programmes.

Regular monthly donations enable us to plan for the future, and legacy donations allow us to develop our long-term strategy to increase the area of native woodland in Scotland.

Our learning programmes

We encourage people of all ages to engage with and enjoy their local woodlands through a variety of different methods. We are most definitely operating a cradle-to-grave approach as the most effective means of promoting greater care of our environment and a healthy future for people and woodlands. We run a number of different programmes that engage with whole communities.

Growing up with Trees

This was our first programme that started over 17 years ago in Kenmore Primary School on Loch Tay. The idea is to introduce children to the full life-cycle of trees. They begin by going out to a local woodland in the autumn and collecting seeds for a variety of trees. They are then shown how to nurture the seeds and protect them over the winter for sowing in the spring. When the young trees have sprouted they are planted in the school's own tree nursery. Tree nurseries often involve more than just the children as they bring parents and grandparents along to help. We have also had volunteers from local firms come out to construct the wooden frames for tree beds.

We provide sessions on how trees grow, how they are harvested and the many uses that the timber provides from fuel to furniture to house building. When the trees are big enough to plant out, the children can either create an area in the school grounds or take them back to the woodland where they collected them. Our first trees in Kenmore are now over 20 feet high and some of the original children are parents themselves – and so the cycle continues.

Forest School

Forest School (FS) is a curriculum-linked programme of regular outdoor learning and has its greatest success among primary school age children. It entails weekly visits to a woodland for a whole term or year. A wide variety of skills is learned by being outdoors, such as shelter building, outdoor cooking on a fire, artwork, nature lessons, play and games, which all add something to the development of the child. In particular, those children who find it hard to assimilate learning indoors and may be disruptive or distracted find they gain more confidence and higher self-esteem when they are in the woods and get the chance to be the leader or be the person to show a younger pupil how to do a task. Some of the schools we are working with are in areas of multiple deprivation and the life skill-enhancing methodology of FS helps towards greater care of the environment and better citizenship.

We cannot meet the demand for FS and are therefore promoting training for others to become FS leaders. This, again, is something that opens up opportunities for the wider community as it is not only teachers who train as FS leaders but community members and those looking for a new career or the opportunity to get back into the workplace.

Earth Education

In essence Earth Education is different from environmental education because it is about being immersed in nature to gain understanding through feelings to transfer learning into *living more lightly on the earth*. Earth Education activities are sometimes used by educators as a bolt-on but they are designed to be used in their purest form, as prescribed by the Earth Education Institute. This cannot happen with isolated activities or as part of another programme. It has to be carefully crafted and structured, which takes time and resources.

Earth Education would ideally take place in woodlands but could also happen in school grounds, however barren, as it is about making the familiar unfamiliar. Our education officer has even carried out an Earth Walk in a car park. This is a highly adaptable programme that can suit all ages, although it is most common from lower primary upwards, and can include high school if there is demand. As well as with schools, it can be run with family groups or after-school clubs. It is cross-curricular and complementary to the Curriculum for Excellence (Scotland's learning standard), embracing the four areas – learning, contributing, responsibility and confidence.

Volunteer opportunities

As part of our core activity we engage with people to undertake practical conservation tasks that will improve a habitat or woodland in their local area. We run volunteering events that offer training in a wide variety of conservation and rural skills. In the past year nearly 90 volunteers have been recruited and learnt skills such as habitat surveying, bridge, path and steps building and restoration, general woodland management, PAWS (Plantation on Ancient Woodland Sites) restoration, tree nurseries and planting, drystane dyking, removal of invasive species, deadwood habitats, use of hand tools, and outdoor health and safety. Many of the volunteers are unemployed people, including some from areas of multiple deprivation, who benefit from many health and well-being outcomes.

The nature of our business means we are mostly working in rural or semi-rural areas in dispersed and small communities that suffer from a lack of access to training and a shortage of networking opportunities. Traditionally, in rural areas, there are more self-employed, more small businesses, more people working two jobs, more seasonal and short-term work and relatively low wages as most jobs are unskilled. The existence of many small local companies means there are fewer opportunities for training or up-skilling, so volunteering can be a very important resource.

Following the economic downturn there is evidence that there are increased mental health issues and greater levels of stress among rural residents as job opportunities become increasingly limited and the cost of living rises. Having social networks such as conservation volunteering can help to remove barriers to employment, as both practical and social skills are learnt and practised. Outdoor working is also known to improve mental well-being.

Learning Woods

This is a project of two strands that engages whole communities in creating or benefiting from local woods. Our aim is to increase knowledge and understanding of Scotland's native woodlands and the opportunities for sustainable woodland management of these woodlands in rural and semi-rural communities.

Strand 1, Learning Woods: creating a community resource

We help communities across the centre of Scotland to create Learning Woods. These discrete new woodland plantings are planned and planted by local people and become lasting community assets, allowing present and future generations to learn about the trees that are found in Scotland and how to look after these woods.

Strand 2, Learning Woods: using a community resource

We also work with groups to help them learn how to use woodlands to create community sustainability. This strand encourages communities to link local woodland management with taking action to reduce their own carbon footprints.

Why is this needed?

Strand 1. Environmental education is now a key theme within the national curriculum, schools increasingly wanting to use woodlands as an educational resource. Evidence of this is seen in the increase in Forest Education initiatives, Forest School and Earth Education activities. Despite this, there remains little more than a superficial knowledge of our full range of native and introduced non-native species. This is in part due to the difficulty schools and other learning organizations have in finding locations where the full range of tree species is available.

Strand 2. Over the last 20 years there has been a heightening awareness of the importance of native woodlands and their management and expansion. This is particularly relevant now with the issues surrounding our need to drastically reduce our level of greenhouse gas emissions. The ability to use locally produced wood fuel to provide home heating is a key component in dramatically reducing domestic carbon emissions from energy consumption at home. Locally produced wood fuel is the lowest embodied energy resource available, with a carbon footprint that is 800 per cent lower than oil (4 g compared with 1100 g of carbon).

The proposal

Learning Woods: creating a community resource

Working across Scotland, Learning Woods will create an environmental resource for schools and the wider public. Each year, we aim to engage with around 10–15 schools or community groups to create educational and volunteering opportunities. The addition of Learning Woods native tree plantings in public parks, school grounds and community open space will further establish and nurture long-term recognition of the plight of native tree species throughout Scotland. These mini-woods will create hundreds of hectares of new woodland, planting thousands of trees and thus expanding woodland habitats and linking wildlife corridors.

Learning Woods: using a community resource

This strand encourages volunteer groups (all ages) to learn more about the ecology and management of their local woods for both conservation and as a potential green energy resource through a series of Learning Woods events. We make use of identified existing woodlands near communities where management for fuel wood production is appropriate. These events work with groups that already have an interest in sustainability but are finding it difficult to make links with their local environment.

Events provide information on the potential for wood fuel, a practical demonstration of how wood fuel production and woodland conservation can be combined and opportunities for hands-on practical sessions related to the production of firewood.

Benefits and outcomes

This project provides essential opportunities to improve knowledge of our native trees, heighten public awareness of sustainable woodland management, local-scale wood fuel production and the contribution to addressing both climate change and energy supply concerns:

- Creation of Learning Woods as long-term outdoor classrooms for all ages.
- Full range of tree species in accessible locations.
- Wildlife corridors and new woodland habitats.
- Production of wood fuel at a local level assists in the stimulation of small-scale rural development.
- Development of local social enterprises linked directly to community involvement promotes sustainability and employment security.
- Woodland management undertaken to produce wood fuel at a local sustainable level balances the requirements of:
  - conservation;
  - natural habitats;
  - energy utilization;
  - the timber resource.
- Small-scale, low-impact woodland management has the potential to allow flexibility in production and so minimize disturbance to the often fragile woodland environment.
- Community involvement in the real tasks of managing local woodlands through the full cycle of wood fuel production activities will promote healthy physical activity with a shared and definite objective.
- A balanced view of these essential elements can foster stronger ties between individuals and communities, and an appreciation of our local natural landscapes.

Beneficiaries

The primary target groups are: schools and the whole school community; young people's organizations; community groups; rural and semi-rural transition towns; social enterprises; and local woodland contractors.

The project activities are open to all to volunteer and subsequently to learn about woodlands and their importance for biodiversity, heritage and economic sustainability. Involvement is encouraged by publishing information on our websites and mailing to schools and community councils, community meetings and demonstration events.

Local contractors are employed to perform wood fuel processing activities that are not suited to volunteer input. This will support local skills development and stimulate rural employment.

CASE STUDY   Camserney Community Garden

Camserney is a community project located just outside Aberfeldy on land donated by the local landowner. At the end of 2009 it consisted of a variety of raised beds, allotments, polytunnels and a greenhouse. Local people have now created five allotments for growing organic vegetables, and the local school, Breadalbane Academy, uses it for training young people in a variety of land use skills including horticulture and arboriculture.

Each year some 30 pupils use the facility for their Skills for Work Course and five of the students won Community Achievement Awards from Perth and Kinross Council for their dedication in both school and free time. The young people have also won four Harris Moore Awards for their efforts in the Community Garden and working in the local community. The students have been involved in projects to help older residents keep control of their gardens and, enthused by their new skills and community spirit, have helped a number of other members of the community.

Local enthusiasm for the project has resulted in many gifts in kind and solid support from local businesses. These have included the greenhouse, a tractor and picnic benches from Dewar's World of Whisky, plastic tubs from a local shopping centre, 20 fruit trees from Forestry Commission Scotland, bags of bark chippings from a local tree surgeon and a further greenhouse, lawnmowers, concrete slabs, tools, wheelbarrows and fence posts from local residents.

The local golf course has contributed summer holiday work experience for senior school pupils based around recreation grass maintenance and associated gardening.

Scottish Native Woods has been instrumental in assisting the community to create and expand on the uses the garden can provide. This includes hedging the perimeter for shelter and as a wildlife corridor, formal and informal education materials for school pupils and volunteers, and a specialist project related to propagating native aspen trees, the constituent tree of Aberfeldy's famous 'Poplar Avenue'.

In summary

Overall, our projects aim to link people back to the woods and stimulate greater care for our natural environment. They also help to meet our charitable objective of restoring and expanding Scotland's native woods. However, charity is the crucial word for all these activities. Although some elements of the programmes can be self-sustaining, it is not the majority. For instance, in days past, schools would have had a budget for extra-curricular activities; that is not the case in the current climate.

Diminishing budgets mean schools and community groups rely heavily on the third sector to provide learning and training. It would short-termist indeed to stop providing our services because of immediate economic constraints.

Scottish Native Woods does not get any direct government support and around 50 per cent of our income is from voluntary donations from either individuals or charitable trusts. We rely on such support to offer our services at affordable rates, or freely, to those segments of society who will benefit the most.

More information about our work, and how to make a donation, can be found on our website, www.scottishnativewoods.org.uk.

PART FIVE
Tangible assets

PASTOR-GENÈVE B.V.B.A.

Building Wealth Today.
Providing Stability for the Future.

Coloured Diamonds......Nature's Most Valuable Asset

For centuries, coloured diamonds have been admired for their beauty and mystique. They are the rarest gemstones in the world. In fact, only one in ten thousand diamonds has a hue. Coloured diamonds are also the most concentrated form of wealth in the world, achieving the highest prices on record at the major auction houses. As the demand for these crystalline works of art increases over the next decade, Pastor-Genève invites you to profit from the three pillars of success the coloured diamond market has to offer:

LONG-TERM GROWTH | PRIVACY | CAPITAL PRESERVATION

TO RECEIVE A FREE SUBSCRIPTION TO OUR MONTHLY NEWSLETTER, PLEASE SEND YOUR CONTACT INFORMATION TO OUR COMPANY ADDRESS BELOW

Pastor-Genève B.V.B.A. • 118 Rue du Rhône • Genève, CH-1204 • Switzerland • Tel: (41) 22-810-3338
Email: info@pastor-geneve.com • Fax: (41) 22-810-3339 • United States Toll Free Tel: 1-866-774-7723

www.pastor-geneve.com

Investing in coloured diamonds

STEPHEN HERSHOFF, PASTOR-GENÈVE

Introduction

Diamonds have long been considered the ultimate form of wealth – a private and easily transportable international currency. The coloured diamond market in particular can be traced back centuries to royalty and the merchant classes. These rare items have always adorned royalty and the wealthy classes as symbols of power and prestige. Elizabeth Taylor and the Sultan of Brunei can be counted among those who have developed a passion for rare coloured diamonds.

Natural coloured diamonds represent one of the most concentrated forms of wealth in the world. After all, you can transport diamonds in your pocket. They are extremely rare, with only 0.001 per cent of diamonds mined in the world each year being coloured diamonds.

Coloured diamonds not only put one in awe of their beauty but they are one of the most valuable gemstones on Earth. According to the *Rapaport Diamond News*, 'Prices per carat have doubled, even during the gloomiest worldwide economic conditions. Someone, it seems, always has the money and the desire to buy these compelling gemstones.'

As sophisticated international investors continue to seek portable, tangible wealth in these uncertain times of huge federal deficits, potential inflation and higher taxes, the potential of investing in rare coloured diamonds has never been stronger.

Coloured diamond prices

In the last couple of years, diamantaires have seen the price of coloured diamonds increase at a rate of more than 10 per cent per annum.

Coloured diamonds offer investors stability, long-term appreciation, portability and privacy. With fancy coloured diamonds, one can choose to invest in small or large stones. The return potential is significant due to their scarcity and the high demand.

FIGURE 5.1.1 Average prices of a highly saturated 1-carat fancy intense blue diamond since 1970, eye clean stones

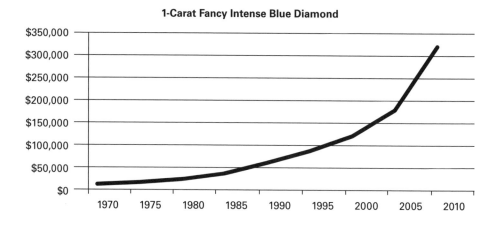

Coloured diamonds are in style – not just among celebrities but also among serious gem collectors and investors. Witness the fact that last year alone major auction houses sold three coloured diamonds at record-breaking prices that made international headlines. Natural coloured diamonds are rapidly increasing in rarity and value, as mines producing them near depletion. In 2010, diamond prices rose 10.6 per cent, according to *Rapaport Diamond News*, with coloured diamonds showing even higher price gains.

Since 1970, natural fancy blue diamonds have doubled in price every five years (see Figure 5.1.1), natural fancy pink diamonds have doubled in price every six to seven years and natural fancy yellow diamonds have doubled in price every eight to 10 years. During recessions, coloured diamonds tend to retain their value and in stable or healthy economies they appreciate in price.

In general, the value of coloured diamonds (whether destined for a private collection or commercial investment) is inevitably driven by the economies of the world. The economic cycles of the past 35 years have seen coloured diamonds reach new heights in value as price records were broken. Then values levelled off as world finances tightened; and then the cycle began again with even newer heights reached. In fact, steady growth with periods of acquiescence continues to be the standard for coloured diamond valuation, all because of scarcity.

There are five main reasons why investors purchase coloured diamonds:

1 *Privacy*. Most countries do not require the ownership of coloured diamonds to be disclosed to any government authority. The certificates are in bearer form, there are no names or serial numbers and there are no registration requirements for coloured diamonds.

2 *Portability*. Coloured diamonds are considered the most concentrated form of wealth in the world, as Figure 5.1.2 illustrates. A multimillion-dollar portfolio can be discreetly placed in a small envelope.

3 *Estate planning.* Consider the acquisition of a small cache of coloured diamonds that can be discreetly passed from one generation to the next. Depending on the number of heirs, more stones with less unit value may be needed.

4 *Price stability.* The majority of the important coloured diamonds are in strong financial hands, whether these be the dealers/jewellers or the investors/collectors who own them. Even in a severe recession, owners of fine coloured diamonds who need money will sacrifice or discount their common merchandise or other assets first. Fine coloured diamonds are so hard to substitute that anything that can be replaced more readily will be sold first.

5 *Long-term growth.* Because of the rarity, decline in supply and the steady increase in demand for quality coloured diamonds, prices should continue to rise for the next decade. It is important to recognize that coloured diamonds are still new to the general public and the potential for new buyers in the next decade is significant, while the supply stream is finite.

Coloured diamond supply

Coloured diamonds appear infrequently in nature. In fact, for every 10,000 carats of colourless diamonds mined, only 1 carat will turn out to be a fancy coloured diamond. Of the estimated 130 million carats of diamonds mined in 2010, only a few thousand carats will be cut and polished coloured diamonds. Furthermore, diamond production is down over 25 per cent from its peak in 2007.

Consider the Argyle mine in Australia. It is the largest source of pink diamonds in the world, producing over 90 per cent of the world's pink diamonds. At their peak, they were recovering 35 million carats of diamonds in a year, of which fewer than 1,000 stones would have been larger than a quarter of a carat before they were even cut and polished. Since then, production has dropped more than 50 per cent, with

FIGURE 5.1.2 An illustration of concentrated wealth

UK pence versus $1 million in coloured diamonds.
Courtesy the 'Colour Variety Collection'

estimated production of only 15 million carats in 2010, so even fewer pinks are coming from the mine today.

You can point to similar supply lines in other parts of the world, where a few carats of blue diamonds come from South Africa each year, a small selection of purple diamonds will appear from Russia and green diamonds will come from the alluvial mines of Brazil as well as Central Africa in small quantities.

For the first time in 25 years, diamond supply is declining around the world and it is primarily declining in areas where they find rare coloured diamonds. At the annual Argyle tender, an annual sale of pink diamonds, production had dropped from almost 65 carats in 2007 to 44 carats in 2009. In South Africa, diamond production has declined by almost 50 per cent in the last three years.

Two recent articles in CNN and the *Financial Times* highlight the supply shortages affecting the diamond market. De Beers has announced they will be paring back production from peak levels in 2008 as their major mines are rapidly experiencing a depletion of supply. Experts predict rough diamond prices should rise at least 5 per cent a year over the next five years, with many expecting prices to rise even more dramatically. Tiffany's has already announced that they will be paying 25 per cent more for yellow diamond rough as of October 2010.

According to Henri Barguirdjian of Graff USA, no matter how profitable the selling price, each sale depletes the available supply. 'We have sold several important stones privately at Graff this year. We thought we had good prices. Then Mr Graff said, "Now that you have sold them, what are you going to do to replace them?"'

Demand for coloured diamonds

Over the last decade, demand for coloured diamonds has increased considerably. This is due to a number of important factors: from the growth of coloured diamond sales at the retail level to the increase in demand from international collectors and investors, coloured diamonds have become the shining light of the gemstone world.

Until very recently an occasional rarity, coloured diamonds have become a staple, taking an increasing share of trade show and independent jeweller counter space, as well as tremendous activity at the auction level. A recent article in the *Globe and Mail*, the most read national newspaper in Canada, stated: 'If you want to focus on the investment side, natural fancy coloured diamonds are the only way to go; they always appreciate in value. In the 40 years since the industry started tracking them, they have always held their value.'

Historically, coloured diamonds have appealed to collectors and investors because they hold their value. According to gemologist Adolfo de Basilio, who heads a new gemological institute in Madrid, the economic crisis has spurred demand for precious stones in Europe, especially large diamonds. 'The price of diamonds and gold is going up, probably because people are worried about the fluctuations of the stock market and prefer to invest in tangible goods,' he said.

One of the strongest trends in the jewellery market is the growth of coloured diamond sales, with several of the top retailers around the world devoting more of their marketing campaigns and display cases to coloured diamonds. Trade

FIGURE 5.1.3 Rough and polished price trends

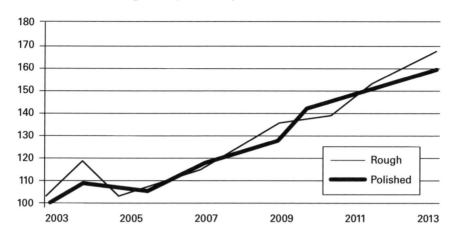

SOURCE www.internationaldiamondconsultants

organizations such as the NCDIA (the Natural Color Diamond Association) have helped educate the general public about the rare coloured diamond market and sales continue to increase as diamond buyers look to add another facet to their jewellery holdings. Coloured diamonds are so on trend that Tiffany & Co's launch of a yellow diamond jewellery line was such a success that their sales are expected to grow well over 10 per cent for 2010.

These factors have led to the first diamond investment fund being offered in London two years ago, with almost $100 million raised in order to invest in rare coloured and colourless diamonds. The fund cashed out with a single-digit return. A new fund has just been opened, which is expected to be even more successful.

François Curiel, Christie's International's head of jewellery, agrees that Middle Eastern and Asian buyers are the biggest consumers of coloured diamonds in today's market, followed by European collectors. In the Geneva jewellery sale in November, a 4.59 carat intense pink diamond sold for over 2.7 million Swiss francs. Good coloured diamonds are so scarce that they fetch multiples of the price of a colourless D-flawless stone. Furthermore, as the supply of diamonds continues to decrease, it is expected that the price of polished coloured diamonds will continue to grow significantly over the next decade, as the projections to 2013 in Figure 5.1.3 indicate.

The auction market

When it comes time to buy and sell rare coloured diamonds, one of the most prominent levels of marketing is the major auctions, held globally in the spring and autumn and selectively throughout the year.

Buyers at auction have been based all over the world and represent dealers and retailers as well as private collectors and investors. The auction houses continue to report a broad-based demand from the United States, Europe and Asia as well as strong growth from private buyers in Russia, the Middle East and Latin America.

Although the auction houses prominently market the truly one of a kind pieces, such as a four carat vivid pink or a true red diamond, they also handle more moderately priced pieces that have inherent rarity and natural beauty. These pieces also sell particularly well and have achieved prices well above estimate. Examples of prices achieved are shown in Tables 5.1.1 to 5.1.3.

TABLE 5.1.1 Recent lot prices 1: Christie's and Sotheby's

Lot no	House	Size	Colour grade	Shape	Estimated price	Actual price
402	Christie's	5.77	Yellowish brown	Marquis	$12,000–$15,000	$27,500
50	Christie's	3.60	Fancy yellow	Brilliant	$21,000–$31,000	$61,500
1957	Christie's	1.66	Vivid orange yellow	Oval	$20,700–$31,100	$40,438
396	Sotheby's	0.80	Light pink	Oval	$20,000–$30,000	$48,000

TABLE 5.1.2 Recent lot prices 2: Sotheby's

Lot no	House	Size	Colour grade	Shape	Estimated price	Actual price
1901	Sotheby's	0.66	Intense pink	Oval	$81,900–$91,000	$104,000
363	Sotheby's	2.15	Light pink	Pear	$75,000–$100,000	$134,500
1955	Sotheby's	8.88	Fancy yellow	Radiant	$101,400–$117,000	$189,800

TABLE 5.1.3 Recent lot prices 3: Christie's and Sotheby's

Lot no	House	Size	Colour grade	Shape	Estimated price	Actual price
212	Christie's	6.89	Vivid purple pink	Radiant	$5.00–$7.00 m	$6.89 m
518	Sotheby's	12.16	Vivid yellow	Heart	$930,000–$1.3 m	$1.87 m

The auction houses will charge a percentage of the selling price, depending on the value of the sale. The higher the selling price, the lower the commission. However, the auction houses have the advantage of getting the kind of exposure that brings out buyers through their global marketing efforts and extensive list of wealthy clients. The minimum offering prices they accept are in the ranges of £3,000 to £5,000, with top lots selling in the millions.

Although the world's 'important and magnificent jewellery auctions' represent a small fraction of global coloured diamond sales, they are an important public record of price performance in the market. The performance at the world's auction houses in the 21st century of rare coloured diamonds indicates a significant increase in prices. Although no two coloured diamonds are exactly alike, when looking at comparable sales, we can gauge the general level of price performance. With even stronger supply and demand fundamentals on the horizon in the rare coloured diamond market, the performance of coloured diamonds at the world's auction houses over the next decade is expected to continue its upward trend.

Acquisition

When purchasing a coloured diamond, consumers have a number of options:

- *Retail jeweller*. Retailers are starting to carry a larger inventory of coloured diamonds in their flagship stores. For example, Tiffany has built a collection of coloured diamonds. Although coloured diamonds are very popular at the retail level, and there is a much better selection than in the past, you will be paying established retail prices.

- *Auction houses*. If you are planning to acquire a piece at one of the major auctions, you are required to provide information of financial suitability in order to enter into the bidding process. Although you may be able to bid on a number of different stones, auctions are a seller's market, and the top pieces usually see a number of buyers competing for the same stone. The auctions have become an important gauge for the coloured diamond market and coloured diamonds are comprising a larger and larger portion of important jewellery sales at the world's auction houses. The recent Sotheby's auction in Hong Kong saw over 90 per cent of the lots on offer sold, with 95 per cent of the lots sold by value. This compares favourably to the historical averages of 75 per cent for lots sold and 80 per cent by value.

- *Coloured diamond dealers*. A third method is through a group of international dealers. Although most dealers work only with the trade, they work exclusively with coloured diamonds and can offer pieces at competitive prices relative to some of the pieces that sell at auction. Dealers have contacts directly with the cutting centres and other diamond dealers and are often in communication with any private sales offering coloured diamonds.

Key trends in the market

Pink diamonds

With demand for pink diamonds growing dramatically and the mine seeing the supply decrease, pink diamonds offer strong fundamental growth prospects. The owners of the Argyle mine have announced they have closed the open-pit mining operation and supply has already declined over 50 per cent in the last two years. If that pace continues, an investment in Argyle pink diamonds today could achieve tremendous returns over the long term. Bubblegum, rose and lilac pinks are the most popular.

Orange diamonds

People don't realize how rare orange diamonds are. They are very undervalued relative to their rarity as they are priced at a deep discount to blue, green and red diamonds even though they are almost as rare. One should attempt to find an orange diamond that looks like a pumpkin, tangerine or a citrus orange.

Chameleon diamonds

These possess the ability to change colour under different lighting conditions. Most chameleon diamonds have a greyish-yellowish-green colour. They are one of the great mysteries of the diamond world. According to Ariel Friedman, 'With chameleons, you will own something clearly unique among the fancy colours.'

Special stones

Any time a red, green, violet or blue can be acquired at the right price, it is always a worthwhile purchase. Only a small selection of these types of stones is available for sale each year.

Taking possession versus offshore storage

Owners have the option of taking possession of their coloured diamond or leaving them in an offshore storage facility. If you take physical possession, diamonds can be delivered to any major city in the world by a bonded and insured delivery service. It is advised that owners have the stone insured. If you choose to leave it in a bonded and insured storage facility, the fees vary from a flat rate every year to a small percentage of the value of the stone annually. In either case, the owner will take possession of the laboratory certificate. Overseas storage facilities are available in the Caribbean, Switzerland, Dubai and the free trade zones in Asia.

Monitoring the market

Monitoring prices is similar to the property market and requires a comparison of prices achieved for comparable stones on a per carat basis. Auction results, retail sales figures and dealer prices are used to gauge the general price level. Individual stones can sell for premiums or discounts depending on the buyer's preference.

The sales process

Like real estate, rare coins or art, the coloured diamond market is considered a decentralized market because there are no specific bids and offers on stones and there is not one central market where the majority of transactions take place. The advantages of a market like this are that buyers working with experts can take advantage of uncertified stones, distress sales and economies of scale to achieve discounted prices of specific pieces. However, it is essential to work with experienced firms who can source top-quality stones at various levels of the wholesale market and who can acquire the relevant certification and documentation to ensure authenticity and quality standards.

There are thousands of participants in the market, from collectors and investors to dealers and jewellery buyers.

However, you should view coloured diamonds as a mid- to long-term investment with a time horizon of five years or longer from acquisition to liquidation. When you do want to sell, you should contact your dealer at least 90 days in advance to remarket your holdings properly. This will give your dealer the chance to accurately gauge the expected market price. Coloured diamonds are similar to real estate and require time to find the right buyer.

Be realistic in your investment outlook; while coloured diamonds have historically been an exceptional investment, they are not as liquid as most securities investments and they are subject to higher markups.

UNLOCKING CANADA'S RESOURCE POTENTIAL

INVEST IN A DEVELOPING EXPLORATION VENTURE AND PROFIT FROM THE POTENTIAL OF CANADA'S NEXT MAJOR RESOURCE DISCOVERY

DIAMINE EXPLORATIONS INC. — BUILDING OUR FUTURE ONE DISCOVERY AT A TIME

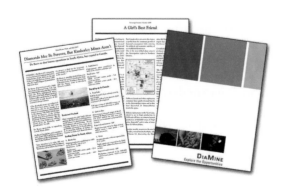

To receive a complimentary copy of our diamond and gold exploration and development plan, along with our company brochure, please send your contact information to our corporate headquarters listed below.

DiaMine Explorations Inc. 675 King St. West Suite 305 · Toronto Ontario Canada M5V 1M9
Tel: 416 847 1524 · Fax: 416 847 1526 · Toll Free: 866 557 8637
Website: www.diamineexplorations.com · E-Mail: info@diamineexplorations.com

The allure of precious metals

H JOHN STOLLERY, DIAMINE EXPLORATIONS INC

Introduction

This chapter explores the relative merits of gold exploration and other precious metals as a significant investment category. First, let us be clear that for all but category experts, diversification is key to investment security. And today, many top investment advisers recommend gold or gold equities (10–15 per cent) as one of four or five main categories of investment for a well-diversified portfolio. (See Figure 5.2.2 later in this chapter, which charts the price growth of physical gold over the past 10 years. Figure 5.2.3 reveals a similarly attractive growth rate for silver.)

Many also note that mining and exploration shares, while higher in risk, can leverage a precious metals investment to much higher percentage gains. In times of economic doubt, such as at the time of writing, gold has traditionally been sought as a safe haven or storehouse of value for preservation of wealth, often driving percentage price gains steeper than in other sectors. For the experienced and savvy investor, gold and precious metal stocks can offer significant investment leverage. Let us begin with a look at some reasons why.

In the beginning there was gold

The element gold, atomic symbol Au, was probably one of the first minerals ever to be collected and used by humans. Incorporated into rock as seams or smaller inclusions, elemental gold is also found in deposits on or near the surface of the earth, and in the gravel of riverbeds. Called 'alluvial' gold, it can be found, essentially pure, in flakes (gold dust) or chunks, up to an ounce or more in weight, called nuggets. Gold tends to shine or glitter, even in its natural state. And aside from its universally agreed visual appeal, gold is malleable and workable enough that even the earliest humans could shape it into simple implements and adornments. Even in humankind's cave-dwelling days, before history was ever recorded, gold was undoubtedly rare and desirable – thus precious. Gold may well have been the first precious commodity.

Many would be surprised to learn that aluminium (or aluminum), the most abundant metal in the earth's crust, was once as valuable as gold.

This was because of the high cost of refining it from ore, which Charles M Hall finally overcame with an electrolysis process in 1888. Now aluminium is used (and tossed away) in every household in the developed world.

On the other hand, gold is becoming increasingly harder to find, even as demand rises. One of the major costs with gold production is that many of the richest deposits have been mostly mined out, and as gold's price rises, lower and lower grades of gold-containing rock are being mined and processed. Yet its continually rising value on world markets makes such gold economical to produce. And therein lies a major factor for investing in gold. Anything above the more or less fixed exploration and production costs per troy ounce, or gram, becomes pure profit.

Golden ages

Throughout recorded history, gold has typically held its lustre the world over. Gold artefacts rank among the most common and persistent to be found in tombs of great leaders and burial sites of the noble and powerful. In Egypt, Rome, the Middle East, China, the Indian subcontinent, Central and South America and the Eurasian countries – virtually everywhere – gold figures importantly in the historical culture, mythology, religion and economy.

In the present day, gold remains the 'gold standard' of beauty, preciousness and value. Expressions such as 'good as gold', 'golden opportunity', 'heart of gold', 'golden age' and 'All that glitters is not gold' persist untarnished and unquestioned in literature and in everyday speech.

Other precious metals, such as silver and platinum (also palladium, rhodium, osmium and iridium) tend to move roughly in concert, proportionately to the price of gold. There tends to be a ratio, for instance, between the value of gold and the value of silver or platinum that varies only occasionally and rarely very much. And exploring for one can lead to the discovery of one or more others. So in broad terms, when we speak of gold as an investment, we speak of other precious metals as well.

Gold as money

As civilization and thus economies emerged on the planet, so did the need for currency (a medium of exchange, so that people didn't have to pay for goods and services with cows, chickens, fruits and vegetables). As societies searched for a common medium, uncommon enough to represent value, various stones and seashells gave way to gold and silver. At a certain level of purity, a certain weight of gold or silver represented an agreed value. To assure both weight and purity, governments began issuing coins, with difficult-to-reproduce markings and engravings. Enter 'money'.

Money representing gold

Next, bankers had the idea of replacing the gold or silver with paper notes and base-metal coins that could theoretically be exchanged for their face value in gold or silver. For example, initially a pound note could be exchanged for a pound weight of silver (specie). Enter 'representative' or 'specie-backed' money.

Money representing nothing

Eventually currencies were backed by only a fraction of their face values in specie (gold or silver). Over time, banking interests pressed for a smaller and smaller percentage reserve, until today the US dollar – like most world currencies – is backed by, frankly, nothing – except the unquestioning faith that it has a certain value. The definition of faith is 'absolute belief in the absence of evidence'. Enter 'fiat money'.

Philip Klapwijk's article 'The decline of the dollar?' discusses the potential demise of the US dollar as the world's reserve currency and its effect on future gold prices.

On 30 November 2009 Arnold Bock wrote an article pondering the demise of the US dollar. One paragraph was headed: 'Supply and demand ratio increasing price of gold. Couple these currency issues with the limited supply of above-ground gold and the fact that mine production has been reducing year over year and the inevitable consequence is demand exceeding supply resulting in gold being bid to ever higher prices.' On that date, gold was trading at or near an all-time high.

Back to gold as money

Inevitably, every so often there is a major economic shock, and the monetary chickens come home to roost. Market faith in the paper promise falters and the 'smart money' moves to another currency or investment category, or gets out of money entirely and into something that represents solid, immutable wealth, such as gold or other precious metals. (Precious stones, too, appear to be gaining credibility, as witnessed by the January 2010 index presence, and recent movement in Canadian junior diamond miners.) Precious minerals are portable, solid, real commodities representing a 'storehouse of value', most likely to gain in value as intangible paper instruments – stocks, bonds and currencies – shed their worth.

A worst-case scenario can occur when fiat currency and other paper financial instruments suffer from rampant inflation (the belief, evidenced in the marketplace, that their value is dropping rapidly relative to the goods one wants to purchase with them). We've all heard stories of Germans during the Weimar Republic needing a wheelbarrow to carry enough cash to buy a loaf of bread. The same type of thing is occurring in the present period.

And here's an astonishing Reuters report, by Robert Bruner, Darden School of Business, Virginia, December 2010:

> The very sad story of Zimbabwe's currency is summarized in a brief but impressive entry in Wikipedia. Suffice it to say, bad government policies and some bad luck ruined the economy of that country. Inflation in Zimbabwe ran at astronomically high rates. In November 2008, inflation in the Z$ was running at 98 per cent per day (according to Steven Hanke of Johns Hopkins) and ceased being used as the medium of exchange in most commercial transactions. *The Economist* reported that since the suspension of the Z$, inflation abated to 5.3 per cent in June 2010.

As of 1 August 2008, the ZW$ was revalued, simply by removing 10 zeroes. ZW$10 billion would be worth ZW$1. At the time of writing, the Zimbabwe currency has been suspended. It is naïve to imagine that the dollar, the British pound, the euro, the yen or the yuan could be immune to collapse. It is common knowledge that the US Treasury is issuing mind-boggling volumes of dollars with nothing – zero – to support them. Many of those dollars do not even exist on paper but on bank computer drives somewhere. As China now holds colossal amounts of US government debt, mainly Treasury bills, imagine the pressure on the purchasing power of a dollar as trillions more flood into the system. And historically, as currencies drop, gold rises.

In 2008 Nadeem Walayat wrote, in relation to Figure 5.2.1:

> The country is now reliant on strings-attached loans to be able to function as an economy to enable it to import goods and services. Whilst Britain is a long way from a similar fate [to that of the Icelandic krona], however, all of the ingredients are there in that Britain has a more or less bankrupt banking sector, with liabilities far beyond the state's ability to guarantee without a loss of confidence in all UK debt and a collapse in the currency.

FIGURE 5.2.1 Pressure on the pound

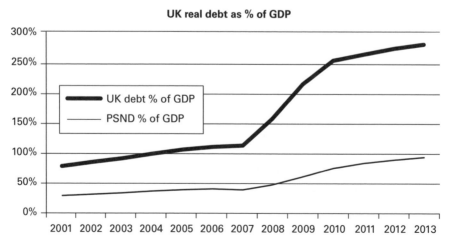

©Marketoracle.co.uk 2008

Hindsight breeds foresight

Bob Irish, investment director of Investor's Daily Edge, is not primarily a 'gold bug' (as diehard gold investing specialists are sometimes called). Still, he asked the question in January 2010: 'What if you had invested in gold at $600/ounce?' As he says, 'You could have as recently as mid 2006. You would now be sitting on over a 100 per cent gain. [Gold's] meteoric rise shows no sign of slowing. Don't let 2011 be the year you look back on and wonder "What if" I had invested in gold at or near $1,300 an ounce?'

These facts are, of course, public knowledge. But it is good to review them for current or future reference. In the first month of 2011, gold traded above $1,400 per ounce.

Goldline.com provided these comments in a recent issue: 'Gold's bull market was recently given extra impetus by concern that $12 trillion of government spending to rein in the worst global recession since the 1930s will trigger inflation... "That's fear and greed at the same time," said Toby Nangle, director of asset allocation at Baring Investment Services Ltd in London. "The fear of inflation is in the gold price."'

Gene Arensberg notes in an article titled 'Got gold report': '[US Commodity Futures Trading Commission] eyes position limits for gold, silver. We reiterate our longer-term view that the world will most likely continue down a path of fiat currency debasement, weakening confidence in all fiat currencies. We see the setup as long-term very bullish for gold metal and extraordinarily bullish for silver, looking well ahead.'

Figure 5.2.2 is an appropriate place to look at the price in US$, with a 10-year chart from Kitco covering January 2000 to January 2011, at the time of writing.

FIGURE 5.2.2 Physical gold price over the past decade

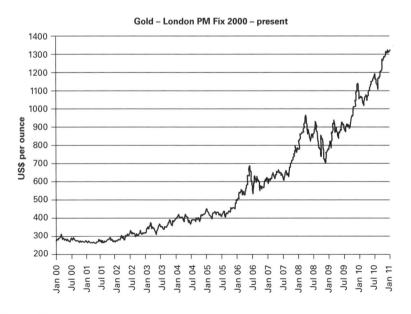

SOURCE www.kitco.com

FIGURE 5.2.3 Physical silver price 2000–11

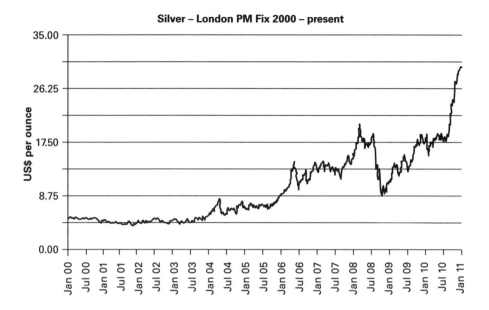

SOURCE www.kitco.com

Silver may currently be under-priced relative to gold.

Platinum follows a loosely similar growth rate in its price range, about 25 or 30 per cent above gold.

Canada's golden opportunity

The majority of Canada's metal mines are on the Canadian Shield, identified in Figure 5.2.4, in an arc stretching southeast from the gold mines of Yellowknife, through Flin Flon, Red Lake, Timmins, Sudbury, Rouyn-Noranda, Val d'Or and Chibougamau, to the iron mines of Labrador City.

Recently, Global Infomine published a total of 982 job vacancies in the Canadian mining sector including positions in management, academic/research, technicians, computers, mining production, audit and legal, health and safety, engineering, auxiliary and support staff, trade and skilled, environmental, human resources, chemical analysts, maintenance/mechanical, marketing and commercial, geology and geosciences, mill and metallurgy, executive and surveying. And this is at a time when unemployment figures are high across North America.

FIGURE 5.2.4 Location of Canada's metal mines

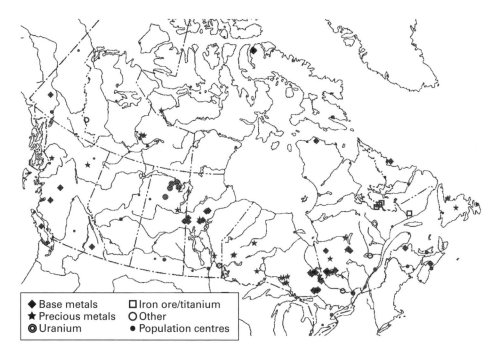

Table 5.2.1, taken from PricewaterhouseCooper's (PWC) 2010 *Global Gold Price Survey Report*, summarizes how the value of gold production in Ontario soared from 2005 to 2008.

TABLE 5.2.1 Value of gold production in Ontario since 2005

	($ billions)
2005	1.24
2006	1.26
2007	1.33
2008	1.50

SOURCE pwc.com

The following press release provides comment:

> Toronto, 17 December 2010. Despite the current strength in the price of gold, mining companies in Canada and globally are predicting high gold prices to continue throughout 2011, according to PwC's 2010 *Global Gold Price Survey Report*, released today.

> Report's key findings:

> - A majority of 82 per cent of gold producers expect their forecasted production levels to increase.
> - Nearly 75 per cent of gold mining companies expect the price of gold to continue to rise in the future. However, the current price of gold is still far below the high of 1980 in real terms.
> - Gold companies predict the price of gold will peak between US$1,400 and US$3,000.

> 'Given the high demand for gold, it will be interesting to see if companies that have located marginal deposits of gold will kick-start their production and move faster than they would under normal circumstances,' says John Gravelle, Canadian mining leader, PwC.

> The survey found 70 per cent of gold producers plan on using their additional cash influx to look for new projects or expand existing ones to replace or replenish reserves. The top three strategies are organic brownfield exploration (78 per cent), organic greenfield exploration (54 per cent), and mergers and acquisitions (37 per cent).

The Mining Association of Canada also released the news item below titled 'Diamond industry principal economic driver in the Territories'. This is significant here because gold, silver and other precious metals deposits may also be discovered during diamond exploration.

> Toronto, 2 March, 2009. A new study by Impact Economics indicates that the Canadian diamond industry has been the principal economic driver within the territorial economy during the past decade...

> [S]ince diamonds were discovered in 1991, the overall impacts to the [Northwest Territories (NWT)] economy have been dramatic, with the territorial gross domestic product tripling from $1.5 billion in 1991 to $4.5 billion in 2007. During the same timeframe, the NWT unemployment rate has fallen from 13.7 per cent to 5.4 per cent.

> Notes Mike Vaydik, General Manager, Northwest Territories and Nunavut Chamber of Mines: 'The size and quality of the territory's labour force [have] expanded dramatically as a result of increased business opportunities, and enhanced skill set and capacity.'

> Bottom line, Canada is good for mining. And mining is good for Canada.

Much more to explore

Canada is already the world's largest exporter of minerals and metals. Canada's mining sector is considered a pillar of the economy. Ranking top, or high, in production of a number of mineral groups, Canada is fifth in gold and silver production and expected to become a major supplier of diamonds, an industry a mere 20 years old in the country. More current figures, when available, will doubtless reflect the remarkable rise in precious metals prices over the past 10 years. At US$84 billion and rising fast as of 2000, Canada is probably just scratching the tip of a very big iceberg. Gold alone contributed US$2 billion in 2000.

Thus it seems obvious that exploration is the name of the game. Timed right, there is 'gold' in gold, in precious metals, and now in Canadian diamonds as well. And exciting high-leverage potential for knowledgeable investors, in well-managed, properly funded mineral exploration company stocks.

Understanding coloured diamonds

STEPHEN HERSHOFF, PASTOR-GENÈVE

Grading diamonds

Like any collectable, the initial price of a diamond and its ability to increase in value are determined by its rarity. The main factors that influence diamond prices are its colour, cut, clarity and carat weight, all being factors of rarity.

Colour

The single most important factor in grading and valuing coloured diamonds is the colour of the stone. The colour hue and tone of the diamond are compared with the lightness or darkness of the colour to determine the grading, or quality, of the stone (see Table 5.3.1). The body colour of a stone greatly affects the appearance of a diamond and its price. Colour is part of the natural composition of the diamond and never changes over time. It is caused by varying quantities of nitrogen and other trace elements present in all diamonds, displacing the carbon atoms within the crystal's structure.

Cut

Cut has the strongest influence on the diamond's brilliance. In a well-cut stone, rays of light entering the diamond reflect back to the eye of the observer. In a coloured diamond, the unique mixture of colour that the viewer experiences is termed 'face up' colour. The cutter of fancy coloured diamonds is an artist using the coloured diamond

TABLE 5.3.1 GIA colour grading scale

Faint	Very light	Light	Fancy light	Fancy	Fancy dark	Fancy intense	Fancy deep	Fancy vivid

FIGURE 5.3.1 Diamond and gemstone shapes

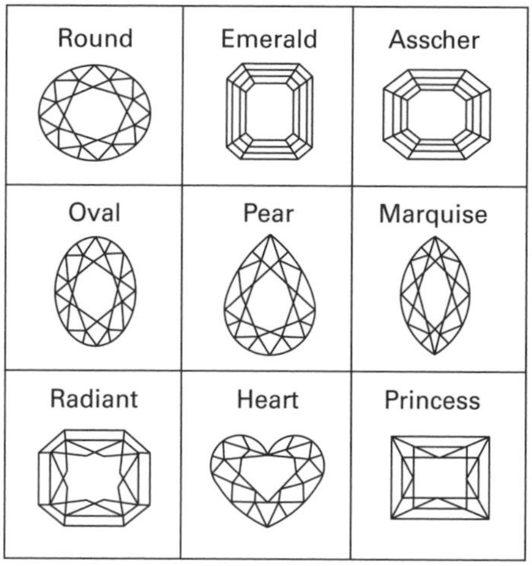

Round	Emerald	Asscher
Oval	Pear	Marquise
Radiant	Heart	Princess

rough material to create individual masterpieces with perfectly faceted dimensions and a vibrant colour composition. Radiant and brilliant cuts in rectangle, asscher, oval, heart and pear shapes are often used to maximize the colour saturation and enhance the viewing of the stone. Ideal proportions, finish and symmetry of a cut are the aim of the cutter, as well as the shape of the stone. The shape of a polished diamond is divided into 'Round brilliant cut', which refers to a round shape, and 'Fantasy cut', which refers to any other shape.

There is a difference between cut and shape. Shape means the outward look of the diamond, such as round, radiant, oval and so on, illustrated in Figure 5.3.1.

Diamond proportion refers to the ratio between the width and height of a diamond. Perfect proportions of an ideal cut affect the three types of light reflected by a diamond:

● *Brilliance:* a white light reflected back to the eye from inside the stone or its surface;

● *Fire:* white light fragmented into the colours it contains: blue, yellow, red and so on; and

● *Scintillation:* a white light reflected back as a result of movement, of either the stone or light source.

Carat weight

The origin of the word 'carat' is in the seeds of the carob tree, which were used for the weighing of precious stones in ancient times due to their weight uniformity. A diamond carat is a measurement of its weight, not its size, and is not to be confused with 'karat', used for determining the purity of gold. Sometimes, a diamond cutter must sacrifice the proportions or symmetry of the stone in order to prevent visible inclusions or to maintain the carat weight of the rough diamond. By compromising cut proportions and/or symmetry, the diamond's diameter can be larger, and thus a diamond's cut can make it appear much larger or smaller than its actual weight. The visible size of a diamond is called 'spread.' Spread is the ratio between the stone's diameter and the crown, girdle and pavilion. Coloured diamonds tend to appear naturally in smaller sizes compared with other diamonds and gemstones. In fact, very few pink diamonds from the Argyle mine in Australia are over one carat in size. At last year's Argyle tender, the largest pink diamond was 2.03 carats and most of the stones were between a half-carat and one carat in size. Because coloured diamonds have a higher price tag and are more readily available in smaller sizes, there is an active sub-carat collector market for these stones. The carat weight scale is illustrated in Figure 5.3.2

Clarity

Most diamonds have natural internal characteristics named 'inclusions' and external features named 'blemishes'. These occur in the volcanic rock where the diamond is created. Clarity, therefore, refers to the nature, colour, number and size of such inclusions or blemishes. Lighter inclusions in fancy coloured diamonds are the cause of a significant drop in clarity grade. The majority of coloured diamonds contain inclusions because of the chemical structure and pressure required to create one. Coloured diamond connoisseurs will acquire a stone based on the colour saturation and consider clarity as a secondary issue. The third most expensive stone ever sold was a 0.95 carat red diamond for $926,000 per carat in 1987. This stone was heavily included but because of its rich strawberry colour, it sold for a world record price. A comparable D-flawless diamond would sell for $20,000 per carat.

The Gemological Institute of America (GIA) has established an internationally accepted grading system, according to which clarity is graded from Flawless to Imperfect as follows:

- *FL (flawless)*: internal and external characteristics not visible to the naked eye. Such diamonds are rare and considerably more expensive than the lower-rated diamonds.

FIGURE 5.3.2 Carat weight scale

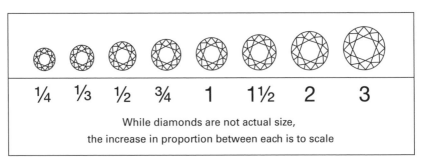

¼ ⅓ ½ ¾ 1 1½ 2 3

While diamonds are not actual size,
the increase in proportion between each is to scale

- *IF (internally flawless)*: the same as FL, except that IF exhibit insignificant minute external blemishes. These diamonds are also rare and expensive.

- *VVS1 (very, very small inclusions)*: inclusions extremely difficult to find under magnification.

- *VVS2*: inclusions quite difficult to find under magnification.

- *VS1 (very small inclusions)*: minor inclusions difficult to see under magnification;

- *VS2*: minor inclusions somewhat easily found under magnification.

- *SI1 (small/slight inclusions)*: imperfections which might not be visible to the naked eye but under magnification inclusions are fairly easily detected.

- *SI2*: inclusions quite easily recognized under magnification.

- *I1 (imperfect)*: inclusions easily detected under magnification and visible to the naked eye when viewed through the top of the diamond.

- *I2*: inclusions easily seen with the naked eye.

- *I3*: evident and prominent inclusions and/or blemishes very easily detected with the naked eye.

Evaluating coloured diamonds

The actual grading of coloured diamonds is very straightforward and simple to understand but it requires sophisticated laboratory equipment and years of experience to become an expert. It is based on both colour saturation and the appearance of colour.

Figure 5.3.3 illustrates the four general categories of colour: pale, bright, dull and deep. These are determined by how light or dark the colour of the stone is and how weak or strong the colour saturation is. Note that the light and faint colour grades will be plotted into the pale quadrant while the brighter stones with stronger colour saturation are classified as the intense and vivid stones. The coloured diamonds plotted in the bright and deep categories (fancy intense, fancy deep, fancy dark, fancy vivid) represent the smallest percentage of coloured diamond supply and are considered the rarest and most sought-after coloured diamonds. According to Stephen Hofer, a polished coloured diamond exhibits a unique impression of coloured reflections that appear deceptive and mysterious as the stone is turned in the light.

It is important to understand that coloured diamonds often appear in nature with a dominant colour and a colour modifier, or secondary colour. On a certificate, colour modifiers will appear with the suffix -ish. For example, a coloured diamond with a dominant colour of green and traces of grey might be certified as follows: fancy deep greyish green. The term 'fancy deep' indicates a very strong amount of colour saturation and a darker colour tone. In this example, the dominant colour green appears last while the secondary trace colour of grey appears first with a suffix.

If the stone is lighter with a moderate amount of colour saturation, and if the secondary colour appears stronger in the stone, ie approximately one-third to one-half purple and two-thirds to one-half quarters pink, the grading will be as follows: fancy intense purple pink. In this case, the purple colour still appears first but has no suffix

FIGURE 5.3.3 General categories of coloured diamonds

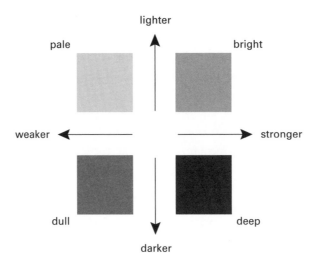

because it appears in stronger amounts while the dominant colour is the last colour, pink.

Over the years, specialists in the coloured diamond market have developed the use of common colour names to help collectors and investors understand and visualize the colour. These common colour names use terms like 'strawberry red' and 'pumpkin orange' to help illustrate the colour to potential buyers.

Stephen Hofer, author of *Collecting and Classifying Coloured Diamonds*, has been using common colour names in his reports since the 1980s as a way to convey the subtle differences between similar shades of colours so that the connoisseur can better appreciate and distinguish the beauty and the rarity of the coloured diamond in their possession.

Coloured diamond rarity

While it is true that all natural coloured diamonds are rare occurrences, the astute investor knows that there are differences in rarity among different colours. In other words, certain colours are more or less rare than other colours. In addition, investors must also understand which diamond colours are perceived in the commercial marketplace as being more rare than others.

Table 5.3.2 is designed to explain different levels of rarity. However, there are exceptions, such as pure orange diamonds, which are almost as rare as reds or blues. Orange is more common with secondary colours of brown or yellow, whereas blue and red rarely appear as secondary colours. Likewise, a pure GIA-certified black diamond is extremely rare because of the treating process used on most black diamonds, making natural blacks quite rare.

TABLE 5.3.2 Different levels of rarity

Extremely rare	Notably rare	Modestly rare
Red	Orange	Yellow
Violet	Purple	Grey
Green	Pink	Brown
Blue	Olive	Black (enhanced)
	White	

It is important to understand that stones that are classified as modestly rare, such as black, yellow and brown diamonds, have also seen dramatic sales increases because of their affordability, beauty and rarity relative to colourless diamonds. Canary yellows and cognac browns are two of the most popular offerings in the market, with sales at the retail and auction level continuing to increase.

Conversely, stones classified as extremely rare are truly one-of-a-kind pieces and are available in the open market only a few times a year. These stones continue to set new record prices at auction on an annual basis and will often see several buyers competing for the same stone. A 5-carat vivid pink just sold at auction for $10.8 million, while a 7-carat intense blue diamond sold at auction for $3.9 million. Both scenarios have a positive impact on the market and add to the continuing demand and appeal of coloured diamonds.

In the coloured diamond marketplace – where buyers compete against one another to own the so-called 'best' stones for their collection and/or portfolio – knowing the order of coloured diamond rarity from 'least rare' to 'more rare' is an important step in determining a diamond's present and potential value.

Certificates and reports

When purchasing a fancy coloured diamond, it is essential that the stone has an origin-of-colour report from the GIA or one of the other qualified gemological laboratories. The most identified laboratory in the world for grading and certifying coloured diamonds is the GIA. The GIA will analyse the stone and create a colour-only report, which identifies the colour, the weight, the measurements and colour grade. This report will also determine whether or not the diamond's colour is natural and unaltered, which is the single most important information on the report. The GIA also produces more detailed full certificates, which include the clarity, a measurement of the fluorescence of the stone and an analysis of the shape and polish of the stone. The other laboratories used for grading and certification are: the IGI (Institute of Gemology), EGL (European Gemological Laboratory), Gubelin and the HRD

(Diamond High Council: Hoge Raad voor Diamant). A Stephen Hofer report from Fancy Color Consultants is also a valuable coloured diamond document. Mr Hofer analyses and measures the colour, provides a historical reference for that type of stone and explains why that particular piece is a rare and unique collector's item.

The science behind coloured diamonds

To help understand the extreme rarity of coloured diamonds, it is important to understand the unusual process behind coloured diamond formation. Created millions of years ago, these colourful gems crystallized under geological conditions relatively similar to those of the well-known, colourless variety, yet with a slight twist of fate, endowing each of them with exciting and unusual colours.

For example, all natural pink diamonds show that they were subjected to a directional pressure in the earth when they were in a semi-solid crystalline state. This is referred to as a plastic deformation, similar to squeezing a deck of playing cards in your hand and having each card slide past the next one by a slight amount along natural parallel directions. In fact, the pink colour seen in all natural pink diamonds is localized along narrowly spaced parallel pink grain lines inside the body resulting from this plastic formation. Researchers are still trying to unlock the mystery behind these structural defects and to understand how slight movements of atoms along octahedral direction can absorb certain wavelengths of light, causing pink colour.

Every coloured diamond has its own story. Green diamonds are exposed to natural irradiation, blue diamonds contain trace amounts of boron and yellow diamonds are created through nitrogen formation under the earth by extreme amounts of temperature and pressure.

It is these unusual circumstances in nature that lead to the creation of coloured diamonds. Only a small percentage of the earth contains diamond deposits. Within these deposits, only ideal conditions of temperature, pressure and chemical exposure will lead to the formation of coloured diamonds. What is critical to understand is that of these coloured diamond formations, very few have the colour saturation, colour composition and consistency of the top-graded coloured diamonds. The science behind coloured diamond formation dictates that very few will appear in nature as the mining cycle continues in the future.

Summary

In these times of world economic and political uncertainty, investors are looking for alternative asset classes. Many turn to investing in collectables as a means of diversifying their portfolios away from traditional investments. A recent Capgemini report indicated that the wealthy have and will continue to increase their holdings in luxury tangible items in anticipation of further economic uncertainty.

The coloured diamond market offers investors the chance to achieve long-term growth, wealth preservation, financial privacy and portfolio diversification. Coloured diamonds have proven to be one of the safest and most profitable long-term investments. They are extremely rare, very durable and have an active market of international buyers and sellers.

However, before you buy your first diamond, research the market. The coloured diamond market is most suitable to certain types of investors who have a strong capital base and a long-term horizon. Always work with a dealer that specializes in coloured diamonds. It is important to learn the subtle nuances of the market so that you can make informed decisions and plan your portfolio to realistically meet your financial goals.

Canadian diamond mining

H JOHN STOLLERY, DIAMINE EXPLORATIONS INC

History of diamonds

The history of diamonds dates back thousands of years to India, where diamonds were valued for their ability to reflect light. The primary purpose of diamonds was for decorative purposes and also as a talisman to ward off evil spirits and to provide protection during battle.

The foundation of diamonds' allure has always been their beauty and mystique as a symbol of value and wealth. Their durability along with their ability to sparkle and reflect light captivates the viewer and drives consumers to purchase these rare and beautiful stones.

This is what leads prospectors and exploration companies to travel to the four corners of the earth, so that they can meet the insatiable demand for these scarce geological formations.

The geology of diamonds

Diamond is a natural crystalline mineral. It is carbon in its most concentrated form and it is widely recognized as the hardest mineral on the planet.

Kimberlite is a rare form of peridotite that can contain diamonds. Although not all kimberlite contains diamonds, all diamonds are found within kimberlite formations called pipes, or in the secondary deposits of washed-away materials called alluvial deposits that are formed in the world's cratons (as illustrated in Figure 5.4.1).

The world's cratons

Cratons are generally found in the interior of continents and formed from lightweight rock (for example, granite) that is attached to a section of the upper mantle. The craton can reach depths of 200 kilometres. Cratons are subdivided geographically and are important formations for diamond exploration, especially the oldest cratons. The location of cratons in North America is identified in Figure 5.4.2.

FIGURE 5.4.1 Alluvial deposits in kimberlite

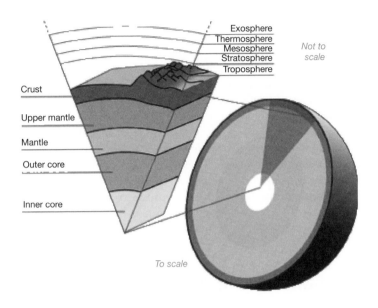

FIGURE 5.4.2 North American cratons

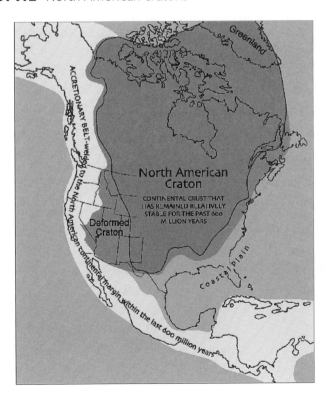

Diamond mining

Diamond exploration requires sophisticated geological analysis using modern exploration and survey techniques and the critical understanding behind the science of diamond formation. From targeting areas with high potential for kimberlite exploration to using air and land magnetic surveys to ascertain the size of the anomaly, the most difficult part of the process is locating the kimberlite.

After critical areas of discovery have been targeted and claims have been staked, explorers look to locate indicator minerals, such as garnet, that were dispersed like volcanic ash in the vicinity of the pipe's surface. Once drill targets are ascertained, mini bulk and bulk samples are taken to ascertain the concentration and composition of the diamonds in the kimberlite. These samples are costly but necessary to determine the grade of the deposit and the quality of the pipe's diamonds.

Investors and mining companies continue to invest in diamond exploration because the returns are considered the highest in the mining industry. A small company with nominal land holdings could be sitting on billions of dollars.

Global diamond supply

The diamond industry is a multibillion-dollar industry at the mining level and a $60 billion dollar industry at the retail level. Global diamond production reached a peak of 176 million carats and a value of $12.1 billion in 2006, with global production in 2010 declining to an estimated 130 million carats and a value of $12.7 billion as the price of diamonds continued to rise. The global breakdown in 2008 of producing countries is identified in Figure 5.4.3.

FIGURE 5.4.3 Global diamond production by country, 2008

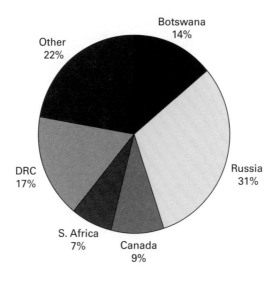

If we examine global production numbers, we see that rough diamond prices have risen approximately 40 per cent in the last three years, as supply around the world declines and rough sales increase.

Global diamond demand

As the price of gold has risen, the demand for diamonds in emerging markets, such as India and China, continues to rise. Although the demand for lower-priced commercial and industrial diamonds declined in 2009 due to the financial crisis, the production declines around the world coupled with the increase in prices for diamond rough helped the diamond market maintain stability on a comparative basis.

In the United States and Europe, the consumer price index (CPI) for jewellery remained positive throughout the duration of the economic downturn, with prices continuing to rise gradually over the last year. The US CPI for diamond jewellery reached an all-time high for three months in a row from October to December 2010. Diamond jewellery sales have been growing at a double-digit rate in emerging markets, and the US and European markets have stabilized. Continued investment demand coupled with expected increases in demand at the retail level means that the diamond market is expected to flourish over the next decade.

According to James Picton, an analyst with WH Ireland, rough diamond demand is expected to grow dramatically in the next decade. Prices will rise by one-third and he estimated that by 2015 there should be a significant shortfall of unfulfilled demand. Trevor Steel and Andrew Ferguson, both City of London analysts, believe diamonds will outperform base metals this decade.

Retail diamond demand is expected to grow by at least 5 per cent a year over the next decade as new buyers from Asia purchase diamonds and US buyers increase their jewellery holdings. That means that a mine equivalent to $500 million of diamond production must open every year for the next 10 years to meet the increasing demand from consumers. Because it takes eight to 10 years to get a mine into full production, a significant increase in exploration must occur to meet the increasing demand for diamonds.

History of Canadian diamonds

The Canadian diamond mining industry began in the late 1980s with two prospectors from British Columbia, Chuck Fipke and Stewart Blusson. In a story that is now folklore, Fipke chartered a helicopter to an unnamed lake about 300 kilometres northeast of Yellowknife. The site, on the shores of Lac de Gras, became Ekati, Canada's first diamond mine.

Among the first on the scene were Grenville Thomas and Chris Jennings, a Welshman and a South African who had been prospecting in the Territories for several years. In the early 1990s, they decided to stake claims southeast of the Ekati mine because De Beers was already staking claims to the northeast of the area. This decision proved a shrewd move for Thomas's company, Aber Resources, because in 1994 a group of geologists headed by Thomas's daughter Eira was examining the last rock-core samples before wrapping up the season when one of the three-inch tubes of kimberlite broke off, revealing a 1.8 carat diamond. It was a phenomenal find, considering that kimberlite normally yields an average of one carat (equivalent to one-fifth of a gram) per metric ton of rock.

This discovery became the Diavik mine owned by Aber Resources and Rio Tinto Mining, worth over $2.5 billion. The Northwest Territories account for over 40 per cent of Canadian diamond exploration, while Nunavut and Northern Ontario are tied for second in prospecting activity.

Canada's overall diamond production has totalled $12 billion, accounting for 13 per cent of global output and ranking Canada third by value of production worldwide. There has been more than $5 billion of initial capital development invested in the industry and Canada has developed four diamond mines and produced 92 million carats of diamonds. Overall, the Canadian mining industry has led in innovative and award-winning environmental and sustainable development practices. The evolution of Canadian annual diamond production and estimated gross revenues are displayed in Figure 5.4.4.

FIGURE 5.4.4 Canadian annual diamond production and estimated gross revenues

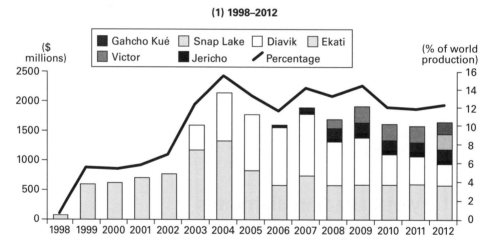

SOURCES Natural Resources Canada; BHP Billiton Diamonds Inc.; De Beers Canada Inc; Diavik Diamond Mines Inc; Tahera Diamond Corporation.
(1) As of August 2008.

Why Canada is an important diamond producer

It has long been known that when a mining company discovers diamonds, its share price will grow significantly. However, investors have had difficulty investing in diamond companies because privately held De Beers used to control over 80 per cent of supply, and new diamond discoveries in the 20th century were in areas of turmoil, such as Sierra Leone and Angola.

Canada offers investors the chance to profit from the enormous growth of diamond consumption while enjoying the political and economic stability of an established democracy.

Political stability

Unlike Africa and Russia, where corruption is rampant and corporate oversight is minimal, companies in Canada, say industry analysts, are held to high levels of accountability and are subject to strict environmental regulations. The high standards, in turn, have earned Canadian diamonds a reputation for being ethically clean.

Profitability

Canadian mines are among the most profitable diamond mining ventures in the world. Bloomberg News reported that every $1 dollar of sales from the Ekati mine in the Northwest Territories results in 56 cents of profits. According to analysts, the Diavik mine is even more profitable, with a gross operating margin of 82 per cent compared with less than 10 per cent for a base-metal mine.

Efficiency

The ratio of diamond-producing kimberlites is also much higher in Canada. It has been reported that 3.1 per cent of the 540 kimberlites found in Canada were worth mining. By comparison, only 0.7 per cent of the 6,395 kimberlites found across the globe were worth mining. That means Canadian mines are four times more likely to be successful.

Pricing

Canadian rough tends to have much better colour, and buyers for these goods are plentiful. Canada produces a consistent supply of large, commercial-quality goods that are most in demand in the major diamond markets. Over 80 per cent of Canadian diamonds are polished in Antwerp, although Yellow Knife has opened up several cutting centres for polishing diamonds. Canadian stones sold in Canada are reportedly garnering premiums of between 5 and 30 per cent over other comparable diamonds. This means that as demand for diamonds increases, it is expected that Canadian diamonds will continue to garner premium prices.

Areas of active exploration

The race to find diamond-bearing kimberlitic pipes remains in full force around the world. But nowhere is it more active than in Canada, which has maintained its position as one of the most promising new locations for diamond mining. The diamond giant De Beers has discovered more than 200 kimberlites in 12 different areas of Canada, identified in Figure 5.4.5. They estimate that well over half of these are diamondiferous.

Ontario

The Victor Mine is located in the James Bay Lowlands of Northern Ontario, approximately 90 kilometres west of the coastal community of Attawapiskat First Nation. It is Ontario's first diamond mine and the second in Canada for De Beers.

FIGURE 5.4.5 Map of Canadian mining activity

Diamond mines and advanced projects in Canada, 2008

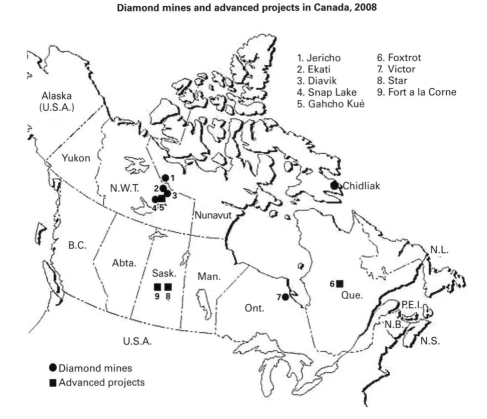

1. Jericho
2. Ekati
3. Diavik
4. Snap Lake
5. Gahcho Kué
6. Foxtrot
7. Victor
8. Star
9. Fort a la Corne

● Diamond mines
■ Advanced projects

The Victor Mine is an open-pit mine and is one of 18 kimberlite pipes discovered on the property. The Victor Mine reached commercial production in 2008 (six months ahead of schedule) and the official mine opening took place in July 2008. It will add about C$7 billion to the provincial economy over the life of the mine. There are several other significant activities in the region. For example, Metallex, owned by Charles Fipke, has been sampling and surveying in the area. Charles Fipke believes the Attawapiskat region has as much potential as the Northwest Territories. The Attawapiskat region lies on the Eastern Canadian Shield, which has recently seen a surge in exploration. The geology indicates strong potential for diamond discovery based on the presence of an Archean craton. Investors who act now may jointly own a part of what is rapidly becoming the main source of diamond supply in the 21st century and reap the benefits of the vast wealth created by diamond mining.

Quebec

The main location for diamonds is the Otish Mountains region, east of James Bay, 400 kilometres from Chibougamau. In 2001, a drill programme on the Foxtrot property discovered Renard 1 and 2, which proved to be diamondiferous. Programmes in 2003 identified an additional eight kimberlite locations. After further testing in April 2008, additional models valued the diamonds at $121 per carat, 11 per cent above the previous model. The discovery of the Hibou dyke, a WNW-trending kimberlite dyke, adds to the diamond exploration frenzy in the area, with several companies very active in the region.

Northwest Territories

The Snap Lake Mine, De Beers's first mine outside Africa, is unique in Canada. Built on the shore of Snap Lake, 220 kilometres northeast of Yellowknife, the mine is Canada's first completely underground diamond mine. The mine began production in late 2007 and is expected to be fully operational for over 20 years, with an expected annual production of 1.5 million carats.

The region can also lay claim to the Gahcho Kué, a joint venture between De Beers Canada Explorations Inc and two Canadian junior exploration companies. Eight diamondiferous kimberlite occurrences have already been found on the property and two of the kimberlite bodies are currently undergoing a $20 million technical study to determine whether or not they are economically viable.

Saskatchewan

Shore Gold and Newmont Mining announced NI 43-101-compliant mineral resource estimates for the Orion South Kimberlite located at the southern end of the Cluster within the Fort a la Corne Joint Venture. The mineral resource estimate includes indicated resources of 84 million tonnes at a grade of 13.83 carats per hundred tons (cpht) and inferred resources of 98 million tonnes at a grade of 12.83 cpht. There have been 73 kimberlites located in the north of Saskatchewan, 63 of which are covered in the Fort a la Corne claims, together forming one of the largest diamondiferous kimberlite clusters in the world. The goal in this region over the next three years is to analyse the most economically feasible way of mining the estimated 70 to 100 million carats.

Nunavut

A large exploration company announced that it has found a 3.6-carat diamond, roughly half the size of a dime, at its property on the Melville Peninsula in Nunavut. The gem, which was found in an 11.4-tonne sample, is the largest diamond found to date on the Aviat project site, company officials have said.

Canada's Peregrine Diamonds Ltd said it made a new discovery of diamonds at the Chidliak exploration property in the northern Canadian territory of Nunavut.

A number of diamondiferous kimberlites have been found on the Melville Peninsula and at the Churchhill Diamond Project, where 10 diamondiferous kimberlites have been found. BHP Billiton has used significant amounts of capital exploring for diamonds in this area because of its potential.

Diamond mining companies: profitability

Diamond exploration companies can take years to develop a viable revenue source, like that of Aber Resources. However, there are a number of proven ways for a new mining company to increase its long-term value and position itself to develop sustainable profitability in the future or be purchased by a large mining company for a premium above the current stock price:

- active exploration;
- surveying; and
- joint ventures.

Active exploration

The first step requires continuous acquisition of claims and properties of merit in proven mining areas along with developing a grass-roots exploration programme in underdeveloped areas. This will develop a diversified and balanced property portfolio in critical areas of discovery.

Surveying

Properties undergo geological mapping, surveying and line cutting in order to establish high-probability targets. Airborne electromagnetic surveys and gravity surveys reveal different physical properties for kimberlites when compared with the surrounding ground in the area. Drilling and sampling are an important way of determining the viability and value of a property.

Joint ventures

Pursuing relationships with other companies is a cost-effective way of gaining a position in an important area of discovery. It gives companies the opportunity to pool their resources through joint financing arrangements and it allows the analysis of experts from both camps to look at projects from different angles and help develop a more thorough long-term plan for surveying and sampling.

Diamond exploration financing

In order to finance exploration, surveying and joint ventures, junior mining companies generally raise capital through brokered and non–brokered private placements. The shares are sold to accredited investors interested in investing in diamond exploration companies. These securities are also usually restricted for a period of time before being sold back on to exchanges.

Diamond exploration investors

There have been numerous success stories in the Canadian diamond business. A number of new junior exploration companies have developed into mature companies, raising millions of dollars on organized exchanges and generating value for their investors. Two examples of successful Canadian diamond exploration companies are:

- Peregrine Diamond Corporation experienced a fivefold increase in its share price from January 2008 until January 2011, rising from 46 cents a share to over $2.47 a share.
- Stornoway Diamond Corporation's share price has risen from 6 cents a share in December 2008 to 62 cents today, a tenfold increase in the last two years.

Investment expectations

Investing in junior diamond exploration companies can potentially be one of the most profitable segments of the equity market. However, investors in exploration companies should be prepared for share price volatility. Because the cycle from exploration to production is a long one and announcements of progress from companies during this period are not made regularly, the share price will fluctuate. Speculation in the junior mining stock sector should be attempted only by experienced traders and only with a limited portion of discretionary trading capital. Further, you should research the company or seek professional advice before making any equity investments.

Investors can purchase private placements of new stock from the company or acquire stock listed and traded on an organized exchange. Private placement stock is restricted from trading for a predetermined period of time. The following is a list of active junior exploration company exchanges:

Vancouver Stock Exchange (Canada);

Toronto Stock Exchange: venture exchange (Canada);

Pink Sheets: over-the-counter market (United States);

London Alternative Investment Market Exchange (AIM) (UK);

NAASDAQ Penny Stocks (United States);

Neuer Markt, Frankfurt Stock Exchange (Germany).

Summary

All forecasts indicate that in 2015 Canada should be mining about 25 per cent of global diamond output by value. This 25 per cent should account for the best-quality stones in one of the most stable sociopolitical environments. Today, diamond rough is rare and Canadian rough is essential for production.

Canadian rough is expected to play a more prominent role because the output from Australia's Argyle Mine is declining, Botswana and South Africa have seen dramatic declines in production and Russia's main pipes are starting to show signs of strain. New growth markets in China and India will continue to drive demand forward at a time when supply restrictions mean that Canada is one of the only viable new sources for consistent diamond supply.

The conditions in Canada are ideal for large-scale mining operations and high-quality diamond deposits. Investors who act now may jointly own a part of what is rapidly becoming the main source of diamond supply in the 21st century and reap the benefits of the vast wealth created by diamond mining.

Sources

http://www.costellos.com.au/diamonds/history.html

http://www.suevematsu.com/famousdia.html

'Diamond' by Matthew Hart. Penguin Canada, Toronto. 2001

http://education.jlab.org/itselemental/ele006.html

http://en.wikipedia.org/wiki/Kimberlite

http://en.wikepedia.org/wiki/Craton

http://www.diamondex.net/s/DiamondExplorationProcess.asp

'Mining Explained' Northern Miner. Toronto, Canada 2004, Glossary of Terms

http://www.nnsl.com/ops/ekati.html

Bloomberg News, August 7, 2006. 'Diamonds to outpace metals'

De Beers Group 2005 Annual Report

www.northernminer.com/Diamonds/pdfs/SourcingCanada.pdf

Rapaport Diamond News, May 26, 2006

Rapaport Diamond News, April 10, 2006

Rapaport Diamond News, April 14, 2006.

China Economic Net. November 3, 2004. 'International giants strive for China's diamond consumption'

Fire into Ice – Charles Fipke, the Great Diamond Hunt, by Vernon Frolick

http://www.canadianarcticdiamond.com/03_history/history.html

www.statcan.ca/english/research/

Sovereign Society A-Letter, February 2006

Rapaport Diamond News, October 28, 2005. 'Ekati earnings to fall to historic levels,' by Ketan Tanna

http://www.diamineexplorations.com/=Diamond_Information/ca_diamond_history.php

Northern Miner News, February 2004

Rapaport Diamond Report, February 4, 2005. 'Canadian rough gives edge in polished'

http://www.diamineexplorations.com/=Diamond_Information/ca_diamond_history.php

Rapaport Diamond Report, February 4, 2005. 'Who's up next?' pp 37–9

Toronto Star, June 19, 2006, by Angela Pacienza

Sovereign Society A-Letter, February 2006

uk.finance.yahoo.com/q?s=ABER

www.tahera.com/Investors/StockPerformance/default.aspx

Rapaport Diamond Report, February 4, 2005. 'Is Canada the answer?' p 87

Art and antiques

JAMES GOODWIN, ARTS RESEARCH

Introduction

'Nearly all the steps upward in civilization have been during periods of internationalism,' noted the celebrated art historian Kenneth (later Lord) Clark (1903–83).

Never has this been truer than in the last 30 years, thanks to the free movement of international capital, with the possible exception of the 19th century, which importantly saw the birth of today's art market and the modern art movement.

The link between art and money is at times perplexing but long-standing, with the first evidence of the art trade 5,000 years ago in the early agricultural communities of Ancient Mesopotamia (modern Iraq). The first well-documented art markets developed in Italy and the Southern Netherlands (modern Belgium) during the early 16th century. Later that century, Portugal developed in the West the long-established international trade in Chinese porcelain that still flourishes today.

Despite its long history, the art market remains one of the last examples of near-unregulated laissez-faire capitalism: one where supply tends to stimulate demand and objects tend to become more highly valued as their original purpose (or even beauty) is lost.

In the wake of the credit crisis that erupted in 2007, as Western investors experience small or negative returns on cash, inflated stock and property markets, commodity price inflation and social tension because of government cutbacks, art remains a safe haven. It tends to hold its value over a longer period while providing lower risk and higher returns if part of a diversified investment portfolio. Thanks to globalization, more buying opportunities are presenting themselves in many emerging markets and some developed economies.

Still, works of art remain what buyers and sellers in the market and the viewing public think they are. The often-repeated advice is to buy an item because it touches your heart and you enjoy looking at it – an aesthetic or emotional investment – and thereby convince others of its value. The majority of art owners consider themselves collectors rather than investors by a ratio of up to 30:1, believing that higher returns are seldom achieved without a genuine love of art.

Whatever the motivation, more sale information, advice and trade opportunities are available, increasingly via the internet, to enjoy this unique and potentially lucrative pleasure on a global scale. The major auction houses are represented in 42 countries, though sales tend to take place in the major financial centres which have diverse cultures, commercial legal systems, low taxation and art expertise. Figure

FIGURE 5.5.1 Emerging market contemporary art indexes

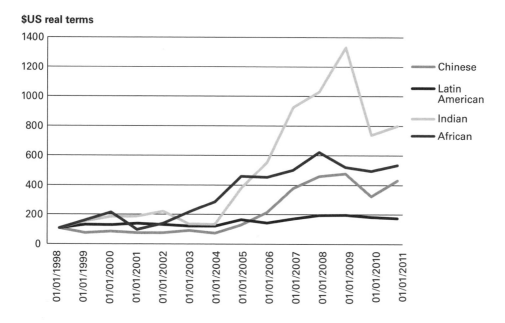

SOURCE Artprice.com

5.5.1 illustrates trends in some major emerging country art sold worldwide at auction since 1998.

The art market

Today's art market grew out of the 19th-century industrial revolution and accelerated in the period up to the First World War, owing to free trade, social and political upheaval in Europe, changes in British property law and the economic awakening of the United States. Until that time decorative arts such as furniture and silver had been more highly prized than fine arts such as painting and drawing.

Like today, the Victorian age was a period when collectors paid record prices for works by living artists, notably English pre-Raphaelites from the 1850s and French Impressionists after the 1870s. Today, some historians draw parallels between 19th-century free trade liberalism and late 20th-century globalization, particularly the emergence of art markets such as China.

As an investment, the market for the 'best' paintings has delivered rising real returns since the 1830s in a pattern following the path of international trade and the economic cycle. Since the 1950s the appreciation in prices culminated in the exceptional records of 1987–90. The bust which followed lasted until the mid-1990s.

Growth returned and accelerated in 2005, causing Western fine art prices to exceed their 1990 peaks in real (inflation-adjusted) terms in 2007–8. The financial crisis afflicting arts' biggest markets in the United States and the UK caused prices there to fall by 35–45 per cent after September 2008. Recovery returned in April 2010.

For the period from 1976 to the end of 2010, a buyer at the top of the market would have seen their $200,000 painting's value rise to $6.5m. Figure 5.5.2 charts how the international trade in works of art, collectors' pieces and antiques has varied over the period 1962–2009.

Globally, it is estimated there are over 32 million fine and decorative art transactions annually, in a ratio of 70:30 by value and 30:70 by volume. Trade is divided equally between auction houses and dealers that total over 80,000 businesses. Figures from the United Nations indicate an art trade of $27 billion in 2009, which was a 34 per cent fall from the 2007 peak. The United States had a 42 per cent market share and the UK 22 per cent, respectively rising by 4 per cent and falling by 8 per cent on the previous two years. Against the worldwide trend, during this period art imports rose in Germany and France, helped in the latter case by the Yves Saint Laurent auction. London remains the preferred location for some international art categories such as Old Master paintings.

Marketing and distributing this trade, 220,000 are employed in Europe and 149,000 in the United States. Salaries average £28,000 (£31,000 in the UK) and productivity among the mostly degree-educated workforce is about the same as other cultural industries but lower than most industries. In Britain, auctioneers employ 9,000 and dealers 42,000. The auction houses Christie's and Sotheby's have a combined international market share of up to 25 per cent. Typical of other industries, 1,000 dealers from a total of 8,500 generate 70 per cent of the UK market's turnover.

FIGURE 5.5.2 International trade in works of art, collectors' pieces and antiques, 1962–2009

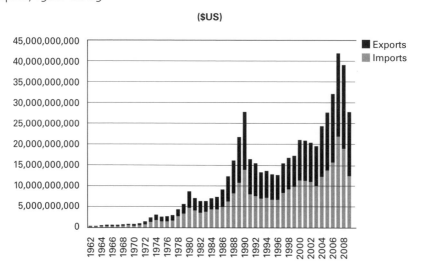

($US)

SOURCE United Nations 2010

Worldwide, in 2009, 527 paintings were auctioned for more than $1 million, falling from 1,103 the previous year. Yet this was nearly double a decade earlier. In 2009 the auction market based on sales at Christie's consisted mainly of Impressionist and Modern art (28 per cent), Asian art (15 per cent), Post-war and Contemporary art (14 per cent), jewellery and watches (12 per cent), Old Masters and 19th-century art (10 per cent), European furniture (7 per cent), 20th-century decorative arts (4 per cent) and American painting (2 per cent). Based on the average prices per fine artwork, the most expensive are Impressionist and Modern art at $3.4 million and $3.3 million, followed by Contemporary at $2.2 million, Old Master paintings at $1.5 million, Post-war art at $1.4 million and 19th-century painting at $393,500.

Photography, which averages $18,500 per work, is up to 25 times cheaper than Western painting. Records for each category in recent years include Raphael's *Head of a Muse* which was sold in London in December 2009 for $47.6 million and a Qianlong dynasty vase which went for £51.6 million ($83.2 million) at a West London auction house, Bainbridge's, in November 2010. The modern art period holds the highest record at auction at $106 million for Picasso's *Nude, Green Leaves and Bust* sold by Christie's in New York in May 2010. Among contemporary records one was established by an Indian artist S H Raza whose *Saurashstra* sold for £2.4 million ($3.5 million) in London in June 2010. Of the contemporary artists that sold well in 2009–10, 19 of the top 50 were from developing countries. This included 15

FIGURE 5.5.3 International trade in works of art by country 2007–9

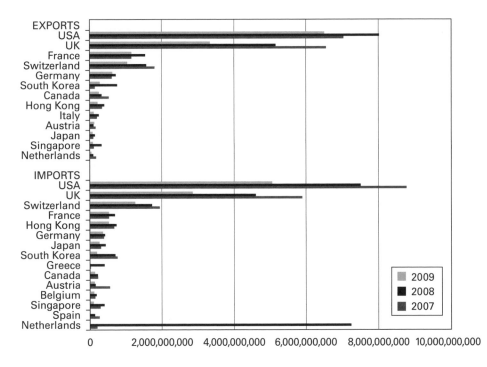

SOURCE United Nations

from China, including Chen Yifei, whose *String Quartet* held the world record contemporary art price in 2010 at $7.85 million. Other emerging artists that sold well came from the United States, Britain, Germany, Italy, India, Spain, Ireland, Japan, Brazil, Indonesia and South Africa. However, for the market as a whole there were only seven living artists among the top 50 artists sold by turnover worldwide. Figure 5.5.3 identifies the international trade in works of art by main trading countries over the period 2007–9.

Today, the market for fine and decorative art trade refers to paintings and drawings (British, Scottish, Irish, European, American, Australian, Canadian, German, Austrian, Greek, Scandinavian, Spanish, Swiss, Israeli, Latin American, Indian, Chinese, Russian, Korean, Southeast Asian, African, South African, Iranian, Turkish, Middle Eastern, sometimes including classical, Old Masters, 19th century, Victorian, after 1850, Orientalist, Impressionist and Modern, Edwardian, 20th century, Contemporary, watercolours, sporting, and maritime painting, and portrait miniatures), prints, sculpture (early European, 19th century), furniture (English, French, European and American), rugs and carpets, tapestries, ceramics, porcelain (European and Chinese), glass, silver, vertu and gold boxes (English, European, American and Russian), clocks, watches, chronometers and barometers, jewellery and diamonds, icons, works of art (antiquities, Chinese, Judaica, Islamic, Indian, Aboriginal, African and Oceanic, pre-Columbian, American Indian, Japanese, Korean, Russian and folk art), garden statuary and architectural items, and decorative art and design.

The smaller market for collectables refers to automobiles, bric-a-brac, scientific instruments, books and manuscripts (English, Continental, American, Russian, music, science, children's, maps, atlases and natural history), posters (19th and 20th century), photographs, sporting guns and memorabilia, arms, armour and militaria, dolls and toys, luggage and other memorabilia, postage stamps, numismatic coins, banknotes, stock certificates, scripts, medals, musical instruments, fashion (costumes and textiles), vintage wines and spirits, playing cards, objets de vertu, entertainment memorabilia, exploration and travel, science and natural history, and popular culture.

Formulating an art investment strategy: the pros and cons

Art's value is intellectually and commercially one of the most mystifying and indispensable concepts. The assignment of monetary value to an artwork is a complex process since there is a myriad of factors affecting art's desirability in any time and place. These range from macroeconomic factors such as currency movements, demographics and tax to those peculiar to the arts such as aesthetics, social value and even art crime! There is good reason to apply the word 'priceless' to the best artworks. In practice, the wide price spreads on the lower and upper price range estimates set at auction indicate the uncertainty about art's value. Technology is now helping to improve attempts at understanding art's value mainly by making prices more transparent but is unlikely to capture the individual appeal of artworks.

Intrinsic factors weighing upon art's value include quality, artistic merit, condition, subject matter and size. Secondary factors include authenticity, attribution, artist's reputation, historical importance, familiarity, provenance, fashion, sale location and sale inducements.

An article in *The Art Newspaper* indicated that certain subject matter could make a difference to the price of a work of art: beautiful young women and children, higher social status, sexiness, horses and figures in landscapes, sunny scenes, flowers, calm water, attractive dogs and game birds, as well as bright, bold and pale colours.

Nevertheless, the economic laws of art supply and demand continue to play the dominant role in the value of art on the market. Studies have shown that the number of best-quality works is usually in the same proportion to the total number offered, with the market tending towards long-term upward price equilibrium based on the amount of net disposable income available.

Naturally enough, demand is driven by new money, with major auctions often an irresistible spectacle of celebrities and millionaires. In the past, higher art price rises were typified by economic booms in Italy and the southern Netherlands in the 16th century, Holland in the 17th century, England and France in the 18th and 19th centuries, the United States in the late 19th and 20th centuries and Japan in the 1980s. In the 21st century, there has been a shift to less familiar art economies. Based on estimated auction sales, China's art market is now the second biggest, ahead of France.

Historically, supply to the art market benefits from debt, divorce and death. During the last 100 years, the average holding period for an established painting was 30 years, but it is now shortening as more wealth enters the art market. Today, sales to meet tax bills provide auction houses with the greatest flow of works. Since the 1980s high prices due to increased individual income have made the best artworks less accessible to public sector museums, with many of the great works disappearing into private collections. Increasingly, market supply has been filled by newer artworks and comparatively undervalued sectors such as the decorative arts and collectables. Yet, typically during the recent recession, older artworks outsold contemporary, confirming the view that people buy contemporary art when they are confident about their future and reminders of the past when they are not. Paradoxically, creativity tends to be stimulated by economic and social strife as much as, if not more than, bountiful economic times when more artists can afford to practise. The relative turnover of international trade in antiques and modern, post-war and contemporary art from 1988 is charted in Figure 5.5.4

Underlying the economic environment, the market's rises and falls are to some extent exacerbated by a consensus of market opinion, in the form of art dealers, critics, art historians and museum curators. Confirming this, every year *ARTnews* and *Art Review* magazines publish lists of the 200 and 100 most influential people in the art market worldwide. To some extent, this consensus guides the market by controlling art's supply using artist contracts and increasing demand via sophisticated marketing aimed at shocking the audience and gaining critical attention.

Economists have found that over time art experts provide an accurate prediction of art prices but with an upward bias. Moreover, art investors should beware of overpaying for art since it leads to lower subsequent returns. By increasing

FIGURE 5.5.4 International trade in antiques and Modern, Post-war and Contemporary art, 1988–2008

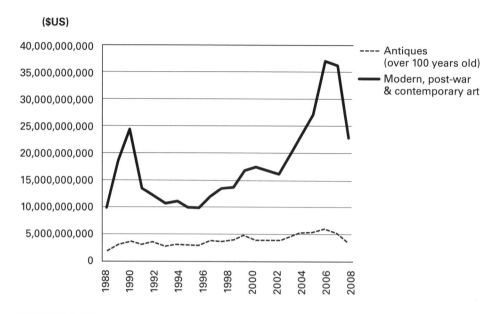

SOURCE United Nations 2010

transparency, the internet may be altering the market's operational dynamics mainly by removing price disparities and reducing transaction costs. In 2010 Christie's sold $114 million online yet this was only 3 per cent of their sales, while in 2011 the world's first virtual art fair, VIP, based out of New York, has been well attended and reviewed.

In terms of culture, studies have shown a correlation between exhibition attendance and art prices and market turnover. Continuing a five-year trend, the most popular exhibitions worldwide in 2009 based on daily totals were in Japan. In Tokyo these were Ashura and Kohfukuji masterpieces, Shoso-in treasures, Imperial treasures and 17th-century painting from the Louvre, according to *The Art Newspaper*. In Britain, the most popular exhibitions were of Chinese Contemporary art by Charles Saatchi and a Banksy exhibition in Bristol, which was ranked 30th in the world. Globally, Impressionist/modern, Contemporary and Asian art exhibitions were the most visited. The most popular exhibition venues were the Louvre, British Museum, Metropolitan Museum of Art, National Gallery and the Tate.

Driving the art market is the growing number of wealthy individuals who are now more evenly dispersed worldwide. According to the latest Capgemini/Merrill Lynch *World Wealth Report*, in 2009 there were 10 million high net worth individuals (HNWIs) globally who qualify as having investable assets worth more than US$1 million, totalling US$39 trillion. In 1996 their numbers were 4.5 million and their assets were worth US$16.6 trillion. The number of ultra-high net worth individuals

(Ultra-HNWIs) or those with over $30 million in assets, grew by 21 per cent. These ultra-rich represent less than 1 per cent of all HNWIs but account for a third of their wealth. The Asia-Pacific has the highest number of the wealthy and is the fastest-growing region. HNWIs are willing to allocate 10–20 per cent of their wealth into alternative investments including 'investments of passion'. Art was 22 per cent of these passion investments (25 per cent for Ultra-HNWIs), adding to the 14 per cent spent on collectables including coins, wine and antiques and the 23 per cent on jewellery, gems and watches. Art was most popular in Europe and Latin America. It is perceived as the most likely passion investment to appreciate in value, and in India, China and the Middle East it is seen as an inflation hedge.

Art is also likely to benefit from the growth of philanthropy among HNWIs. In the United States around $200 billion a year is donated to charities, with other regions of the world now increasing their allocation. This is for reasons of social responsibility, networking and tax benefits. In the arts this generosity means donations for public museums to buy art or bequests for which there are tax benefits. On account of their intellectual independence, museums underpin art's value and are thus vital for the operation of the market. The United States is widely regarded as the model for arts philanthropy worldwide. In Britain, private investment accounts for 15 per cent of art's income, of which 55 per cent comes from individuals, amounting to £363 million in 2009. In 2010 three-quarters of art organizations increased their funding activities but, so far, less than 10 per cent source their donations from legacies estimated to be worth £1.9 billion a year, owing to the 2007/8 financial crisis now afflicting the public sector in many countries, it seems likely that museums will begin a process of deaccessioning or selling their unseen and unused surplus art.

In Figure 5.5.5, the dispersion of HNWIs is recorded for the years 2003–9.

FIGURE 5.5.5 High net worth individuals by country, 2003–9

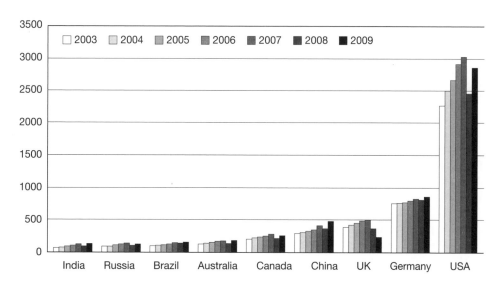

SOURCE Cap Gemini/Merrill Lynch 2004-10

In future, ageing populations and shrinking workforces in many countries will have an effect on supply and demand in the art market until about 2050. Like Japan today, where the economic and art boom ended in 1990 and the working-age population turned negative after 1998, regions and countries that will be particularly affected after 2020 will be Russia, Europe, especially Germany and Italy, China, South Africa and South Korea. Regions and countries least affected because of higher working-age populations include Turkey, Africa, the Middle East, especially Iran, Brazil, Argentina, India and Malaysia. During the next 10–15 years it seems likely that art buying will increase as more people reach the peak of their earning power pre-retirement. After that prices seem likely to fall in the West unless demand for art grows in more populous, developing countries. However, ageing populations and a passing generation are likely to increase donations to the museum sector.

Meanwhile, if history is used as a guide, creativity seems likely to increase in countries with large youthful populations and in some declining economies. Moreover, the arts are likely to benefit from ageing populations' preference for cultural tourism, as in Japan today.

Art as investment

There are two main schools of thought on art investing: specialization in new styles or artists/craftspeople with the aim of building a market for these, or specialization in art and artists that have remained unfashionable for years.

Unlike most investments, art is based only on the capital gain when the investment is realized, since there is little or no interest, dividend or rent on the capital invested. The profit on sale must be greater, therefore, than other capital gains including these less inflation. The theory is that as the number of buyers in the market goes up, art supply stays static or declines, so promising a long-term upward movement in prices.

The capital appreciation has to be substantial to make up for the initial cost of acquisition and disposal, valuation and provenance research fees as well as insurance, conservation, storage and transport. Even without these costs, a painting bought at auction for £1,000 in 2000 would have needed to fetch £2,158 in 2010 to produce an 8 per cent gross annual return including an inflation rate of 3 per cent.

Added to this, place of purchase, mainly referring to taxation, has a substantial influence on price. From 1998 to 2001, according to a TEFAF survey, the average price of a painting sold advanced 54 per cent to $22,039 in the UK and 75 per cent to $69,736 in the United States, while declining by 39 per cent to $6,761 in the EU. *The Art Newspaper* found that for a typical Contemporary work sold from the United States where there is no added taxation as in Canada, you would need to add 5 per cent in the UK and Dubai, and between 5.5 and 10 per cent in Europe, rising to 28 per cent and 29 per cent in Russia and China. Figure 5.5.6. shows the indexes for Western painting sold worldwide at auction since 1998.

UK art importers have been adversely affected by EU legislation introduced in 1999 and 2006. At the earlier date, import VAT was set at 5 per cent and more recently, *droit de suite*, or artists' resale rights tax (a tax paid to living artists which in other EU

FIGURE 5.5.6 Fine art indexes

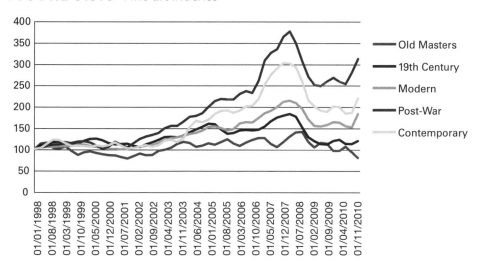

SOURCE Artprice.com

countries includes the sale of works for artists who died within 70 years of the resale date, from which the UK was allowed a six-year derogation), has been payable at 0.25–0.4 per cent on artwork, up to a maximum of €12,500. However, the effects have been mitigated by at least 50 per cent of artworks now being imported on a temporary basis, which makes them VAT exempt.

The British Art Market Federation reckons that *droit de suite* will affect those buying art in the £50,000–£100,000 range. In 2012 the 70-year rule affecting other EU countries will be introduced in the UK. This will include frequently traded modern artists such as Picasso and Matisse. Altogether, these measures disproportionately affect the UK art market worldwide wherein less than 10 per cent of its trade is with EU countries.

Assisting the collection of art in the UK, about 85,000 objects qualify for so-called heritage tax relief under inheritance tax (IHT) rules, if you choose to give items of national interest to the state on your death (IHT is otherwise levied at 40 per cent). These include certain types of books, manuscripts and scientific collections of national, scientific, historical or artistic interest. Capital gains tax (CGT) relief is also available on heritage property transfer under stricter criteria than for IHT.

For the benefit of the investor, the art market has price data going back hundreds of years. Collection of the data since the 1960s has increased the number of economic studies on the art market.

Research on the British art market from the second half of the 18th century to date by Goetzmann *et al* (2009) shows prices tracking the path of economic development, boosted by the Industrial Revolution and worldwide trade liberalization. Another study by Wolfgang Wilke (2006) about Chinese ceramic prices indicates four major cycles lasting 12–20 years since 1820.

One of the earliest art investment studies, by R C Anderson (1974), was based on the repeat sales of artworks found in Gerald Reitlinger's chronicling of the British art market 1760–1970. He calculated that the annual real return on paintings was 3 per cent and higher for Impressionist and 20th-century paintings. In his study of Post-war art, John Stein (1977) concluded that paintings were no more or less attractive than other assets, yielding the going rate for their systematic risk. He also found art prices susceptible to stock market performance. These views have been borne out by other studies. For example, William Goetzmann (1993) noted that investing in art is 10 times more risky than shares.

Today, the best-known study is by Jianping Mei and Mike Moses (2002), using data from 5,000–8,000 repeat art sales at New York auctions since 1875. These provided investors with a real return of 4.9 per cent. Moreover, like all investments, buying art is about timing as well as market knowledge. They calculated that from 1954 to 2003, art returned an annualized 12.6 per cent, which was slightly ahead of the S&P 500's 11.7 per cent and well above Treasury bonds. They also demonstrated that the art market never really crashes. Art prices have experienced only moderate declines during the 27 recessions since 1875. Moreover, in the last four major wars, art outperformed the S&P 500, growing by 108 per cent during the Korean War (1950–3), compared with 67 per cent for shares.

Further study by Mei and Moses showed that, as with other investments, the more you pay, the lower the return. A 10 per cent increase in price reduced returns by 1 per cent. This is contrary to traditional advice suggesting you should buy the best you can afford and buy fewer pieces. Their research has been confirmed by a similar study of the prints and sculpture market. They also found that holding objects for over 20 years increased return and reduced risk by 75 per cent. See Figure 5.5.7.

Research into diversification by Rachel Campbell (2008) showed that art has a low correlation with equities and other financial asset classes. Adding fine art to a diversified portfolio is likely to produce a slightly greater return for each unit of risk and a significantly better return with less volatility than stocks and bonds on their own. Based on data from 1980 to 2006, Campbell found that Contemporary art offered the highest returns and Old Masters the lowest with the least volatility. She recommended an optimal asset allocation of 4.19 per cent including transaction costs, and 2.82 per cent when hedge funds are part of the portfolio.

Another study by Clare McAndrew and Rex Thompson (2005), based on a study of Impressionists sold between 1985 and 2001, concluded that by ignoring unsold (bought-in) art, the downside risk was understated by as much as 50 per cent. Buy-in rates in the fine art market averaged 30–35 per cent in the last decade, peaking at 43 per cent in the second half of 2008 before falling to 37 per cent in 2009, according to artprice.com.

Among emerging art market studies, Henry Mok *et al* (1993) found that Modern Chinese paintings resold between 1980 and 1990 had an average holding period of less than four years, and concluded that they were an unattractive investment alternative. Sebastian Edwards (2004) found that Latin American artists followed different patterns from US artists, offering a very high rate of return and a very low correlation to international equities. A paper by Aylin Seckin and Erdal Atukeren (2006) on returns for Turkish paintings sold in 1990–2005 showed a return of 6.8

FIGURE 5.5.7 Mei and Moses art index and the US S&P 500 share index 1960–2010

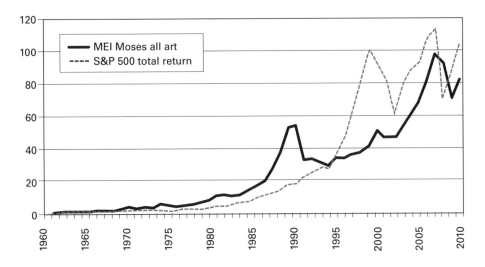

per cent compared with 10 per cent for the Istanbul Stock Exchange main index. Returns on Islamic art, sold in 1998–2007 as investigated by William McQuillan and Brian Lucey (2008), found that they delivered 13 per cent, which was more than the S&P 500's 8.49 per cent. Higher oil prices were shown to have a positive effect on prices and Islamic terrorism in the West a very negative outcome. In their study of Modern Russian art, Luc Renneboog and Christophe Spaenjers (2009) found that it returned 4 per cent in 1967–2007 and 12 per cent since 1997. Nineteenth-century Russian art provided the best returns. A study of the emerging art markets of Russia, China and India in the 21st century by Roman Kraeussl and Robin Logher (2008) suggested limited portfolio diversification potential. During this period Indian art created the highest returns and Chinese art offered some hedging potential during financial downturns.

Among collectables, a recent study by Elroy Dimson and Christophe Spaenjers (2009) on the investment performance of catalogue-priced stamps sold in 1900–2008 indicated a return of 6.7 per cent in nominal terms, which was more than bonds but less than equities.

Ongoing research into art's value could also prove useful for investors. The method known as hedonic regression, which has origins in the early 18th century, deconstructs art into its constituent characteristics and obtains estimates of the contributory value for each characteristic. One of the earlier studies by Bruno Frey and Werner Pommerehne (1989) based on Willi Bongard's study in the 1970s of Contemporary artists, indicated that the most important factors in art prices were: real per capita income, real rate of bonds and shares, as well as one-man exhibitions, group exhibitions, years since those exhibitions, art prizes, technical variety of the art and past prices. They used this to predict future prices of Robert Rauschenberg's art sold at auction and were accurate within 10 per cent. In emerging art markets, John

Wei-Shan Hu and Juo-Han Tseng (2005) found that the prices of Modern Chinese art were increased by colourful appearance, silk material, handscroll and album leaf mounts, artistic fame and auction house reputation.

Other research demonstrates that art is more closely correlated with the real estate market than other assets, as Guido Candela and Antonello Scorcu (1997) first found in their study of Italian Modern and Contemporary art and property and stock prices. Takato Hiraki *et al* (2003) experienced similar findings in a study of Japanese land prices, art and stocks during the late 1980s. In 2009 many of the world's property markets rose again, particularly in Singapore, Hong Kong/China, Australia, and Germany and France. According to the *Economist,* based on long-run house prices to rents, they are overvalued in most countries but undervalued in Japan, Germany and Switzerland and about the right level in the United States.

Added to this, there is an obvious but often neglected caveat. Art is a lagging indicator, which responds slowly to recovery and recession. In a study of the UK art market, Rachel Campbell *et al* (2005) found that art price returns tend to be higher during the upward consumption phase of a business cycle. Following that, when asset prices fall, people feel less rich and eventually stop buying art, which is usually between four and 18 months after a stock market crash.

In response to the growing interest in art investment, a Barclays equity and gilt study in 2004, for the first time since 1956, included art as a medium- to long-term investment based on the Mei and Moses research. Their research demonstrated that, since the Second World War and 1970, art performed best relative to other investments under conditions of above-trend inflation and growth, and worst under conditions of above-trend inflation and below-trend growth. They suggested a portfolio weighting over 10–20 years of 10 per cent in art, 17.4 to 18.0 per cent in equities, 0 to 16.8 per cent in gilts, 39.6 per cent to 0 in inflation-linked gilts, 5 per cent in cash, 3.1 to 25 per cent in commodities and 24.9 to 25 per cent in property.

In 2004, ABN Amro Bank Private Wealth Management suggested expanding the range of alternative assets to include art. Their analysis supports an allocation of 4 to 6 per cent in art investment into a medium- to high-risk portfolio, believing art funds could capture 10 per cent of a $300 billion alternative investment market in the next 10 years.

The resurgence in art collecting for investment purposes is a phenomenon last experienced in the 1970s but with origins in the early 20th century. In 1904 the Peau de L'Ours group of 13 Frenchmen bought 145 Contemporary artworks for investment purposes, including works by Picasso and Matisse, and 10 years later sold them for four times what they paid. In 1974 the publicly owned British Rail pension fund invested £40 million, or 5 per cent of the fund, in art. This was the first time a collection had been formed specifically for that purpose due to the adverse economic climate. At the end of 1974 in the UK inflation and tax were high, stock and property markets had fallen heavily, the pound was weak, exchange controls were in operation and index-linked gilts were unavailable. Advised by Sotheby's, the fund made 2,525 purchases across a wide range of art sectors. However, political pressure, along with 1980s financial deregulation, a booming stock market, high costs and no accurate measure for art precipitated the fund's gradual art sales after 1987.

In 1989 a quarter of the art was sold, indicating a better return than property and a worse performance than equities. By 1997 the fund had yielded a real annual return of 4.3 per cent, including 11.9 per cent for Impressionist and Modern art and 7.7 to 8.5 per cent for Chinese works of art. It was concluded that the fund had met the primary objective of at least safeguarding pensions by matching inflation over time.

Following this example, several attempts have been made since the late 1980s to establish art funds that resemble private equity closed-end funds. The reputation of art funds has often been marred by financial scams and in most cases failure. Nevertheless, some economists have likened the growth of art funds today to US real estate investment trusts (REITs), first started 30 years ago, which allow small investors to invest in large buildings.

One of the first and still most successful art funds is the Fine Art Fund established in 2004. Advised by a 'Who's Who' of the art and financial world, the fund now has four funds in operation, which have invested in Old Masters to Contemporary art and on a region-specific basis including China and the Middle East. The minimum investment is $100,000–$250,000 with investment targets of $100 million–$350 million. The aim is to achieve returns of 10 to 15 per cent a year over 10–13 years. The fund charges a 2 per cent annual management charge and takes 20 per cent of the profits over a 6 per cent hurdle rate. Other costs include legal costs and capital-raising fees. Costs are kept to a minimum mostly by buying – often from distressed sellers – and selling privately, and by cutting out the auctioneers. The appeal of the fund is that it can act quickly, knows the inner workings of the market and can take a long-term view of the market. In October 2009 the Fine Art Fund reported annualized returns of 30.15 per cent, with the best results coming from its first fund.

There are nine other art funds now operating worldwide but 23 that had to be abandoned in the last five years or whose status cannot be determined. One of the most successful has been Merit Alternative Investments art photography fund, which returned 17.7 per cent in its first year since its launch in March 2008.

Added to this, an increasing number of financial companies are accepting artworks as collateral against loans, especially during the credit crisis. At the very least, art tends to hold its value against inflation though art loans aren't a cheap form of financing. Loan rates range from 3 per cent over the prime interest rate to 15 per cent for between 40 and 50 per cent of the estimated art value because of the risk involved. Owing to this high interest, art loans suit less liquid and high, long-term borrowers or those requiring bridging loans. At Sotheby's the minimum loan is $1 million, rising to a total $3 billion, and is mostly used by estates to pay inheritance taxes. In 2006, they made $208 million art loans, more than doubling over the previous two years. Loans at Citibank, which have been offered since 1979, saw a 50 per cent increase in clients leveraging their art last year. Art loans are also a practice long offered by Christie's and by Bank of America. Contemporary art accounts for much of the current interest in this field, owing to greater liquidity, frequent trades and a growing belief in some of its long-term value. Evolving these activities, some have proposed an art exchange as a mechanism for the issuing of securities, with art or collections as the underlying asset.

A related development has been the continued growth in rental income from art. In 1972, the Canadian government was the first to set up an art rental project aimed at government agencies. It allocated $5 million over five years. With some 18,000 paintings, prints, photographs and sculptures by over 2,500 artists, the Canada Council Art Bank is now home to the largest collection of Contemporary Canadian art and the most important player in the Canadian art market. Art is available for rent to corporations, institutions, government departments and agencies. From 2002 it was entirely self-funding and is now worth over $60 million. In the commercial sector the world-renowned collector Charles Saatchi recently published a catalogue of 600 works offered at a cost of £7,000–£20,000 per year for 5–20 works. The aim is to bring in £150,000 a year to defray the costs of running his gallery.

How to invest in art and antiques

JAMES GOODWIN, ARTS RESEARCH

Art and antiques journals, guides and price indexes

Linking the finance and art worlds is a new breed of specialist advisers that have experience in either or both. They have access to leading experts, valuation, investment research, marketing and other operating procedures. UK-based companies specializing in this include ArtTactic, which provides a full international research service and Fine Art Wealth Management, which liaises between art funds and the art trade. In between is a growing number of art advisers such as Mcintyre Art Advisory, which won the Spear Wealth Management award in 2009, 1858 Ltd, Locus Capital Art Advisory and the longer-established Seymours Art Management. Several banks, such as HSBC, Deutsche Bank, Citi and ING, also offer this service.

Before taking further professional advice, this author's recent book *The International Art Markets – The Essential Guide for Collectors and Investors* offers for the first time a comprehensive guide to the world's 42 leading art markets from the viewpoint of locally based experts, including an introduction to the market.

There are also a number of art market courses and degrees by Christie's Education, Sotheby's Institute and Kingston University in London offering a rounded and art insider's view of the industry. From a mainly financial perspective, London Business School and other international business schools are beginning to offer short courses.

Elsewhere, there is no shortage of information on art and the art market, albeit fragmented, sometimes confusing and challengingly objective. Britain, in particular, is blessed with a large number of auctioneers, dealers, galleries, trade organizations, museums, art libraries and bookshops. Information on the UK and international art markets is available from the weekly *Antiques Trade Gazette* and the monthly journals *The Art Newspaper, Apollo, Antique Collecting, Art Review, Art Monthly, Modern Painters* and *Contemporary* from the UK and *Art and Auction, ARTnews, Art Forum, Art in America, Art Investor, Flash Art, Arts of Asia, Orientations* and *Asian Art Newspaper* from the United States, Europe and Asia. This is supplemented by regular information, updated online, in some daily newspapers and periodicals. Trade associations such as the Royal Institute of Chartered Surveyors (RICS) publish a regular magazine and do a quarterly survey of the art trade. The major auction houses Sotheby's, Christie's and Bonham's publish a monthly magazine promoting their sales.

Among the best-known price guides published since 1985 are *Miller's* antique guides, which cover 60 subjects and 10,000 items from 20 auctioneers. Prices include buyer's premium and VAT. Their other buyer's guides cover the individual collecting areas in more detail and are available in pocket size.

Based on similar data, art indexes are the closest thing to an objective, statistical analysis of the art market. Now mostly available online, they are an invaluable tool for understanding art market trends. However, it should be noted that most are based on auction prices excluding dealer prices, which are usually more than 50 per cent higher and represent the other half of the market.

One of the oldest is John Andrews's ACC Index, which is based on the average prices for 35 types of 1,200 typically good-quality pieces of British furniture from seven periods dating from 1650 to 1860. These are illustrated in a book and discussed in a monthly magazine, *Antique Collecting*. The index has been published annually in January since 1968, and is compared to the FTSE 250, house prices in the Southeast excluding London and UK inflation. Results for this 40-year period show the steepest price declines during the last decade for early Victorian furniture and Regency furniture and relatively stable prices for walnut furniture. Oak and country furniture remain the most popular. The most recent index is reproduced in Figure 5.6.1.

Also dating from 1968 but measuring the fine art auction market is LTB Gordonsart Art Sales Index, which is published every August in three languages and updated continuously on the internet. By 2010 the Index included 3.5 million pieces of data

FIGURE 5.6.1 Antique British furniture index 1969–2010

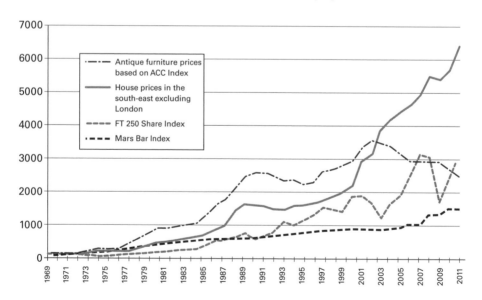

SOURCE Antique Collector's Club 2011

on 300,000 artists, covered by 2,400 auctions. Bought-in (unsold) items are excluded, and the figures are net of auction premium and tax.

Offering the broadest range of art prices are Robin Duthy's Art Market Research indexes. The 500 indexes, which are internet-based and include most fine and decorative art categories sold at auction, have been compiled annually since 1976 with the help of Christie's. Data on stock markets, UK property markets and other forms of investment are also available. Each graph can be calculated in five different currencies, adjusted for inflation, segmented into five parts, eg top 10 per cent, and measured by compound interest. Their clients include the US and UK revenue services, banks, insurers, galleries and newspapers.

Located abroad but also available in the English language are a number of fine art websites used by the art auction market, journalists and academics.

From France, artprice.com, created in 1987, provides 29 million data entries by 405,000 artists including bought-in works sold at 2,900 auction houses in 40 countries. Its website provides analysis of artworks, artists and their works, market segments and market overviews. In 2005, it added a database for the decorative arts and in 2006 launched an art valuation service. One of its latest innovations is an online confidence index.

From Italy, Art Investments, founded in 1996, provides 950,000 artworks sold at auction since 1980, subdivided into Old Master paintings, 19th-century, Modern and Contemporary art. It also publishes a confidence and liquidity index adjusted for inflation. Art Investments' intention is to bridge the gap between fine art and finance via a quarterly magazine and distribution on the Bloomberg media network. Art Investments has been one of the pioneers in measuring emerging art markets.

Similarly, Artnet.com, founded in the United States in 1989, links works sold by each artist in order of ascending value. Its database includes 4 million illustrated auction prices from 500 international auction houses. Its website and magazine provide general market information about the market, including dealer locations and events. It is favoured by a large number of Society of London Art Dealers (SLAD) members and Sotheby's in London. Lately it has transformed itself into an online auctioneer.

Also from the United States, ArtFact, founded in 1989, contains over 5.5 million public auction sale results and is one of the few archives that include decorative art as well as fine art. It is referred to by a number of leading auction houses and museums.

Buying and selling art: artists, the internet, dealers, fairs and auctioneers

There are several routes to buying and selling art: artists, galleries, auctioneers, online auctioneers and dealers. The primary market is where original works are sold for the first time – art schools, artists' studios, art fairs, galleries, etc – and has been the fastest-growing area for the last 10 years. Long term, their price returns can be higher but so are the risks of finding the right artist among many. The secondary market is for the exchange of previously traded works, where participants are likely to have more historical information.

Dealers in the primary market tend to take a longer-term view of their art and artists by establishing a firm market for their work, helped by close relations with the creator and their customers. They do this by controlling supply of the art, sometimes through contracts, and influencing demand by selling to dedicated long-term collectors or institutions induced by a range of discounts. In the secondary market the auction system is a key determinant of the cost of creating and distributing works of art, and of understanding what is good and bad historically. However, a key consideration is that auction prices often rise above 'true value' when two or more people are determined to bid for them. Dealer prices in the secondary market tend to stay higher for longer during a downturn. Based on return on capital between 2006 and 2009, Contemporary art and antiques dealers performed best. Auctioneers tend to do better during prolonged downturns. Other areas of the art market that recently had higher returns are some artists and research organizations.

Still, there remains an interdependence between all areas of the art market, demonstrated by a third of auction sales being made to dealers. Consequently, major sales and promotions are often coordinated between all the main players, including museums, which underpin values in the art market. The main selling months in the art calendar are May, June and July, October, November and December, and to a lesser extent January, February, March and April.

In the UK the auction market is represented by the big four of Sotheby's, Christie's, Bonham's, and Phillips de Pury and 94 regional auctioneers. The *Antiques Trade Gazette* lists a further 26 online auctioneers including eBay.

Both Sotheby's and Christie's were founded in the 18th century and are the world's oldest and most prestigious art auction houses. Collectively, they have 85 offices (14 salerooms) in 43 countries and hold over 700 auctions every year at prices ranging from $200 to $80 million. The third auction house, Bonham's, from its base in London, has 600 international sales annually in the UK, the US West Coast, Australia and Hong Kong. The fourth, Phillips de Pury, was formed in 2003 loosely based on the highly regarded 18th-century British auctioneer Phillips. It operates in 12 countries, mainly in the United States, mostly selling Contemporary art. In 2008 it was bought by a Russian-based company for $60 million. The UK's largest regional auctioneer is Dreweatts with nine salerooms offering 24 categories, followed by Scotland's oldest auctioneer, Lyon & Turnbull, which operates in the United States under the name Freeman's. The Society of Fine Art Auctioneers and Valuers (SOFAA) is the UK's only professional body that exclusively covers the valuation and sale by auction of fine art and antiques. The Society's 48 UK members offer services including: inspection and preliminary advice, removal, cataloguing and reporting, reserves, marketing, catalogues, viewing and settlement. It is also advisable to buy from auctioneers or valuers who carry the RICS mark, since they will be governed by the Institution's codes of conduct, such as holding clients' money in a designated bank account separate from their own business.

Today, the presence of high-end works in provincial salerooms is more commonplace with £1 million-plus sales including internationally prestigious works. This is partly thanks to online catalogues that project works worldwide though their transaction charges match those of the international auctioneers. Despite great pockets of expertise, 'sleepers' or grossly undervalued artworks are more likely to emerge at the lower end of the market. For example, a painting now entitled *Rembrandt Laughing*, which is a self-portrait by the Dutch artist, painted in 1628, was estimated at £1,000–£1,500 when sold at a small English auctioneer in the Cotswolds based on the belief that it was from the school of Rembrandt. After testing and verification by the Rembrandt Research Project it was believed to be by the artist and sold for £2.6 million at an auction in October 2007.

The maximum sales commission at Bonham's in the UK is 15 per cent up to £5,000 and 10 per cent thereafter. Lyon & Turnbull charges 15 per cent on the first £3,000 and 10 per cent thereafter. Buyer's fees at Christie's are levied at 25 per cent up to £25,000, falling to 20 per cent up to £500,000 and 12 per cent above that, all including VAT. The threshold for all consignments at Sotheby's is £3,000. At Dreweatts charges are 20 per cent on the first £250,000 and 12 per cent thereafter.

As mentioned, technology is beginning to transform the art market. The advent of online auctions since the mid-1990s has made sought-after items even more accessible and is transforming the traditional art market by offering greater price transparency. It is estimated that it is five times more expensive to sell a painting at a traditional auction house than online. Today, many dealers consult the online auctioneer eBay for price information to buy ceramics, silver and jewellery. What's more, attempts to sell expensive art works online have met with success, with some being bought physically unseen. eBay was founded in September 1995 and floated in September 1998. It registers 88 million active users in 38 countries, turning over $8.6 billion in 2008. Half of these sales in 2006 were for art, antiques and collectables such as jewellery, watches, coins and stamps. For 1.3 million eBay sellers it is their primary or secondary source of income. For items sold for £600 or more eBay charges 8.75 per cent on the initial £29.99, 5.25 per cent up to £599.99 and 1.5 per cent thereafter, plus a £1.90 advertising fee.

Exploiting this opportunity, in July 2006 Christie's launched its live auction website in New York and London. In the first year, 25 per cent of the internet bidders were new customers to Christie's. In 2009, there were 49,343 online bids, which amounted to 30 per cent of all bids at Christie's and 14 per cent of all winning bids. The most active online categories are interiors, photographs, prints, watches, jewellery and wine, music and pop culture. The most expensive lot sold online was in September 2010 for a late Shang Dynasty wine vessel which went for $3.3 million to an American via a New York auction. Sotheby's has now also introduced a similar live online bidding platform.

Technology for authenticating art is now also becoming more widely available. Scientific authentication is an objective evaluation based on assorted scientific tests, which is used in conjunction with art history. The many scientific methods range from thermo-luminescent analysis to X-rays.

Buying and selling through a dealer can represent a more straightforward transaction than at auction since artworks can often be viewed online and purchases can mostly be made on sight without purchase pressure. The most reputable dealers are typically those belonging to the Society of London Art Dealers (SLAD), the British Antique Dealers' Association (BADA) and the Association of Art and Antique Dealers

(LAPADA). As well as organizing fairs and exhibitions, these trade organizations offer a wide range of services including restoration, valuation and consumer information, such as lists of packers and shippers. Internationally, some of these associations and their best dealers belong to the International Confederation of Art and Antique Dealers' Associations (CINOA), based in Brussels.

In the UK, antique shops and collectors' fairs are still the preferred trading place for collectors, thanks to increased dealer specialization. In any given week you could expect to find no fewer than 25 British general fairs listed in the *Antiques Trade Gazette*. In the Contemporary market, art fairs provide the opportunity to see the work of hundreds of different artists under one roof and are good for judging what's on the market. For SLAD members the most popular fairs are the 20/21 British Art Fair, Grosvenor House and TEFAF, New York International Fine Art Fair, Art Islington, and Palm Beach Art and Antiques, with Art Basel the most highly rated. The majority of SLAD dealers trade in Post-war and Contemporary art, Impressionists and 19th-century European pictures. According to a LAPADA survey, 54 per cent of their turnover is from shops or galleries, 39 per cent at fairs, 4 per cent on the internet (58 per cent have sold and 39 per cent bought via the internet) and 2 per cent at auction. Fifty-four per cent of their sales are to the 40–50 age group and 40 per cent of all sales are when people are furnishing their houses.

The internet is also likely to transform the market for dealers in the Contemporary art market. For example, the website artsource.org claims to trade art at prices 20 to 30 per cent below those at most galleries. To help buying and selling decisions, the market now benefits from online confidence indicators. Artprice.com has been offering a real-time index for two years and ArtTactic has been regularly surveying the world's top dealers since 2005.

Many collectors are also buying directly from artists. For the more adventurous, the MA degree shows, often in June, are worth considering, following the successful promotion of the Young British Artists in the 1990s.

It is estimated that 3,700 graduates leave art school every year, adding to the 60,000 or more practising artists. The best UK colleges are the Royal College of Art, Goldsmith's College, Central Saint Martin's College, Slade School, Camberwell College, Chelsea College of Art, Glasgow School of Art and the Ruskin School of Drawing. Students at these colleges elected the following artists as the most influential: Marcel Duchamp, Pablo Picasso, Francis Bacon, Henri Matisse and Lucian Freud, according to a survey in *The Art Newspaper*. The internet is also improving the market for aspiring artists. The dealer Charles Saatchi is using his website to attract, promote and sell new art talent at a lower cost based on his reputation. In 2008, 35,000 artists signed up to his website from which he will choose works in the £500–£5,000 price range.

The return on capital employed for 168 UK art market companies for the period 2006 to 2009 is plotted in Figure 5.6.2.

FIGURE 5.6.2 Return on capital employed for 168 UK art market companies in 2006–9

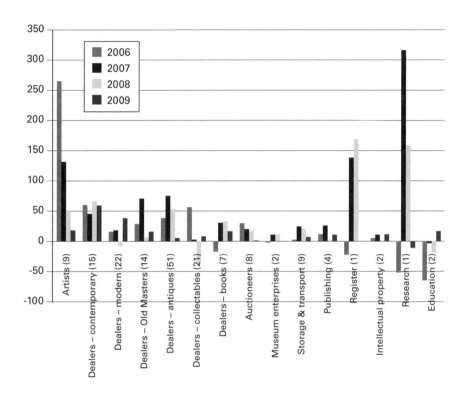

SOURCE FAME 2010

Conclusion

'Buy today's painting: it may go up. Buy yesterday's painting: it won't go down' is a maxim that should lie at the heart of any art investment strategy.

In April 2010 the art market began to recover after falling by over 40 per cent during the previous 19 months. It is again at its mid-2006 levels in real terms.

The present art market cycle which began over five years ago is very different from the late 1980s when trade was dominated by buyers from the United States, Britain, Western Europe and later Japan. Throughout history, the art market has followed the path of trade, which in the 21st century is more widespread than ever. In fact, newly developed countries, especially Hong Kong, South Korea and Singapore, now appear among the main international art traders. However, international trade in art in most developing countries is far behind them and even further behind many countries in the West. For example, imports and exports in mainland China in 2009 were only $10 million and $45 million. Therefore, the transition from the large and long-established Western markets to the smaller and culturally different Eastern ones remains uneven and for now uncertain. Though some wealthy Eastern buyers are now showing a taste for prestige Western art, a greater supply than can be consumed by these new collectors is likely on the market during the next decade as a populous and rich Western generation passes. For those wishing to sell their art in the coming 10 years, it will be important to understand past and present economic developments and follow cultural trends before acting decisively.

For buyers the choice of art at relatively low prices from developing and some developed countries has never been greater. However, choosing from this bewildering range of art, as more familiar work once used as a benchmark becomes scarcer, represents a major challenge. For this reason, buying art from countries associated with future economic growth and a strong national culture that fit into the international art history canon may reap the best rewards. The logic being that as the wealthy proportion of a population reaches a certain income level they tend to buy their own art at home and then abroad before exploring art from other countries, eventually leading to a taste for the international avant garde.

Aiding this development, an increasing amount of multilingual advice on up-and-coming artists, especially from emerging markets, is being offered by the art trade's internationally published magazines.

FIGURE 5.6.3 International trade in art in new developed economies in 1998–2009

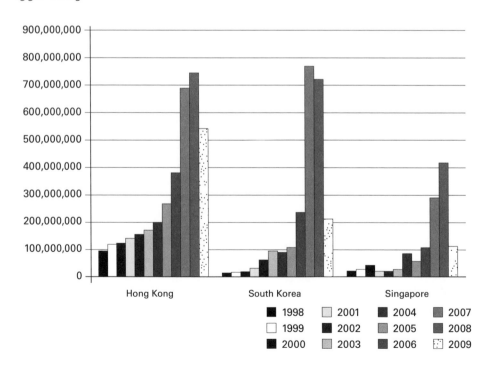

SOURCE United Nations 2010

Nevertheless, the best advice as always is to buy something you like and hope your enthusiasm is shared with buyers of the future wherever they may be.

As Kenneth Clark wrote, 'I believe that the majority of people really long to experience that moment of pure, disinterested, non-material satisfaction which causes them to ejaculate the word "beautiful"; and since this experience can be obtained more reliably through works of art than through any other means, I believe that those of us who try to make works of art more accessible are not wasting our time.' Figure 5.6.3 charts the value of the imported art trade in three newly developed countries.

Bibliography for Chapters 5.5 and 5.6

ABN Amro (2004) Art Investment Advisory Group

Anderson, R (1974) Paintings as an investment, *Economics Enquiry*, 12, 13–26

Antique-acc.com (2010) Antique furniture price index

Artbank.ca (2010) Canada Council Art Bank

Arts & Business (2010) Arts Philanthropy – the facts, trends and potential, October

Artfact.com (2010)

Art Investor (2006) Wolfgang Wilke art economics column

Artmarketreport.com (2010) Art indexes

Artnet.com (2010)

ARTnews (2010) 200 top collectors, Summer

Artprice.com (2010) Art market trends 2009

Artprice.com (2010) Contemporary art market review 2009–10

Artprice.com (2010) Art market insight

Art Review (2010) Power 100, October

Artsalesindex.artinfo.com (2010) Art sales index

Bada.org (2010) British Antique Dealers' Association

Bonhams.com (2010)

Bureau van Dijk (2010) *Financial analysis made easy* (FAME)

Campbell, R (2005) *Art as an alternative investment*, Maastricht University, Working Paper

Candela, G & A Scorcu (2001) In search of stylized facts on art market prices: evidence from the secondary market for prints and drawings in Italy, *The Journal of Cultural Economics*, 25: 219–31

Capgemini & Merrill Lynch (2010) *World Wealth Report* 2009

Christie's (2010) *Annual Review – 2009*

Christies.com (2010) Specialist Departments

Clark, K (1969) *Civilisation – a Personal View*, John Murray

Dimson, E & Spaenjers, C (2010) The investment performance of collectable stamps, *Journal of Financial Economics*, 15 December

Economist (2010) Global house prices, October

Economist (2009) A special report on ageing populations, 27 June

Economist (2006) London's art market, June

Edwards, S, (2004) *The economics of Latin American art: creativity patterns and rates of return*, NBER Working Paper No. W10302

Frey, B & Pommerehne, W (1989) *Muses & Markets – Exploration in the Economics of the Arts*, Basil Blackwell

Ginsburgh, V & Weyers, S (2005) *Persistence and Fashion in Art: Italian Renaissance from Vasari to Berenson and Beyond*, Poetics

Goodwin, J (2008) *The International Art Markets – The Essential Guide for Collectors and Investors*, Kogan Page

Goodwin, J (2004) How Old Masters paid for old age pensions, *Financial Times*

Goetzmann, W, Renneboog, L & Spaenjers, C (2009) *Art and money*, Working Paper, 3 November

Goetzman, W N (1993) Accounting for taste: art and the financial markets over three centuries, *American Economic Review*, 83(5), pp 1370–6

Hiraki, T, A Ito, D Spieth & N Takezawa (2003) *How did Japanese investments influence international art prices?* Working Paper, Graduate School of International Management, International University of Japan

Horowitz, N (2011) *Art of the Deal – Contemporary Art in a Global Financial Market*, Princeton University Press

Hu, J W S & Tseng J H (2005) *Returns on the Portfolios Containing Modern Chinese Paintings*

Investors' Chronicle (2003) AXA art – art buying survey

Kraeussl, R & Logher, R (2008) Emerging art markets, SSRN, December

Lapada.org (2010) The Association of Art & Antique Dealers

Magnus, G (2009) *The Age of Aging*, John Wiley & Sons

McAndrew, C & Thompson, R (2005) *The collateral value of fine art*, Dublin Global Finance Conference

McQuillan, W & Lucey, B (2008) *The Validity of Islamic Art as an Investment*

Mei, J & Moses, M (2005) Vested interest and biased price estimates: evidence from an auction market, *The Journal of Finance*, Vol. LX, No 5

Mei, J & M Moses (2002), Art as an investment and the underperformance of masterpieces, *American Economic Review*, December 2002, 92(5), pp 1656–68

Mok, H, Ko, V, Woo, S, & Kwok, K (1993) *Modern Chinese Paintings: An Investment Alternative*

Munus.com (2010) Art investments

Reitlinger, G (1961) *The economics of taste: the rise and fall of the picture market, 1760–1960*, London: Barrie & Rockliff Ltd

Renneboog, L & Spaenjers, C (2009) *The Iconic Boom in Modern Russian Art*, 17 November

Rics.org (2010)

Seckin, A & Atukeren, E (2006) *Art and the Economy: The First Look at the Market for Paintings in Turkey*, 5 September

Simmonds, J (2001) *Art and Taxation: a Guide*, Institute of Art and Law

Slad.org (2010) Society of London Art Dealers

Society of London Art Dealers (2006) Survey of Members

Sofaa.info (2010) Society of Fine Art Auctioneers & Valuers

Sothebys.com (2010) Departments and Services

Stein, J (1977) The monetary appreciation of paintings, *Journal of Political Economy*, vol 85, no 5

TEFAF (2007) *The International Art Market*, ed McAndrew, C, The European Fine Art Foundation

TEFAF (2002) *The European Art Market in 2002*

The Art Newspaper (2006) Tax and art, September

The Art Newspaper (2010) Exhibition attendance figures 2009, March

UN Comtrade (2011) *Works of art, collectors' pieces and antiques* – SITC 896, United Nations

Wallace, P (1999) *Agequake*, Nicholas Brealey

Watson, P (1992) *From Manet to Manhattan*, Hutchinson

Racehorse ownership and investing in bloodstock

5.7

AMY BENNETT, BRITISH BLOODSTOCK MARKETING

Introduction

The ownership and breeding of racehorses may be a time-honoured investment opportunity but it is also first and foremost a sport.

Those who view horse racing as a means of increasing their wealth would do better to seek other ventures. Anyone who has ever risked even a £1 bet on the Grand National can attest that there is no sure thing in racing.

There are certainly more secure investments to be made – after all, a work of art never suffers an injury on the eve of a big race, and property investments rarely decide they are simply not in the mood that day.

But that same hapless punter watching his horse falling at the final fence in the Grand National or being passed by his rivals in the home straight at Royal Ascot can also assure investors that there is no bigger thrill than being involved in almost any manner in the high-octane sport of horse racing.

Racing and breeding are a global industry worth billions, where fortunes are won and lost throughout the year, but it is also an industry in which even a small interest can pay dividends at the races or in the sales ring. And above all it is a sport fuelled by passion, dreams – and money.

What is it all about?

Not for nothing is horse racing called the Sport of Kings.

Modern racing can be said to have had its birth in 1604 when King James I found a pleasant spot near Cambridge to go hunting. The monarch was so pleased with his find that he returned repeatedly to hunt and race his own horses in the area that soon became known as Newmarket, even going so far as to establish a very modest palace in the fledgling town.

James's son Charles I followed in his father's footsteps, regularly competing in races in Newmarket, but it was his own son, Charles II, who put the town on the map as the headquarters of racing in the 1660s. Twice a year, the Merry Monarch, as he was known, would move the royal court to Newmarket and enjoy competing in races.

Since that time, royalty has maintained a keen interest in racing through to the modern day as Queen Elizabeth is herself a successful owner and breeder of racehorses.

Racing is not, however, solely the pursuit of the wealthy and titled. Thousands of people are involved in owning and breeding at all levels, from those with a tiny share in a racehorse through to those who own outright 100 racehorses of their own. In 2010, there were around 14,340 horses in training in Britain (monthly average), with almost 9,000 trained for Flat races and over 4,700 racing over jumps.

Plenty of owners are also involved in breeding racehorses, while many people focus entirely on the ownership of bloodstock – that is, stallions and mares for the production of future generations of racehorses. The progeny are then sold either privately or at public auction or else retained for racing. In 2010, over 9,800 broodmares were bred in Britain, with around 70 per cent of those bred for Flat racing.

Racing and breeding have their own particular jargon, which can seem confusing to the uninitiated but it is quick to learn (see Table 5.7.1).

Racehorses in Britain are divided into two disciplines, Flat and National Hunt. Although Flat racing takes place all year round, the season 'proper' runs from mid-March to the first weekend in November, and takes in such high-profile meetings as the 2,000 Guineas and 1,000 Guineas at Newmarket, the Derby and the Oaks, Royal Ascot, Glorious Goodwood, York, and Newmarket and Ascot's championship races in September and October.

National Hunt is the name given to jump racing, which also takes place year-round with the best action traditionally taking place between October and April and including such iconic events as the Grand National and Cheltenham Festival.

Racing in Britain takes place seven days a week, with Good Friday and December 23–25 the only guaranteed 'empty' days on the calendar. A total of 9,566 fixtures were held in 2010, with over 6,000 taking place on the Flat and the remainder over jumps.

For key racing dates, visit the British Horseracing Authority's website (see useful website addresses at end of chapter).

Racehorse ownership

Horse racing has a long and illustrious involvement with the world's aristocracy. Increasingly however, the 'man in the street' is becoming involved in ownership, and it is not always necessary to have access to a hedge fund or an oil well to fund your purchase.

TABLE 5.7.1 Glossary of handy terms

Term	Meaning
Foal	a horse under one year of age
Yearling	a one-year-old horse
Colt	a male horse under five years of age
Filly	a female horse under five years of age
Entire	an uncastrated male horse over five years of age who is still racing
Gelding	a castrated male horse
Mare	a female horse over five years of age who is still racing
Broodmare	a female horse of any age who is being used to breed foals from
Stallion	a male horse used for breeding purposes
Dam	mother of a horse
Sire	father of a horse
Store	an unraced jumps horse
Training yard	the stables where a horse is trained
Stud farm	the place where broodmares, foals and stallions are kept
Break in	the method of teaching a horse to be ridden; usually done at 1–2 years of age with horses who will race on the flat, and at 3–4 years for horses who will race over jumps

The aptly named Dream Ahead, winner of two Group 1 races in 2010 and among the favourites for some of racing's biggest contests in 2011, was bought for £36,000 at Doncaster Bloodstock Sales as a two-year-old in 2010, while Makfi, one of the leading horses in 2010 and now in his first season as a stallion, was bought for around £27,300 at Tattersalls Horses in Training sale and went on to earn over half a million pounds in prize money.

Bargain buys are not just confined to the Flat, however. Hell's Bay, a Grade 2 winner at jump racing's biggest venue, Cheltenham, on New Year's Day 2011, was bought for only £3,000, while one of the season's most exciting horses, Diamond Harry, was purchased for approximately £11,550.

Of course, for every cheap successful horse, there are dozens who cost thousands of pounds more. The highest price paid for a yearling in Britain in 2010 was approximately £1.26 million. Price is largely dictated by the pedigree of the horse – that is, what its immediate family has already achieved – as well as its looks, and while money is no guarantee of success, it certainly helps.

Those seeking to invest in a racehorse must ask themselves one simple question – How much am I willing to spend?

For those who can afford it, there is no greater thrill than outright ownership of a successful racehorse. In 2010, of the 8,774 registered owners in Britain, 2,342 were sole owners. However, along with sole ownership comes the responsibility of all the expenses as well. The average cost of having a horse in training in Britain is approximately £20,000 a year, although costs vary with location.

It is well worth bearing in mind that owners registered for VAT, whether alone or in a partnership, can reclaim some of the costs of purchase and training fees. Members of the Racehorse Owners Association (ROA) in Britain can also register for the Totesport owner-sponsorship scheme, allowing them to recover VAT on their racing activity. Full details of this scheme are available from the ROA (see useful contacts).

If you do decide to take the plunge on your own, you will need to select the trainer you want to have charge of your horse. The National Trainers Federation (see useful contacts) can advise you of trainers in your local area and give you useful contacts.

A trainer may be able to sell you a horse already in his yard, or else can accompany you to the sales or advise on a bloodstock agent to help you purchase a racehorse.

The other alternative is to share ownership either with a group of friends or by joining a syndicate. There are numerous racing clubs and syndicates and the return on your investment will vary depending on the terms, but many syndicates offer several shares in different horses for a set sum of money each month or year, allowing you to spread the risk and the enjoyment.

Syndicates have enjoyed numerous high-profile successes in recent years, and 2010 was no exception. One of the hugely successful Highclere Thoroughbred Racing syndicates was rewarded with a breathtaking victory in the Group 1 King George VI and Queen Elizabeth Stakes at Ascot in July with Harbinger – bought for approximately £189,000 as a yearling – who went on to be crowned the best horse in the world.

The Elite Racing Club has also enjoyed numerous successes over the years, including at Royal Ascot in 2010 with Dandino, a horse bred by the Club as part of its very successful breeding programme that allows members to experience bloodstock as well as racing.

Investing in bloodstock

Investing in bloodstock is every bit as risky as buying a racehorse, but as a long-term investment the risk is spread over more time and so therefore there is more chance of recouping your initial investment.

All thoroughbred horses trace their ancestry back to three stallions imported into Britain in the 17th century – the Byerly Turk, the Darley Arabian and the Godolphin Arabian. The General Stud Book, a meticulous record of every thoroughbred racehorse born between the late 18th century and the modern day, is kept by Weatherbys, a family firm based in Northamptonshire, allowing you to trace each modern racehorse to his forefathers around 300 years ago.

Sales

Britain has three thoroughbred auction houses, catering to every level of the market throughout the year.

Bloodstock sales in 2010 were:

Yearlings:
- –3 February: Tattersalls February sale
- –31 August–1 September: DBS Premier Yearling sales
- –8 September: DBS St Leger Festival sales
- –4–7 October: Tattersalls October Yearling sale Book 1
- –10–12 October: Tattersalls October Yearling sale Book 2
- –13–15 October: Tattersalls October Yearling sale Book 3
- –31 October–1 November: DBS Autumn Yearling and Horses in Training sale
- –21 November: Tattersalls December Yearling sale

Breeze-up:
- –12–14 April: Tattersalls Craven Breeze-up sale
- –19–20 April: DBS Breeze-up sales
- –7 May: Ascot Breeze-up sale
- –26 November: DBS Breeze-up sales
- –9 December: Brightwells Cheltenham Breeze-up sale

Horses in training:
- –25 January: DBS January sales
- –3 February: Tattersalls February sale
- –13 April: Brightwells Bloodstock sale
- –21 April: DBS Horses in Training sales
- –4 May: Brightwells Cheltenham Bloodstock sale
- –17–18 May: DBS Spring Horses in Training sale
- –5–8 July: Tattersalls July sale
- –2–4 August: DBS August sales
- –14 October: Brightwells Cheltenham National Hunt sale
- –24–27 October: Tattersalls Autumn Horses in Training sale
- –2–4 November: DBS November sales
- –11 November: Brightwells Cheltenham National Hunt sale
- –28 November–2 December: Tattersalls Breeding stock sale
- –5–6 December: DBS December Horses in Training sales

Breeding stock:
- –25 January: DBS January sales
- –3 February: Tattersalls February sale
- –25–28 July: Tattersalls July sale
- –28 November–2 December: Tattersalls Breeding stock sale

Foals:
- –22–26 November: Tattersalls December Foal sale

National Hunt:
- –25 January: DBS January sales
- –29 January: Brightwells National Hunt sale
- –5 March: DBS NH Festivals sales @ Newbury
- –13 April: Brightwells Cheltenham Bloodstock sale

–21 April: DBS Horses in Training sales
–4 May: Brightwells Cheltenham Bloodstock sale
–17–18 May: DBS Spring Horses in Training sales
–25–26 May: DBS Spring Store sales
–2–4 August: DBS August sales
–14 October: Brightwells Cheltenham National Hunt sale
–24–27 October: Tattersalls Autumn Horses in Training sale
–31October–1 November: DBS Autumn Horses in Training sales
–11 November: Brightwells Cheltenham National Hunt sale
–26 November: DBS Hennessy sales @ Newbury
–5–6 December: DBS December Horses in Training sales
–9 December: Brightwells Cheltenham Breeze-up sale

Tattersalls is the oldest, having been founded in 1766 at Hyde Park Corner, London. Tattersalls subsequently moved to Knightsbridge and has operated from its present site in Newmarket, Suffolk, since 1965, although Tattersalls had held sales in Newmarket since the early 20th century.

Tattersalls uniquely sells in guineas – that is, £1.05. This retention of the imperial rather than metric currency is handy for deducting the 5 per cent commission taken from the vendor by the sales company. Tattersalls is the largest of the three British auction houses both in terms of revenue and numbers sold. It holds 10 sales throughout the year and in 2010 produced a turnover across all its sales of £162,155,700 for 4,483 horses sold.

Doncaster Bloodstock Sales (DBS) is based in Doncaster and has its sales offices in Hawick, in the Scottish borders. It also holds two sales a year of jumps horses in training at Newbury racecourse. DBS was founded around 40 years ago, merging with the Irish bloodstock company Goffs in July 2007.

Although it sold in guineas until as recently as 2007, DBS converted to selling in pounds sterling at all its sales from January 2008. DBS caters to both the Flat and jumps markets in Britain, holding 11 sales throughout the year, and generated a total turnover across all sales of £27,563,800.

Brightwells is the third of Britain's auction houses. It holds eight sales of bloodstock at the lower end of the market at its Ascot venue, although 2010 saw the introduction of a breeze-up sale for two-year-olds to be held at Ascot in May, which is sure to raise both quality and profile. In addition, Brightwells hosts six 'boutique' sales of jumps horses at Cheltenham throughout the year, which have proved both popular and profitable. These are sales of hand-selected jumps horses, whether horses in training or breeze-up horses.

Bloodstock investment

There are around 125 stallions at stud in Britain to which it costs £1,000 or more to send a mare for breeding in 2011. The most expensive of these is the leading young stallion Oasis Dream who stands for £85,000 at Banstead Manor, the breeding operation owned by the Saudi prince Khalid Abdullah.

Banstead Manor is also home to the second most expensive, Dansili, at £65,000. Sheikh Mohammed, the ruler of Dubai, stands seven stallions in Britain including Dubawi at £55,000, while Cheveley Park Stud, also in Newmarket, stands five stallions, including Pivotal for £55,000.

Standing stallions can be big business. For example, Oasis Dream was bred to 149 mares in 2010 at a fee of £85,000 each. While some of those mares will have been owned by Khalid Abdullah himself and several others will not have produced a live foal, he produced an income on paper of over £9 million before tax. Oasis Dream is 11 years old and, if health and good results continue to go his way, he could theoretically cover mares for another 15 years.

The northern hemisphere breeding season takes place between mid-February and July, and most studs require a stud fee to be paid in October once the mare has been successfully scanned in foal. At present, with studs competing for business, some will offer terms and conditions allowing payment to be delayed until the foal is born, or even until it is sold at public auction.

Of course, for every stallion whose progeny shine on the racecourse there are many more who do not succeed, and it is also very rare that an opportunity arises to buy into a stallion prospect.

Bloodstock investment opportunities are therefore more likely to be limited to breeding foals from a mare each year and selling these at auction, or else 'pinhooking'. Few people in bloodstock could explain the origin of the term, but put simply, pinhooking is the practice of investing in a horse at the sales and reselling it for profit at a later date.

The most common of these opportunities are buying foals to resell as yearlings, buying yearlings to resell as two-year-olds and buying broodmares to resell. The initial cost of buying the horse at whatever stage and the ongoing keep costs are then deducted from the end sale price. Added to this is the cost of preparing the horse for its return to the sale ring.

If this is an attractive investment idea, then it is vital to secure the services of a bloodstock agent who can guide you through the process. The Federation of Bloodstock Agents (see useful contacts list) can provide you with a list of suitable agents who focus on the area in which you wish to invest. Bloodstock agents usually charge a commission of 5 per cent but it is vital to arrive at the sales with an expert.

Pinhooking is not without risks. Horses have an uncanny knack of seeking out trouble and even a minor bump can knock several noughts off a sale price once it ventures into a sale ring. One way of spreading the risk is to join or set up a syndicate and pinhook several foals or yearlings together, thereby spreading the risk among both the number of horses and the number of investors.

Bloodstock agent David Redvers, who also runs Tweenhills Farm & Stud in Gloucestershire, has run several profitable bloodstock Enterprise Investment Schemes since 2003, with Tweenhills Pinhooking Ltd returning a 70 per cent net profit on all stock sold in 2009. Some of the most profitable investments included a colt bought for €26,000 as a foal and resold the following year for €80,000, and a colt bought for around £30,450 who was resold for around £89,250 a year later. This is just one example of syndicates available; there are several others in operation pinhooking foals, yearlings and mares.

Another popular form of pinhooking is to invest in a young filly or mare whose racing career has just ended, breed her to a popular stallion in February and then resell her, hopefully at a profit, at the breeding stock sales in December. Again, this requires the assistance of an expert to first identify a mare with an attractive pedigree and/or racing record, and then to select a mate for her who will enhance her value when she returns to the sale ring.

An outstanding example of this was illustrated at the Tattersalls December Mares sale in 2010 by a mare called Diary. Now aged 12, Diary has led an interesting life. She was bought as an unraced two-year-old in October 2001 for around £7,350 and was sent to race in the minor racing nation of Greece.

In 2005, having won three races in Greece, she returned to Tattersalls where she was bought for around £11,500, having produced just one foal to date. Diary then produced a colt foal who failed to find a buyer on his two trips through the sale ring. However, Total Gallery, as he was named, proved everyone wrong once he began racing, going on to win one of the season's leading sprint contests, the Group 1 Prix de l'Abbaye in France in October 2009. Just a week earlier, Diary's third foal, Lady Darshaan, finished runner-up in a top race for two-year-old fillies, and their dam's value skyrocketed.

When Diary returned to Tattersalls in December 2010, she did so as the dam of two Group 1 performers, and in foal to the champion stallion Galileo. She was subsequently bought for around £1,365,000 – an astronomical return on that initial £11,500. At the same sale, her daughter Lady Darshaan was bought for around £630,000, while Diary's foal of 2010 was bought for £210,000.

Those with the capital to do so may prefer to keep their broodmare purchase and breed from her each year, either selling the resulting foals or retaining them to race. This is obviously a more expensive option, requiring ongoing keep costs for both the mare and her progeny as well as the yearly outlay on stud fees.

For the lucky few, the resulting foal offered at auction will possess the right combination of good conformation, the right sire and the right dam, and will prove popular in the sale ring. Plenty of others will have to wait for a big return at the sales until some of the mare's progeny have raced and hopefully proved their worth. The wait for a return from a jumps-bred mare will be even longer as jumps horses are older before they make their racing debut, and a mare could easily have produced four or five foals before her oldest progeny makes his racing debut.

Summary

No investment is made without some form of risk, but racing and bloodstock must surely be one of the most risky investment avenues available. It is possible to get the best advice, buy the best horse and ensure it receives the best care, and still come away empty-handed.

Where racing and bloodstock stand head and shoulders above other investment opportunities, however, is in terms of the enjoyment they offer. Whether it is a day at the races, a day at the sales or simply watching your horse in training at whatever stage of its life, racing is a hugely absorbing and satisfying sport to be involved in.

Investing in racing and bloodstock is not an easy get-rich-quick scheme, but with sound advice, sensible investment – and luck – profits can be made.

Useful websites for anyone seeking to invest in racehorse ownership or bloodstock

British Bloodstock Marketing: www.bbm.gb.com

National Trainers Federation: http://www.racehorsetrainers.org

British Horseracing Authority: www.britishhorseracing.com

Racehorse Owners Association: www.racehorseowners.net

Thoroughbred Breeders' Association: www.thetba.co.uk

Weatherbys – central administration for British horseracing: www.weatherbys.co.uk

Tattersalls: www.tattersalls.com

Doncaster Bloodstock Sales: www.dbsauctions.com

Brightwells: www.brightwells.com

Berry Bros. & Rudd Review: Wine Investment

By Joss Fowler, Berrys' Wine Investment Expert

Investing in wine is by no means a new phenomenon. Many years before fine wine became truly global in the mid-1990s, wily buyers would often buy more than they intended to drink, selling the excess at a later date to fund new purchases.

In the 1990s demand for the best wines from Bordeaux boomed. The 'traditional' market for the best wines, Europe and North America, was joined by the new Far Eastern markets. Prices moved up and though the prices of some top Bordeaux châteaux dropped in 1998 due to the Asian economic collapse the general trend in wine prices has been up. Whilst it is difficult to find totally accurate records and therefore data, it is fair to say that the prices for the very best wines have risen by an average 15% per annum over the past 25 years, with quiet periods (e.g. 1998 to 2002) being more than balanced out by the busy ones (e.g. 2005 to 2007).

It is undeniable that the best wines have proved to be sound long term investments over the past 20 years, though it is important to remember that one has to take the long term view. While the fine wine market had an exceptionally buoyant couple of years from 2005 to 2007, and Berrys' customers who bought top end 1996 and 2000 Clarets at the right time will have done very well indeed, wine prices are not immune to economic malaise and the global financial crisis did finally bite in October 2008 and prices – notably those of the top 2005s – dropped off from their early 2007 peaks. That said, confidence and demand came back to the fine wine market throughout 2009 and 2010 saw the market back at full strength; demand for the top wines, notably Châteaux Lafite-Rothschild, Latour and Mouton-Rothschild, is as strong, if not stronger, that it was during the boom of 2005 – 2007. To put this in perspective, 2005 Château Lafite-Rothschild was released en-primeur in June 2006 at £3,760 per case in bond. By the summer of 2008 it was fetching just under £10,000 per case in bond. In November 2008 brave buyers could buy the same wine at just under £6,000 per case in bond. The wine is currently trading (May 2011) for more than £12,500 per case.

The correlation between the financial and fine wine markets is relatively small. Prices for a few wines, such as 2005 Lafite discussed above, have shown some volatility, but

advertisement feature

the market as a whole has been resilient when compared with more traditional investment markets. The reason for this is relatively easy to explain: fine wine is a tangible asset, it is a luxury product that we aspire to own, consume and know more about. For many people it's much more useful than gold, and easier to enjoy than art. Interest in wine is growing at all levels. Most important is supply, which is limited; the supply of any particular vintage of, say Ch. Margaux, is constantly diminishing and in the case of younger vintages is constantly improving.

Key to investing in wine is buying the right wines (at the correct prices). The wines that have exhibited the best performance historically are the top 30 or so châteaux of Bordeaux. These are often best bought at their opening price en primeur but because supply is so restricted at the moment selected older vintages are looking to be good bets for the next five years. To put this in some kind of perspective and illustrate the problem of supply and demand, Ch. Latour made approximately 10,500 cases in 2003 and this production has to be allocated around the world. In the past, around 20% of Bordeaux wine was imported into the UK, which in this case may have accounted for around 2,000 cases of this château's production. This is already a restricted supply, but the UK now takes a far lower proportion of Bordeaux's production and less and less wine is released at opening prices. The opening price for 2003 Ch. Latour (if one could get hold of a case in June 2004 as this was available only on an allocation basis at most merchants) was around £2,250 per case. The wine currently trades (as at May 2011) at around £10,500 per case.

The practical advantages to wine investing are fairly straightforward. Wine is an easily transferable asset, there is an established fine wine market and a thriving auction market. There are no limits to wine investing, though the current prices of the top wines are such that one really should start with £5,000 to £10,000.

Berry Bros. & Rudd
3, St James's Street
London
SW1A 1EG

www.bbr.com
0800 280 2440

PART SIX
Ethical investment

Sustainable and responsible investing

PENNY SHEPHERD, UKSIF

What is sustainable and responsible investing?

Sustainable and responsible investing looks at the wider impact of investing on society and the environment when seeking financial returns. It takes into account social or environmental criteria in addition to financial criteria. It is a different way of looking at any investment opportunity, not a particular set of investments.

Sustainable and responsible opportunities are now available across an increasingly wide range of investment types. Established ethical investments are being joined by new options like climate change funds, sustainable property and microfinance funds.

You may sometimes hear the terms 'ethical', 'green' or 'socially responsible' investing used interchangeably with 'sustainable' and 'responsible', but they usually mean the same thing. Some people use the phrase 'green investments' specifically for investments in renewable energy or environmental (or 'clean') technologies.

Why choose sustainable and responsible investing?

Today, a wide range of people choose Fairtrade and organic products part of the time because they are great products in their own right and they help society and the environment at the same time. Similarly, it can make sense for all investors to consider sustainable and responsible investing for at least part of their portfolio.

It can also make good financial sense. 'Sustainable investing was once regarded as only of appeal to those that were ethically minded. However, with the world undergoing significant change, the issues around sustainability have become so fundamental to today's global society that the mainstream investment community is increasingly citing sustainable investment themes as the ones that offer the best potential for significant growth,' according to one experienced fund manager.[1]

In addition to this focus on social and environmental trends, the field also includes more traditional approaches like avoiding investments in the defence industry or pornography on moral rather than financial grounds. As with any investment field, it is important to understand the approach being offered by a specific investment and not to make assumptions.

Who uses sustainable and responsible investing?

2010 research by the European Sustainable Investment Forum[2] (Eurosif) found that an estimated 11 per cent of the portfolios of high net worth investors across Europe were already invested using sustainability criteria. According to Eurosif, this reflected both interest from successful entrepreneurs and inherited wealth that has moved to a younger generation, with the majority influenced most strongly by the financial opportunity offered by sustainable choices.

Experienced advisers in the UK report that, as well as more traditional ethical investors, a wide range of clients are now demanding investments that fit with their personal values. Indeed, over half of British investors want their investments not only to make money but also to make a difference in the world, according to consumer research in autumn 2010.[3]

What types of techniques are used?

Sustainable and responsible investing techniques used to select investments include the following.

Thematic investing

Picking investments using social and environmental themes where there are business opportunities in helping people or protecting the environment. These themes could include education, climate change or ageing society. Often, they are in areas where social or political pressures may create better business opportunities in the future than in the past. The new area of 'impact investing' described below is one specific type of thematic investing.

Positive screening

Selecting those investment opportunities that deliver better social and/or environmental performance than ones that are otherwise similar to them. This might mean picking the mining company with the best health and safety record, the energy company with the lowest carbon emissions or the commercial property investment that uses the least energy or most contributes to urban regeneration.

Engagement or responsible ownership

Rather than focusing on selecting investments, engagement aims to improve the social and/or environmental features of an investment while it is owned and to ensure that it is well managed so that its long-term value is protected. Engagement is therefore sometimes known as 'responsible ownership'. This may be achieved by using the power of being an owner to encourage, lobby for or support better business behaviour. It may also include publishing research or rankings of investments to encourage change.

For shareholdings in listed companies, voting at AGMs can be one part of this. Shareholders may also put forward shareholder resolutions to instruct or encourage companies to change if more informal influence is unsuccessful. In the UK, there are usually only a small number of socially or environmentally motivated shareholder resolutions each year but they are much more common in the United States.

Following the financial crisis, financial regulators are concerned to encourage responsible ownership. The world's first 'Stewardship Code' was launched in the UK in 2010. All UK investment managers are now required to state whether or not they follow the Code.[4]

Negative screening

This describes the traditional approach of avoiding particular investments altogether – for example, shares in tobacco manufacturers or publishers of pornography.

What types of sustainable and responsible investments are available?

There is an increasing range of investment types offering sustainable and responsible investing choices for private investors. Active and passive strategies are available. Asset classes include shares, bonds and property.

Collective investment funds and discretionary portfolio management services

Subject to your social and environmental interests, collective investment funds such as unit trusts and open-ended investment companies (OEICs) are available in at least a dozen of the investment sectors classified by the Investment Management Association. (See Table 6.1.1 for details of the investment sectors including ethically screened funds.) Discretionary portfolio management services are also available for those with larger amounts to invest.

TABLE 6.1.1 Investment Management Association: investment sectors with ethical funds

Active Managed
Balanced Managed
Cautious Managed
Europe excluding UK
Europe including UK
Global
Specialist
UK All Companies
UK Equity Income
Unclassified sector
£ Corporate Bond
£ Strategic Bond

Investment sectors containing at least one screened collective investment fund from a member firm of the Investment Management Association at 7 February 2011. This investment sector classification is defined and managed by the Investment Management Association. For current information, visit www.investmentfunds.org.uk/fund-sectors/find-a-fund and select 'Ethical'. This list demonstrates the range of options available and does not necessarily include all investment sectors in which ethical funds are available.

Exchange traded funds

A wide range of indexes with sustainable and responsible themes has been launched over the last few years. Examples are given in Table 6.1.2. Exchange traded funds (ETFs) are available to track some of these indexes. There are ETFs for clean energy companies, water-related businesses, large companies with low carbon emissions compared with others in their industry sector and Sharia-compliant (Islamic) investments.

TABLE 6.1.2 Environmental, social and governance (ESG) indexes: examples

Dow Jones Sustainability **Korea** Index
MSCI **Europe ESG** Index
S&P ESG **India** Index
FTSE4Good **Global** Index
Saudi Arabian Responsible Competitiveness Index (SARCI)
ECPI Global Longevity Winners Equity Index
Opportunities for the Majority (OM) Index
S&P CNX 500 **Shariah** Index
MSCI USA **Catholic Values** Index
Dow Jones **Dharma** Indexes
FTSE CDP **Carbon Strategy** All-Share Index
HSBC Optimised Global **Water** Index
MSCI Global **Green Building** Index
FTSE **Environmental Opportunities** All-Share Index

These examples of ESG indexes have been selected to give an illustrative range of the topics covered. They have not been selected for investment purposes, and any associated investment products may not be suitable for all investors. For details about each index and any associated investment products, please consult the index provider where specified or search online.

Property

The sustainable property investment area has ranged from pioneering eco-buildings to healthy low-energy offices and social housing with different products available at different times. Sustainable property funds may have a focus on issues such as environmental performance, urban regeneration, social housing or other societal impacts.

Other

Other investment options include some forestry investments, bond funds to raise capital for social projects and microfinance funds. And some investors are 'green business angels', investing directly in new small businesses delivering social and/or environmental benefits.

Investment structures

Tax-efficient structures like ISAs and Enterprise Investment Scheme (EIS) investments are available. Vehicles like Venture Capital Trusts (VCTs) and Real Estate Investment Trusts (REITs) may also be used.

Many stakeholder pensions and personal pensions offer sustainable and responsible options. A wider choice of sustainable and responsible investments may be held within a self-invested personal pension (SIPP).

Give me examples of sustainable and responsible investments available today

Examples of investments tackling particular social and environmental priorities include the following.

Climate change and environmental markets funds

There is a range of different investment techniques described today as 'climate change funds' or 'environmental markets' investments.

Some funds invest in 'environmental solutions', eg companies providing the environmental technologies and services likely to benefit from tighter regulation of carbon emissions and/or other environmental issues. There is a variety of such funds, including those with a broad remit and others with a specific focus such as sustainable water funds.

Other climate change funds invest in large companies that are leaders in managing their environmental impacts.

A climate change or environmental markets fund's investment strategy may or may not include any further negative or positive screening. For example, if you particularly support or object to nuclear power, you may wish to consider whether a particular climate change or environmental technology fund will include or exclude this form of energy generation. Similarly, you may wish to understand whether a fund investing in companies that are 'low carbon leaders' assesses performance on wider issues such as child labour. The fund literature should make this clear – if no information is provided then it is reasonable to assume that no specific criteria exist.

In the future, there may be a wider range of climate change investments. Significant capital will be needed for energy-efficient upgrades to existing housing and other property, and for low-carbon infrastructure such as smart electricity grids and charging points for electric cars. This may result in governments and companies issuing fixed interest 'climate bonds' either directly to private investors or to fund managers who may then offer fixed income climate change funds. And policy makers are looking for ways to give financial returns from sustainable forestry by valuing the 'ecosystem services' and 'carbon capture' that forests provide as well as their value when felled.

Sustainable thematic funds

Sustainable thematic funds invest across a wider range of themes than climate change or environmental management funds. These usually include both social and environmental trends.

Fund titles vary but may include words like 'future', 'sustainable' or 'eco'. Fund managers say that using a breadth of themes gives greater flexibility in selecting industries or, where appropriate, geographical regions offering the most attractive investment prospects over time. If pricing in some industries or technologies becomes unattractive, then they can rebalance the relative emphasis on different themes until the situation changes.

Screened collective investment funds ('ethical funds')

Broadly based 'ethical funds' use a selection of environmental, social and/or ethical issues together with conventional financial criteria to select suitable shares, bonds and/or other investments. They will usually use both negative screening and positive techniques, and may also use engagement.

It is possible to select a fund that takes a broad approach to responsible business behaviour. Alternatively, you can use the detailed information available about these funds to pick ones tailored to your specific priorities.

A list of the issues addressed by different funds is available at www.yourethicalmoney.org. A form used by an experienced financial adviser to ask clients about their detailed concerns is available at www.uksif.org. Some funds provide more detailed information about their investment approaches by using the European SRI Transparency Code.[5]

But can sustainable and responsible investments deliver good financial returns?

It is now widely recognized that well-managed sustainable and responsible investments can deliver excellent financial performance.

Specialist financial advisers say that, as with any other investment, the skills of the fund manager are key. According to the Investment Management Association, 'the performance of ethical funds is just as reliant on good management techniques as that of conventional funds'.[6] And 90 per cent of wealth managers responding to a 2009 survey said that their sustainable and responsible investing portfolios had performed the same as or better than their other portfolios.[7]

Some sustainable and responsible investments have a track record going back over 25 years, demonstrating that they can perform across a range of market conditions. Over short time periods, like other portfolios run according to investment convictions, a sustainable and responsible investment portfolio may vary above or below a conventional benchmark for a period of time.

Because sustainable and responsible investing is an investment style or philosophy and not restricted to a particular investment sector, the financial performance of a particular sustainable and responsible investment product should always be compared with another with equivalent financial characteristics. As with other investments, it does not make sense to judge a fund manager by comparing the performance of, say, a fund seeking dividend income from UK companies with another investing globally for capital growth.

There are strong arguments for thinking that sustainable and responsible investments may deliver superior financial performance in the future. This is because they address the implications for business of tomorrow's key social and environmental drivers. For example, the shift to a low-carbon economy will result in major changes to how companies operate and the products and services they sell. There will be winners and losers. Managers of sustainable and responsible investments are already considering where the profitable opportunities lie in this shifting landscape. They are assessing which companies manage their social impact well today and how easily they can respond to tomorrow's challenges.

What should I do if I am more concerned about social and environmental impact than financial return?

In the past, investors usually aimed to make as much money as possible from their investments – and then perhaps gave some of this away to good causes. Recently, a middle way is starting to emerge where some investors are putting aside a proportion of their wealth to invest mainly for the social and environmental impact achieved. This new area of 'high social impact investing' or 'impact investing' is attracting attention from individuals who have, for example, sold businesses or inherited wealth and wish to put some of their money to work doing good in a different way from charitable donations.

One impact investing adviser says: 'In addition to offering considerable social and environmental benefits, these investments are also appealing on a number of financial fronts. Impact investments often operate in geographic areas and sectors outside the financial mainstream, which are thus less correlated to other asset classes. Incorporating impact investment strategies into portfolio management can lead to better diversification. They can also appeal because these are not volatile instruments requiring delicate market timing or active portfolio management.'[8]

TABLE 6.1.3 Considering sustainable and responsible investing: a five
-step process

Step 1 – your investment aims. Consider why you are interested in sustainable and responsible investing. Is it to make money or to make a difference in the world – or a combination of the two? Do you want to have a positive impact or are you more concerned to avoid activities that you dislike – or both? Is this something that you want to consider for all your investments or just for a proportion of them?

Step 2 – your social and/or environmental priorities. Consider what aspects of society and the environment you want to take into account. Your response to the first step may affect this. Are you most interested in the impact of your investments on people or the planet? Are you particularly attracted to new business solutions to today's problems? Are your interests fairly general or do you feel really passionate about some things, like opportunities for young people, climate change or the treatment of animals?

Step 3 – your preferred approaches. Consider what type of investment strategy most attracts you as the way to put your priorities into action. Is it backing certain investment themes? Is it picking bigger companies that are most committed to doing their bit? Is it using ownership power? Is it avoiding some investments? Is it a mixture of these?

Step 4 – your financial objectives. Having thought through what you want to achieve and how, it is important to consider all those financial criteria that are relevant for any investment decision. For example: What are your financial performance objectives? What return are you looking for – and over what timescale? What is your attitude to risk and volatility? What asset mix are you seeking in your portfolio and how might your sustainable and responsible investments best fit into this? How will your sustainable and responsible investments help to address your diversification needs? If these questions are unfamiliar to you, it is worth learning more about financial planning in general or seeking independent advice.

Step 5 – your judgement of best fit. Having identified all of the above, you then need to research the marketplace and pick the investments that best meet your range of needs. The good news is that there is an increasing range of opportunities available – and there are likely to be more in the future.

This process is not intended as a substitute for professional financial advice. If you are considering making a significant investment, we recommend that you consult an independent financial adviser or wealth manager with skills and experience in advising on sustainable and responsible investing.

How should I get started with sustainable and responsible investing?

If you use an independent financial adviser or wealth manager, it makes sense to start by asking how they can help. Do explore what knowledge and experience they have in the field. For example, they might have done UKSIF's online investment advice course. Or they might be certified to the international standard for personal financial planning (ISO 22222), which requires them to ask clients about whether they should take any social, ethical, environmental or religious issues into account. Check how up to date they are – the area has developed a lot in the last few years.

If you don't wish to use an existing adviser, you might consider a financial adviser who is a member of the Ethical Investment Association (EIA). Advisers in this association are committed to increasing access to sustainable and responsible investment advice for individuals, businesses and charities, and to increasing and improving their own professional knowledge.

Private client investment managers and stockbrokers who manage sustainable and responsible investments may be members of UKSIF, the sustainable investment and finance association, listed at www.yourethicalmoney.org and/or accessible through Ethical Screening's services for private investors.

If you want to understand the social and environmental characteristics of the stocks in your existing portfolio, Ethical Screening's private investor service might be appropriate.

Of course, it is important to blend your social, environmental and ethical priorities with your financial requirements to get a diversified range of investments that is suitable for you. If you want to explore sustainable and responsible investing without an adviser, you may wish to consider the five-step process given in Table 6.1.3, which is based on UKSIF's free online training course for financial advisers.

What about other financial services?

As well as investments, there are bank accounts, savings, mortgages, credit cards, insurance and other financial services designed to take into account their wider impact on the world. For example, visit www.yourethicalmoney.org (an initiative of the EIRIS Foundation, a charity) to find out more.

How can I find out more?

To explore sustainable and responsible investing and consider how you can get started, there is a range of useful information sources online. See Table 6.1.4 for more details. If you want to read a longer introduction with further useful links, try *Green Money: how to save and invest ethically* (A & C Black Publishers Ltd, 2009) by respected consumer journalist Sarah Pennells (or visit www.savvywoman.co.uk to buy it online).

TABLE 6.1.4 Sources of further information

www.neiw.org
The site for National Ethical Investment Week, which is run annually by UKSIF, the sustainable investment and finance association, to raise awareness about sustainable and responsible investing. This includes information for private investors that is available throughout the year, although its main function is as an information clearing house for details about what is going on each year during the Week.

www.yourethicalmoney.org
A non-profit site that aims to provide you with objective, independent information on sustainable and responsible finance, including investments. It is run by the EIRIS Foundation, a charity with over 25 years of experience in the field.

www.ethicalscreening.com
To check your existing investments against sustainable and responsible investment criteria.

www.holden-partners.co.uk
This financial adviser firm offers a detailed *Guide to Climate Change and Ethical Investing* for free download from their site.

www.eurosif.org/research/sector-reports
For general overviews of environmental, social and governance risks and opportunities faced by companies in a range of industry sectors.

www.thegiin.org
Internationally, the Global Impact Investing Network is at the cutting edge of supporting the emerging specialized field of 'impact investing' that puts social and environmental impact ahead of financial return. Today, impact investing is of particular interest to charitable foundations and those seeking business-driven alternatives to charitable donations. Those active in the UK in impact investing include Triodos Bank (www.triodos.co.uk), ClearlySo (www.clearlyso.com) and, for professional advisers and charitable foundations rather than private individuals, Investing for Good (www.investingforgood.co.uk).

www.ethicalinvestment.org.uk
To find a financial adviser specializing in sustainable and responsible investment.

www.eurosif.org/sri-resources/sri-transparency-code
For signatories to the European SRI Transparency Code.

www.uksif.org
The general website of UKSIF – the sustainable investment and finance association. This includes information on financial organizations that are UKSIF members, tools for financial advisers and other resources.

These websites do not provide financial information about sustainable and responsible investments. Such information is available from standard financial information sources.

This chapter offers a general overview and should not be taken as financial advice or seen as an endorsement of any particular company, organization or individual. While we have sought to ensure this information is correct at time of print, the author and UKSIF do not accept liability for any errors.

Notes

1 Michael Fox, The Co-operative Asset Management (see www.ftadviser.com/FinancialAdviser/Investments/Sector/EthicalAndSRI/Features/article/20090910/ec701584-97aa-11de-b57d-0015171400aa/Profit-with-principles.jsp).

2 See www.eurosif.org/research/hnwi-a-sustainable-investment.

3 See www.neiw.org/about/media-centre/greed-good-green-good-2010s-set-become-decade-financial-responsibility.

4 See www.frc.org.uk/corporate/investorgovernance.cfm and www.frc.org.uk/corporate/stewardshipstatements.cfm.

5 See www.eurosif.org/sri-resources/sri-transparency-code.

6 See PDF at www.investmentfunds.org.uk/consumer-centre/consumer-factsheets/ethical-investing.

7 See www.eiris.org/files/press%20releases/HNWIsurveyoct09.pdf.

8 Geoff Burnand, Chief Executive, Investing for Good. See www.ftadviser.com/FinancialAdviser/Investments/Sector/EthicalAndSRI/Features/article/20091015/e152d6f6-b289-11de-b38a-00144f2af8e8/Brace-for-impact.jsp.

Mission possible: how the wealthy can help charities during the economic downturn

STEFAN VELVICK, CHARITIES AID FOUNDATION

These are tough times for charities, although demand on many charities' services has never been higher. Demands on housing, mental health, debt counselling and drug rehabilitation charities, to name a few, are more pressing than perhaps they have ever been.

The UK still has one of the most favourable tax regimes for charitable giving in the world, making it the most attractive place to make gifts of any size, from small cash donations to substantial gifts of shares or property. Donations through the Gift Aid scheme alone reached £4,578 million[1] in 2009/10, according to HM Revenue and Customs.

As the world economy has started to recover from the 'Great Recession', there has been a recovery in the value of assets held by the super-rich. The 2010 Merrill Lynch Capgemini Survey reported an 18.9 per cent increase in the global wealth of high net worth individuals between 2008 and 2009[2] to US$39 trillion. However, this is still below the 2007 peak of US$40.7 trillion.

The amount donated by the Top 100 philanthropists, according to the 2010 *Sunday Times* 'Giving List', was £2,493 billion in 2009; this is £324 million or 11.5 per cent down on 2009.[3] Despite this decline the amount donated, as a proportion of the total wealth of the richest 1,000, increased, as overall their total wealth declined by 37.4 per cent in the same financial year (see the 2009 *Sunday Times* 'Rich List'). In 2008–9, 201 donations of at least £1 million or more were made, with a combined value of £1.5 billion,[4] according to a report by Coutts.

But for some sections of the wealthy, giving their money away to recognized charities is not enough. They want to set up their own charitable foundation where they can exert the same level of control as they do in their business ventures. These types of donors are often attracted by the concept of 'entrepreneurial giving', viewing their donations more as investments than gifts.

A more cost- and time-effective option for other well-off donors is setting up a trust with the Charities Aid Foundation (CAF). The 2,807 wealthy donors who use CAF's Trust service gave away £81.6 million in 2008–9.

CAF has over 80 years' experience of helping people make their donations go further. That experience has taught us that the best way to start making a difference is to be clear about what it is you want your support to achieve.

Developing your giving strategy

At CAF we can help you to maximize the impact of your philanthropy by developing a strategy that meets your aims.

Defining aims and objectives

What are the causes that matter to you? Who do you want to help? What do you hope to achieve? By talking to you about your charitable interests, we can help you clarify your aims and objectives and suggest a strategy to help you achieve them.

Designing your portfolio

Do you want to support a range of causes or focus on a single project? We can create a giving portfolio for you which suits your needs and can be regularly reviewed to ensure it is still making a difference to the causes that matter to you.

Refining your strategy

Philanthropy works best when you have a clear and costed strategy for achieving your goals. This means applying business thinking to your philanthropy. We can work with you to design a personal giving plan to help you to be strategic in your choice of causes.

Measuring your impact

It's natural to be concerned about how much of your gift will ultimately reach the people and projects that you wish to support. Using benchmarks, we can assess the impact of each donation you make and report on what your support has achieved.

Supporting your community

If you want to support people or projects close to home, we can help you identify local charities working in your local area. Whether that's by finding a local project that matches your interests or by identifying an organization with a track record of delivering results, we can design the right solution for you.

Providing international solutions

If you want to support international projects, you may want to consider donating to organizations based overseas. CAF is well placed to advise you on the impact of your international giving. With offices in seven countries and projects in six continents, we can provide you with quality information and research on charities' work across the world.

Taking advantage of the tax breaks

To help you adopt a planned and informed approach to your giving, you need to be aware of the available tax incentives for charitable gifts.

Gift Aid

Make sure every gift you make to charity is a Gift Aid donation. Using Gift Aid means the charity will receive an extra 25 per cent.[5]

When you make a Gift Aid donation to charity, it is treated as net, ie after basic rate tax has been deducted. For example, if you give £100, tax can be reclaimed and added to your donation, making it worth £125 to the charity. The calculations for basic rate and higher rate tax payers are detailed in Tables 6.2.1 to 6.2.3.

TABLE 6.2.1 Basic rate taxpayer

Your donation to charity	£1,000
Amount reclaimed by charity from HM Revenue & Customs	£250
Transitional relief[6]	£32
Total amount received by charity	£1,282
Cost to you to give £1,282	£1,000

TABLE 6.2.2 Higher rate taxpayer (40%)

Your donation to charity	£1,000
Amount reclaimed by charity from HM Revenue & Customs	£250
Transitional relief	£32
Total amount reclaimed by donor in tax return	£250
Cost to you to give £1,282	£750

TABLE 6.2.3 Higher rate taxpayer (50%)

Your donation to charity	£1,000
Amount reclaimed by charity from HM Revenue & Customs	£250
Transitional relief	£32
Total amount reclaimed by donor in tax return	£375
Cost to you to give £1,282	£625

Who can use Gift Aid?

Anyone who has paid enough income tax or capital gains tax in the current financial year to cover the amount reclaimed by the charity can use Gift Aid. So if you give £100, you need to have paid at least £25 in income tax or capital gains tax.

In addition, if you have not submitted your tax return for the previous tax year (ending on 5 April), you can elect for charitable donations to be related back to the previous year so as to take advantage of any unused income tax or capital gains tax in that year.

How does it work?

You need to complete a simple declaration for the charity. This can be done in writing, over the phone or online. The declaration can apply to past donations you have made and to all future donations you make.

What can I receive in return for a Gift Aid donation?

You cannot use Gift Aid to pay for goods or services, eg school fees. However, Gift Aid can be used to pay certain charitable subscriptions and membership fees, eg for heritage charities.

If you are a higher-rate taxpayer you can claim the difference between the basic rate and higher rate personally or give it to charity on your annual tax return.

How can I plan my giving more effectively?

There are several ways CAF can help you plan your giving. We offer a number of specialist services that help you tailor your giving to your circumstances.

CAF Charity Account

The CAF Charity Account is a brilliantly simple way to plan your giving throughout the year. It works like a current account, but it's exclusively for your charitable giving. By ensuring that you always have a pool of funds to draw from, your Charity

Account enables you to respond to emergency appeals as well as provide regular support to a portfolio of your favourite charities.

For every pound you pay into your Charity Account, we will reclaim the tax and add it to your balance. Charities don't always find it cost effective to reclaim Gift Aid on every donation; but with a Charity Account you can rest assured that every penny you give is tax efficient.

Other benefits of using a CAF Charity Account include:

- You can make anonymous donations.
- You can give to charities based overseas.
- You only need to make one Gift Aid declaration.

Payroll giving

If your employer (or pension payer) offers payroll giving, this is one of the simplest ways to make regular tax-efficient donations. Money is simply taken from your gross salary (before tax is deducted) and passed on to your chosen charities. This makes it especially attractive for higher-rate taxpayers, as Table 6.2.4 demonstrates.

CAF offers payroll giving through its Give As You Earn Scheme, which gives the donor the option to change the charities they support and respond to emergency appeals. You can also fund a Charity Account through Give As You Earn.

TABLE 6.2.4 The tax benefits of payroll giving

Your monthly pledge	£1,000
Cost to basic-rate tax payer (20%)	£800
Cost to higher-rate taxpayer (40%)	£600
Cost to higher-rate taxpayer (50%)	£500

Charitable trust

A charitable trust or foundation is a structure that can be set up by anyone who has decided that they want to set aside some of their assets or income for charitable causes. Setting up your own trust provides a framework for planning your charitable giving in a systematic and thoughtful way.

Normally you would need to appoint your own trustees and pay up to £1,500 plus VAT in legal fees and yearly accountant fees of up to £1,000 plus VAT.[6]

However, if you set up a CAF Charitable Trust you will not need to appoint your own trustees or employ the services of a solicitor or accountant. A CAF Trust allows you to donate a sum upwards of £10,000 which will form an invested fund. You will then be free to give away the income (and the capital if you choose) to any charity of your choice. You can also share the grant-making decisions with your partner or family members.

David Pitt-Watson, Director of Hermes Focus Asset Management, is an enthusiastic advocate of the CAF Trust. He uses his trust to support a wide range of charities. David said: 'I wanted the flexibility to give to a range of charities in an enduring way. The advantage of a CAF Trust is that it's so easy. You can do something with it now, or you can park it during a busy time – you don't have to worry about it. The CAF Trust was recommended to me, and I would absolutely recommend it to others. It's a great system.'

Giving shares

When people think about supporting charity they usually think of giving cash. But a gift of stocks and shares can be an even more effective way of benefiting the causes you care about.

A gift of shares to charity is exempt from capital gains tax and when the shares are sold by the charity, once again this is tax free.

A gift of quoted shares has the advantage of a double tax benefit; not only is it exempt from capital gains tax, it can also enable you to reduce your income tax bill. However, to receive the income tax relief, the shares have to be a qualifying investment listed by HMRC.

If you donate shares to CAF we will sell them and place the proceeds in your CAF Charity Account or CAF Charitable Trust. You may prefer to sell shares at less than their market value to CAF and claim relief against your taxable income on the discount.

Gifts of land or artworks

If you wish to give land or works of art, CAF can sell them and place the proceeds in your CAF Charity Account or CAF Trust. This would allow you to avoid capital gains tax and it may be possible (in the case of land) to obtain relief from income tax.

Leaving money to charity in your will

You can leave money or property to charity by making provision for this in your will. This is known as a legacy or bequest. You may leave a specified sum of money to charity or leave the residue of your estate, that is, the amount left once the executors have paid all the necessary outgoings and other legacies or bequests.

Normally once you have written your will you can't change the charities you wish to leave money to without contacting your solicitor to amend the will. But with a CAF Legacy Account you can change the charities you wish to support at any time during your lifetime, without changing your will.

Social investment

As well as giving money away, you may be interested in becoming a social investor. Venturesome, our social investment initiative, provides smaller charities with loans and investments when they can't access mainstream funding. In contrast to a one-off gift, when you make a gift through Venturesome we aim to recycle it three to four times. This offers you a unique opportunity to make your money work harder to achieve a social impact.

Balancing your commitments

As well as cash you may want to give your time and share your skills with your favourite charities too. We can source volunteering and mentoring opportunities which match your skill set. That way, not only will your financial support achieve the maximum impact, your time will be used to best effect too.

Conclusion

This five-step action plan is designed to help you ensure that your giving is as targeted and effective as it can be.

1 Commit to a timetable
Plan your giving over a longer timescale. At CAF we offer a range of giving solutions specially designed to help you to start seeing giving as a permanent fixture in your life.

2 Structure your gift:
- How do you want to give?
- Do you want to provide regular support or donate a capital sum?
- Would you prefer to release your donations in phases?
- Do you want to include a loan as part of your gift?
- Or offer your skills and expertise to the project?

3 Make your giving tax efficient
Plan your giving tax efficiently to increase its value. At CAF we offer a range of solutions to help you take advantage of the available tax incentives for charitable giving.

4 Choose carefully
Before jumping in with both feet, think carefully about what you want your giving to achieve. Create criteria of things that matter to you. Then develop a strategy that can help you make a difference to the people and projects you wish to support.

5 Know your impact
Once you know what your charitable goals are and have developed a strategy to achieve them, you can measure the impact of your giving. We at CAF can use benchmarks that produce tangible evidence of what your giving has achieved.

About CAF

Charities Aid Foundation is a charity whose mission is to create greater value for charities and social enterprise. We do this by transforming the way donations are made and charitable funds are managed. Our core activity is to provide innovative financial services to charities and their supporters.

Notes

1 http://www.hmrc.gov.uk/stats/charities/table10-3.pdf
2 http://www.capgemini.com/insights-and-resources/by-publication/world-wealth-report-2010/
3 http://features.thesundaytimes.co.uk/richlist/live/
4 www.kent.ac.uk/sspssr/cphsj/documents/mpdr2010.pdf
5 As from April 2008.
6 The government brought in transitional relief until April 2011 to compensate charities for the reduction in Gift Aid following the 2% reduction in basic rate tax.
7 *A Guide to Giving*, www.PhilanthropyUK.org

The impact of epilepsy

ROPINDER GILL, EPILEPSY SOCIETY

Epilepsy Society

Epilepsy Society (the new name for The National Society for Epilepsy) is a national charity that makes a lasting contribution to the treatment and understanding of epilepsy. It does this by raising awareness, undertaking pioneering medical research and providing specialist medical services, information, support, and respite and residential care.

The impact of epilepsy

Epilepsy is one of the most distressing conditions imaginable. In the UK it is the most common serious disorder of the brain, affecting nearly half a million people and with 30,000 new cases every year. It kills more than 1,000 people annually and in extreme cases it ravages physical, emotional and mental health.

Epilepsy can have a far-reaching psychological impact; it often means coping with many uncertainties, in practical and emotional terms and in the social impact on everyday life. There is also the physical impact of seizures: knocks, bruises, black eyes and concussion. Reducing the frequency and severity of seizures is usually the key to managing epilepsy.

Trying to control seizures can mean a lifetime of medication. In a third of people who develop epilepsy, the medication doesn't work and seizures continue. When they do work, anti-epileptic drugs are a lifeline. However, getting the right medication is a matter of trial and error, often involving long stints on unsuitable drugs with severe adverse effects, until the right one is found.

Nationwide support and information

Epilepsy Society offers nationwide support and information to everyone affected by epilepsy. It provides information leaflets that deal with many aspects of epilepsy from diagnosis to driving regulations. In 2010 it gave out over 535,000 information leaflets and resources such as seizure diaries and ID cards. Our website has a wealth of information for people about epilepsy and how to manage the condition. We also provide a specialist website for health professionals.

The Epilepsy Information Network (EIN) provides support throughout England. By recruiting and training volunteers to deliver information and support to people with epilepsy, Epilepsy Society reaches out to families and carers within their own regions. There are currently over 188 such services in operation, of which 37 are in paediatric units, with around 216 trained volunteers around England. EIN distributes our information resources and also delivers our schools awareness programme. This increasingly popular programme was developed in conjunction with teachers and aims to raise awareness of epilepsy amongst school children to reduce bullying.

Helpline and forum

Our helpline receives around 6,000 calls every year from people with epilepsy, and from their family and friends, GPs, nurses, pharmacists, employers and schools, all wanting to know more about epilepsy. For many it is a lifeline when they need to talk or have concerns that they would like to talk through.

For those people who want to connect with others with epilepsy, Epilepsy Society hosts a web forum that currently has almost 6,000 members. It provides a self-support system amongst a community of people who have all been affected by epilepsy in one way or another.

Medical services

At our site in Buckinghamshire, we offer world-class medical facilities and see thousands of patients every year. Epilepsy Society provides the best in assessment, diagnosis and treatment. Its reputation as a centre of excellence, recognized by the World Health Organization (WHO), has been gained through its working partnership with the National Hospital for Neurology and Neurosurgery (NHNN) and the Institute of Neurology (part of the University of London). Together Epilepsy Society and NHNN provide clinics for new patients, diagnostic tests such as EEGs and MRIs, and dedicated neurological and neurosurgical intensive care units.

Medical research

Our expertise in medical assessment means that it is uniquely placed to research the causes of epilepsy and the best possible treatments. Our consultant neurologists, including its medical director Professor John Duncan, are experts in brain imaging, genetics, pharmacology, epidemiology and psychology and have been at the forefront of epilepsy research since the 1960s. Professor Ley Sander leads our international effort researching epilepsy in China and countries in Africa, and Professor Sisodiya leads our work in the field of genetics, working in collaboration with the United

States' Duke University. With 50 million people living with epilepsy worldwide the impact of our research is vast.

The goals driving our research are to be able to understand what has caused the epilepsy in each person who develops the condition, to be able to identify the best individualized therapy from the outset and to make this expertise widely available. Epilepsy Society is currently raising funds for a new epilepsy research centre in Buckinghamshire in which to continue our research.

Through medical research our award-winning neurologists are looking for the answers that will help us to understand epilepsy better, to improve medication and surgery, and ultimately to eradicate epilepsy.

Making an impact

Epilepsy Society is unique in the breadth of services it provides and it has been developing these services for people with epilepsy since 1892. Epilepsy Society also provides a range of options to meet the needs of the people coming to stay in its residential care homes in Buckinghamshire. For a small group of very vulnerable people with severe and complex epilepsy, this kind of specialist residential care is essential, and many of the ancillary therapies offered are funded wholly by our supporters.

Through our services we hear about how epilepsy has affected people, their families, their work and their relationships. We hear from parents, siblings, grandparents, employers, teachers, partners and friends. By providing up-to-date information and support we arm them with the knowledge needed to help them cope with epilepsy. And by undertaking research we offer them hope for the future.

Despite the prevalence of epilepsy, stigma and misunderstanding are still rife. People do not realize that epilepsy can affect anyone at any time and can be caused by so many different things. Outdated beliefs about epilepsy still prevail.

An Epilepsy Society survey showed that two-thirds of people with epilepsy worry about the reaction of others to their seizures. This backs up the many stories that we have heard concerning a woeful response to the sight of someone having a seizure. We know of instances where purses have been stolen or people have been arrested or assumed to be drunk or drugged. Many people also have little or no understanding of epilepsy and necessary treatment during a seizure.

Despite the strides that we have made in making epilepsy more acceptable, people still lose their jobs and children continue to be bullied because of their epilepsy. Others are scared to do the normal things in life for fear of having a seizure that frightens those around them.

Why we need your help

For the vast majority of people with epilepsy, it just becomes a part of their life, which for the most part can be controlled and managed. However, there is a huge demand for Epilepsy Society's services. We get so many positive responses to the services we provide, but the need is greater than we can currently meet. There are more people trying to get through to our helpline than we can deal with, and there are so many places in the UK that do not have an epilepsy information point or an epilepsy information volunteer. There are topics that we know people would like us to cover with our information leaflets, but with our current resources this is not always possible. And there are not enough funds for all the threads of epilepsy research that we do.

We know that within the NHS there are not enough neurologists, epilepsy clinicians or specialist nurses. There is not enough information on the risk of sudden unexpected death in epilepsy (SUDEP) and how to manage that risk. Apart from tackling these issues we also want a better deal in employment and better education provision for children with epilepsy. We raise awareness not just through our media work but also through our campaigns.

We want people affected by epilepsy to know that we are here so that they don't feel as though they have to deal with their epilepsy on their own. We understand their experiences, and through NSE expertise, research and knowledge we want to provide support and hope for the future, but we need help from others to achieve this.

How you can help

Whether you have a personal experience of epilepsy or are just inspired by our work for others, you can be sure that we will make your gifts go as far as possible. There are many ways to support our work, including:

- *A major gift*. The decision to make a large annual donation, of say over £1,000, or a large regular donation usually requires some research and planning. We would be delighted to work with you to ensure that your gift is making a difference in the way that you want it to. We will take the time to answer any queries that you have and discuss which areas of our work you would like to contribute to, whether research, our helpline or our other support services. You may be happy to contribute to our running costs or you may want to support our capital appeal for a research centre. Perhaps you have set up a foundation or trust and would rather make a gift from that. Whatever your interest we want to involve you so that the process is as rewarding and enriching as possible.

- *A payroll gift*. A regular gift through your salary means that we are able to depend on a regular, stable source of income. Payroll giving (also known as Give As You Earn or GAYE) is a highly efficient way to support Epilepsy Society and is a particularly attractive option for higher-rate taxpayers. If you earn a salary or if your occupational pension is paid through PAYE, then you could make regular contributions to Epilepsy Society through a payroll-giving scheme. Or perhaps you own or manage a business and would like to offer your employees the opportunity to support Epilepsy Society by setting up a GAYE scheme. If you sign up to a payroll-giving scheme, a donation will be deducted from your salary (or pension) before tax. However, a monthly pledge of £250 will cost a basic-rate taxpayer £200 (20 per cent relief) and a higher-rate taxpayer £150 (40 per cent relief).

- *Leaving a gift in your will.* Making a will is about helping others to live and is a positive recognition of the people you care about and the causes that inspire you. Please remember the Epilepsy Society when you come to making or updating your will, and we will use every penny to make a difference. Gifts to Epilepsy Society are also exempt from inheritance tax, so not only can you be sure that we will get the full benefit of your gift but the gift can also be used to reduce your overall tax burden. Ask your solicitor for advice on inheritance tax planning.

- *Other types of planned giving.* Leaving a legacy is one type of planned giving that does not require immediate financial commitment. Another way is to make Epilepsy Society a beneficiary of your life insurance or pension scheme funds or a proportion thereof.

- *Share giving.* Whether you have a few windfall shares sitting gathering dust or a more sizeable investment portfolio, it is simple to give shares to Epilepsy Society as long as they are listed or dealt with on a recognized stock exchange in the UK or elsewhere. Share gifts benefit from income tax relief and exemption from capital gains tax. You are also entitled to claim tax relief for any related costs, such as brokers' fees. Tax relief applies whether it is a company or an individual giving the shares. Your personal circumstances will affect the tax benefits to which you are entitled. For a higher-rate taxpayer, for example, who donates shares worth £1,000 to Epilepsy Society, the income tax relief will be £400. You will not have to pay any capital gains tax on these shares. You may find it helpful to take professional advice to ensure that your donation to Epilepsy Society is structured in the most efficient way. To find out how to donate shares, please visit our website, or phone 01494 601313.

- *Giving land or buildings.* There are different ways in which people can support Epilepsy Society, and a very small number may wish to give a gift of land or buildings. Although this type of gift is rare, it can be very significant in value. If this is something that appeals to you, it's worth bearing in mind that you can give land or buildings in their entirety or a proportion of the holding and that either way there is generous tax relief available on such gifts. The tax relief available to people giving land or buildings is very similar to that on the gift of shares; there is income tax relief and exemption from capital gains tax. Tax relief is given for the market value of the property in the tax year when the gift is made, and it is deducted from the donor's income tax liability with any incidental costs of transferring the property, such as a solicitor's fee. It is important to get professional advice from an accountant or financial adviser when making a gift of land or buildings, and your tax office may be able to help with other questions that you might have.

Helping you to decide

Any gift to the Epilepsy Society is very gratefully received. We want to help donors understand our work and see the difference that their support can make first-hand. So if you would like to see our services then please arrange a visit to our site in

Buckinghamshire by calling Ropinder Gill on 01494 601313. Alternatively you can e-mail fundraising@epilepsysociety.org.uk.

By coming to visit us you can see, amongst other things, Epilepsy Society support services, medical services and our medical research work. NSE consultant neurologists and medical staff can answer specific queries on research and medical services. You can also see the plans for our epilepsy research centre. If you are able to consider a six-figure gift or above, we can discuss naming rights with you.

Epilepsy Society is happy to provide any information that will help you make a decision to support us, including our annual review, statement of accounts or supporter newsletters. Our regular e-newsletter is also a great way to keep up to date with our work, so please sign up on our website.

Epilepsy Society website

Our website at www.epilepsysociety.org.uk is an excellent resource for learning more about epilepsy, about the work we do and about the various ways to support us.

CASE STUDY

'I was discovered having that first seizure slumped over a hi-fi in my bedroom banging my head against a desk and a large wooden box. Since then I've had seizures in McDonalds, on a dance floor, sitting next to my wife on the sofa, even in the office. A seizure on the edge of a railway platform could prove fatal. But thanks to the Epilepsy Society, I am now free to live my life to the full.'

For over a decade Mark was on the wrong mix of anti-epileptic drugs. It wasn't until he was referred to specialists at the Epilepsy Society that a new drug regime achieved control of his seizures. He is now part of research programmes at Epilepsy Society, undergoing MRI scans to provide data for specialists working on advances in diagnosis and treatment of the condition.

Philanthropy matters

DAVID WARNER, NATIONAL ANIMAL WELFARE TRUST

The job satisfaction is tremendous from philanthropy. It makes me more than someone who has just made money.

Alec Reed, Chair, The Big Give (from FT.com)

The rise of the new philanthropists

Philanthropy has grown in the UK over the past decade. Some influencing factors are undoubtedly the rise in personal wealth (the *Sunday Times* Rich List has shown that the ratio of inherited wealth to self-made wealth has completely reversed from 75:25 to 25:75 in the past 15 years), as well as a move towards donors becoming more active in their giving, offering a more strategic approach to how their money is spent.

Riding the wave is a greater support network for philanthropists from within the business world, the charitable sector and government. One recent example is the new post of Ambassador for Philanthropy that was established in 2009, under the guidance of Dame Stephanie Shirley, to advance philanthropic ideals in Britain. Its website gives a 'voice' to philanthropists, and there are many useful interviews on all manner of topics associated with the subject.

The new class of philanthropists, such as Darcey Bussell, Martha Lane Fox and J K Rowling, is young and largely self-made, and includes a growing proportion of women. Experts in the sector say the increasing female influence has made a difference to the types of causes and the nature of giving on offer, adding to the diversity and complexity of the subject.

With such high-profile names willing to talk openly about their giving, less well-known philanthropists are now also being given a mass market platform on such TV shows as *The Secret Millionaire*.

This increasingly open attitude to giving has also resulted in the charity world being asked to be more transparent, leading to a greater flow of information from the sector.

What is philanthropy?

The *Oxford Dictionary* describes philanthropy simply as the desire to help others, especially through donation of money to good causes. It is also perceived as the act of giving assets, encouragement and expertise to create a social or environmental impact.

How to give

You may give some of your money to charity already, and your style of giving is probably built on personal values and motivations that might not be too dissimilar to some of your own business motivations. *Dragons' Den* judge and entrepreneur James Caan was struck early on in his career by how his business was successful because of its people, and that has shaped much of his charitable giving. J K Rowling's Volant Foundation is another example of how charitable donations often match the personal values and experiences of the benefactor. It gives to a wide range of institutions dealing with social deprivation affecting women and children in particular, as well as research into multiple sclerosis, the disease from which her mother died.

When it comes to choosing your preferred cause, there is an increasing range of information available to potential donors. Organizations like the Charity Commission, the Charities Aid Foundation (CAF) and New Philanthropy Capital give plenty of advice on specific charities – their websites offer clear and easy guidance on financial performance, reporting and, in some cases, environmental attitudes.

Sitting alongside the wealth of online information are a host of professional advisers and third parties that help individuals devise a strategy, scope out a specific charity sector and identify their preferred route to giving.

Teaming up

When Warren Buffett, the world's richest man, decided to give 85 per cent of his estimated $61 billion wealth mainly to a foundation set up by the world's second richest man, Bill Gates, it signified another trend that seems to be emerging – that of investors teaming up, or pooling their donations, in order to make more of an impact with their finances. Absolute Return for Kids (ARK), the Funding Network and the Big Give are examples of this – or, if giving back to your local community is your priority, Community Foundations is a network of local charities that work with philanthropists to give money to local causes in a structured and unbiased way. The advantage of foundations is that they have already built up a track record in giving, have established networks, are knowledgeable on matters regarding impact and how to give and are therefore an easy and very helpful route to explore.

Getting involved

It's noticeable when reading or studying views on philanthropy that all donors, be they the richest people in the world or the rest of us, feel they get more out of giving when they become actively involved in the charities to which they contribute. You may prefer not to do too much of this, but understanding to what degree you wish to be involved is an important part of your strategy.

What risks do you want to take?

This again might be aligned to your own personal style. Are you prepared to take some high risks? It's notable that the rise in individual donors in the charity sector is making it easier for them to take some higher risks with some initiatives, but you may prefer a more tried-and-tested method of making an impact. It is worth taking some time to reflect on whether you want to be involved with quick results, or slower approaches that are more tolerant of process.

What about the reward?

It's unquestionable that donors feel the rewards are great, but do consider what will give you the greatest reward. Is it how many people you will be reaching, your own personal recognition or the personal stories that you will inevitably encounter?

Giving tax efficiently

Without doubt philanthropists are also motivated by the idea of giving tax efficiently, and the UK has a range of incentives to make that transaction run as smoothly as possible. Just as it takes time and thought to decide to whom and how you want to give, you will also need to review your financial situation with your financial adviser and/or philanthropic adviser, to decide what is the most efficient method for you. There is a wide range of methods and models, from payroll and gifts of assets for the corporate donor to charitable trusts. If you decide on a portfolio of giving, then you'll need to plan your best method of approach to maximize the gift.

Legacies remain the highest contributor to the charity sector in the UK. According to Remember a Charity (which promotes leaving legacies to charity), more than £1.9 billion is left in wills every year. Most charities, foundations and trusts will offer you advice on how to arrange wills and can even act as executors. Bodies like the Big Give also offer matched funding for legacies.

A charity with community roots at its heart

Like philanthropy the charity sector has undergone several changes over the past decade. There is increasing pressure on transparency and accountability and for organizations to provide evidence on how they measure their impact both in their day-to-day operations and across the wider community in which they serve. The National Animal Welfare Trust (NAWT) provides one such example.

The NAWT is one of the top 10 animal rescue and rehoming charities in England, and runs centres in Watford, Berkshire, Essex, Somerset and Cornwall. The NAWT is home to a surprisingly wide variety of animals, primarily dogs and cats, but also farm animals, horses and donkeys, ducks, poultry and small domestic pets. It cares for around 500 animals at a total cost of £8,000 per day (equivalent to £16 per animal). Although animal care is its primary focus, the NAWT also serves an important function within the wider community, providing opportunities for human interaction with animals in a safe and controlled environment. Hundreds of volunteers and fundraisers become involved with the NAWT for a diverse number of reasons, whether they are a local group of people with learning difficulties or young people wishing to gain work experience for a career in veterinary nursing.

The NAWT's main areas of concern are:

- Rehoming strays or neglected or unwanted pets. Careful attention is paid to matching the animal with the prospective owner, and no animal is refused. A considerable amount of rehabilitation and behavioural tutoring time is spent on animals where needed, in order to give them the best chance of finding a new home.

- A non-destruction policy. If no suitable home is found and providing the animal is in good health, it will remain with the Trust for the rest of its natural life. The Berkshire centre at Trindledown Farm provides an environment for elderly pets and other animals that need special care.

- A pet care scheme to reassure owners that the Trust will care for their pets in the event that they are no longer able to do so.

- Education on animal welfare and promoting the benefits of animal and human companionship.

The Trust is a non-political and non-campaigning organization – it concerns itself simply with looking after some of life's casualties. It receives no money from the government and relies entirely on voluntary contributions to carry out its work. For every £1 donated, 89 pence goes directly into charitable activities, with the rest of the money spent on fundraising and administration.

As a pioneering charity in the animal sector it is currently in the middle of a capital investment programme to modernize and improve the accommodation for the pets, while at the same time making the environment better for staff and visitors to the centres. At the heart of this upgrade scheme is the commitment to use as many environmentally sustainable measures as possible in order to save money on day-to-day running costs – but also to contribute to the future of the planet. The award-winning Cornwall centre is the first animal centre in the UK to have incorporated a wind turbine, solar panels, heat recovery and rainwater reclaim.

The Somerset centre has been using a natural water treatment system by running sewage through reed beds, extracting the harmful waste and turning clean water back to the Somerset Levels. A new cattery has just been opened at the centre that is using low-energy systems that are similar to those of its Cornwall sibling.

There are plans to carry out similar work at other centres, but the economic downturn has meant there hasn't been a large enough donation inflow to invest in the next phase of capital works in Watford and Somerset. An investment of £5 million would help to realize further the NAWT's commitment to sustainability and to secure the long-term future of these highly valued community resources.

CASE STUDY   Twiglet's night-time plight

When nine-year-old miniature pot-bellied pig Twiglet developed an infection complicated by hypothermia over the Christmas break, her prognosis wasn't good. But that didn't stop NAWT London and Home Counties staff members Tania Mazzoni and Stevie Dempster from extending their seven-day shift to care for the sick animal. On that very cold night, every hour on the hour both women, armed with just a torch and a fresh hot water bottle, made their way through a muddy field to syringe and hand-feed Twiglet and warm the sty a bit. Offering pain relief and antibiotics prescribed by the vet, they also tried to encourage the pig to move about to improve her circulation.

NAWT veterinary nurse Liz Yallop explained: 'If they hadn't spent the night caring for Twiglet, she really would not have made it.'

The pig has made an excellent recovery, and Tania and Stevie have demonstrated the NAWT team's dedication towards the animals in its care.

CASE STUDY   The dog with the blog

When NAWT staff favourite Buffy finally found a new home in Wiltshire after two-and-a-half years at first the Watford and then the Berkshire centre, new owners Pam and David Kearns felt compelled to start a blog about Buffy, to stay in touch with the dog's large network of fans.

'Buffy spent so much of her life at the NAWT that she was part of the family there. It just seemed to be such a good way of keeping everyone up to date on Buffy's progress,' explains Pam.

The six-year-old springer spaniel collie cross has a rare heart condition called patent ductus arteriosus, which means she has to live life at a slower and quieter pace than most dogs of her age.

Although she is attractive and friendly, her illness put many prospective owners off rehoming her – until, that is, Pam and David spotted her after recently losing their own pet dog after a long illness.

'When we started looking around for a new dog we saw Buffy on the website and immediately fell in love with her, but we didn't dare go and meet her until we had spoken to the NAWT a few times first,' added Pam.

Visit www.buffy-buf.blogspot.com or look for the link on the NAWT Facebook page.

We hope this chapter has inspired you to think about your motivations for giving and the huge changes you can make with your wealth.

Useful resources

TheBigGive.org.uk
IntelligentGiving.com
New Philanthropy Capital, www.philanthropycapital.org
Philanthropyuk.org
Institute of Philanthropy, instituteofphilanthropy.org
Community Foundations, communityfoundations.org.uk
Remember a Charity, rememberacharity.org.uk
Absolute Return on Kids, arkonline.org

APPENDIX 1

Contributors' contacts

Atkinson Bolton Consulting Limited
Cheveley House
Fordham Road
Newmarket
Suffolk CB8 7XN
Tel: +44 (0) 845 458 1223
Contact: Simon Gibson
e-mail: simon.gibson@atkinsonbolton.co.uk

Bestinvest
6 Chesterfield Gardens
Mayfair
London W1J 5BQ
Tel: +44 (0) 20 7189 9999
Contact: Martin Rooks
Tel: +44 (0) 20 7184 7904
e-mail: Martin.Rooks@bestinvest.co.uk

Brewin Dolphin
12 Smithfield Street
London EC1A 9BD
Tel: +44 (0) 845 213 1000
Contact: Stephen Ford
e-mail: stephen.ford@brewin.co.uk

British Bloodstock Marketing
British Bloodstock Marketing
190 High Street
Newmarket
Suffolk CB8 9W1
Tel: +44 (0) 1638 676940
Contact: Anna Powell
e-mail: info@bbm.ab.com

Charities Aid Foundation (CAF)
25 Kings Hill Avenue
Kings Hill
West Malling
Kent ME19 4TA
Tel: +44 (0) 3000 123 338
Contact: Stefan Velvick
e-mail: svelvick@cafonline.org
website: www.cafonline.org

Citi Private Bank
Citigroup Centre
25 Canada Square
London E14 5LB
Tel: +44 (0) 20 7508 8690
Contact: Anna Wooldridge
e-mail: anna.wooldridge@citi.com
website: www.citiprivatebank.com

Davis Arnold Cooper LLB
6-8 Bouverie Street
London EC4Y 8DD
Tel: +44 (0) 20 7293 4801
Contact: Ian Lane
e-mail: ILane@dac.co.uk

Deutsche Bank Private Wealth Management
1 Great Winchester Street
London EC2N 3DB
Tel: +44 (0) 207 545 8000
Contact: Michael Darriba
e-mail: michael.darriba@db.com

DiaMine Explorations, Inc
675 King Street W #305
Toronto
Ontario M5V 1M9
Canada
Tel: +001 4167 847 1524
Contact: H John Stollery
e-mail: info@diamineexplorations.com

Epilepsy Society
Chesham Lane
Chalfont St Peter
Buckinghamshire SL9 0RJ
Tel: +44 (0) 1494 601300
Contact: Ropinder Gill
e-mail: ropinder.gill@epilepsysociety.org.uk

Forsters LLP
31 Hill Street
London W1J 5LS
Tel: +44 (0) 20 7863 8588
Contact: Patrick Harney
e-mail: patrick.harney@forsters.co.uk
website: www.forsters.co.uk

James Goodwin
Street Farm
Newbourne
Woodbridge
Suffolk IP12 4PX
Tel: +44 (0) 794 707 3939
e-mail: arts.research@gmail.com
website: www.artsresearch.org.uk

Grant Thornton UK LLP
Enterprise House
115 Edmund Street
Birmingham B3 2HG 2HJ
Tel: +44 (0) 21 232 5171
Contact: Eric Williams
e-mail: eric.williams@uk.gt.com

Hamptons International
32 Grosvenor Square
Mayfair
London W1K 2HJ
Tel: +44 (0) 207 758 8468
Contact: Alan Challis
Mobile: +44 (0) 7833 058 741
e-mail: challisa@hamptons-int.com
website: www.hamptons.co.uk

Kleinwort Benson
14 St George Street
London W15 1FE
Tel: +44 (0) 20 3207 7400
Tel: +44 (0) 20 3207 6024
Contact: Sarah Fernandez
e-mail: enquiries@kleinwortbenson.com

KMS Baltics
Woodland Place
West Street
Belford
Northumberland NE70 7QA
Tel: +44 (0) 1668 213693
Contact: Felix Karthaus
e-mail: felix_karthaus@msn.com

Mattioli Woods
MW House
1 Penman Way
Grove Park
Enderby
Leicester LE19 1Y
Tel: +44 (0) 116 240 8700
Contact: Adrian Mee
e-mail: Adrian.mee@mattioli-woods.com

Moore Stephens
P.O. Box 146
Town Mills South
La Rue du Pré
St Peter Port
Guernsey GY1 3HZ
Tel: +44 (0) 1481 721769
Contact: John Pickles
e-mail: john.pickles@msgsy.com

National Animal Welfare Trust
Tyler's Way
Watford By-pass
Watford
Hertfordshire WD25 8WT
Tel: +44 (0) 20 8950 0177
Contact: David Warner
e-mail: d.warner@nawt.org.uk

Octopus Investments Limited
20 Old Bailey
London EC4M 7AN
Tel: +44 (0) 207 710 2800
Contact: Claire de Sousa
e-mail: CdeSousa@octopusinvestments.com

Pastor-Gèneve BVBA
118 rue du Rhone
Genève, CH-1204
Switzerland
Tel: +41 (0) 22 810 3338
Contact: Stephen Hershoff
e-mail: info@pastorgeneve.com

PricewaterhouseCoopers LLP (PwC)
1 Embankment Place
London WC2N 6RH
Tel: +44 (0) 207 583 5000
Contact: Clive Mackintosh
Tel: +44 (0) 207 804 5614
e-mail: clive.mackintosh@uk.pwc.com
website: www.pwc.co.uk

Jonathan Reuvid
Little Manor
Wroxton
Oxfordshire OX15 6QE
Tel: +44 (0) 1295 738070
e-mail: jreuvidkoganpage@aol.com

Scottish Native Woods
1 Crieff Road
Aberfeldy
Perthshire PH15 2BJ
Tel: +44 (0) 1887 820392
Contact: Dianne Laing
e-mail: dianne.laing@scottishnativewoods.org.uk
website: www. scottishnativewoods.co.uk

UKSIF – the sustainable investment and finance association
Holywell Centre
1 Phipp Street
London EC2A 4PS
Tel: +44 (0) 207 749 9950
Contact: Penny Shepherd
e-mail: info@uksif.org
websites: www.uksif.org and www.neiw.org

APPENDIX 2

Directory of investment managers and independent financial managers

Disclaimer

This directory is published solely for information purposes and does not form the basis of any contract or commitment whatsoever. Nothing in the following pages should be construed as investment advice, either on behalf of particular investments or in regard to overall investment strategies.

Neither Kogan Page nor the Institute of Directors are liable for damages caused by actions taken as a result of any information contained within this directory. No information included here constitutes a recommendation to buy, sell or hold any stock, share, financial product or instrument discussed therein.

Appropriate advice should be obtained before making any such decision. Any arrangements made between you and any third party are at your sole risk and responsibility. Past performance is not indicative of future results: prices can go up or down. Investors investing in investments or products denominated in foreign (non-UK) currency should be aware of the risk of exchange rate fluctuations that may cause loss of principal when foreign currency is converted to the investor's home currency. Readers should understand that it is his/her responsibility to seek legal and/ or tax advice regarding the legal and tax consequences of his/her investment transactions.

Region: East Anglia
Atkinson Bolton Consulting (Head Office)
Cheveley House
Fordham Road
Newmarket
Suffolk
CB8 7XN
Tel: 0845 458 1223
Fax: 0845 458 1224
Contact: Simon Gibson
E-mail: simon.gibson@atkinsonbolton.co.uk
General enquiries e-mail: info@atkinsonbolton.co.uk
Web: www.atkinsonbolton.co.uk
Chartered financial planners, corporate benefit consultants and wealth managers.

Region: North East
Barclays Wealth (Newcastle-upon-Tyne Office)
Cross House
Westgate Road
Newcastle-upon-Tyne
NE1 4XX
Tel: 0191 260 4000
Fax: 0191 232 4674
Contact: Andrew Miller
E-mail: andrew.miller@barclayswealth.com
Web: www.barclayswealth.com

Region: West Midlands
Barclays Wealth (Birmingham Office)
1 Colmore Square
Birmingham
B4 6ES
Tel: 0121 200 2244
Fax: 0121 683 7300
Contact: Ben Gulliford
E-mail: ben.gulliford@barclayswealth.com
Web: www.barclayswealth.com
In Birmingham the Barclays Wealth team consists of 24 private bankers and investment managers providing bespoke wealth management solutions to clients across the Midlands. Being closer to our clients allows us to forge stronger relationships with them, the result is a personal service, tailored precisely to the individual.

Region: Scotland
Barclays Wealth (Glasgow Office)
Aurora Building
120 Bothwell Street
Glasgow
G2 7JT
Tel: 0141 240 4000
Fax: 0141 204 4281
Contact: Craig Jamieson
E-mail: craig.jamieson@barclayswealth.com
Web: www.barclayswealth.com

Region: South West
Brewin Dolphin Ltd (Cheltenham Office)
The Lypiatts
Lansdown Road
Cheltenham
Gloucestershire
GL50 2JA
Tel: 01242 577 677
Fax: 01242 586 822
Contact: Edward Mawle
E-mail: edward.mawle@brewin.co.uk
General enquiries e-mail: info@brewin.co.uk
Web: www.brewindolphin.co.uk

Region: North West
Brewin Dolphin Ltd (Keswick Office)
42 St John Street
Keswick
Cumbria
CA12 5AG
Tel: 01768 781 960
Fax: 01768 781 961
Contact: Peter Martin
E-mail: peter.martin@brewin.co.uk
General enquiries e-mail: info@brewin.co.uk
Web: www.brewindolphin.co.uk

Region: Channel Islands
Brewin Dolphin Ltd (Jersey Office)
Kingsgate House, 2nd Floor
55 The Esplanade
St Helier
Jersey
JE2 3QB
Tel: 01534 703 118
Fax: 01534 731 910
Contact: Stuart Sangan
E-mail: stuart.sangan@brewin.co.uk
General enquiries e-mail: info@brewin.co.uk
Web: www.brewindolphin.co.uk

Region: Scotland
Brewin Dolphin Ltd (Inverness Office)
Lyle House
Fairway Business Park
Inverness
Scotland
IV2 6AA
Tel: 01463 225 888
Fax: 01463 226 777
Contact: Elaine McLachlan
E-mail: elaine.mclachlan@brewin.co.uk
General enquiries e-mail: info@brewin.co.uk
Web: www.brewindolphin.co.uk

Region: West Midlands
Brewin Dolphin Ltd (Hereford Office)
35 Bridge Street
Hereford
HR4 9DG
Tel: 01432 364 300
Fax: 01432 354 193
Contact: Clive Loader
E-mail: clive.loader@brewin.co.uk
General enquiries e-mail: info@brewin.co.uk
Web: www.brewindolphin.co.uk

Region: Channel Islands
Brewin Dolphin Ltd (Guernsey Office)
1st Floor
10 Lefebvre Street
St Peter Port
Guernsey
GY1 2PE
Tel: 01481 736 682
Fax: 01481 729 910
Contact: David Smith
E-mail: david.smith@brewin.co.uk
General enquiries e-mail: info@brewin.co.uk
Web: www.brewindolphin.co.uk

Region: South West
Brewin Dolphin Ltd (Exeter Office)
Vantage Point
Woodwater Park
Pynes Hill
Exeter
EX2 5FD
Tel: 01392 440 450
Fax: 01392 440 451
Contact: Richard Pike
E-mail: richard.pike@brewin.co.uk
General enquiries e-mail: info@brewin.co.uk
Web: www.brewindolphin.co.uk

Region: Scotland
Brewin Dolphin Ltd (Edinburgh Office)
7 Drumsheugh Gardens
Edinburgh
EH3 7QH
Tel: 0131 225 2566
Fax: 0131 225 3134
Contact: Bryan Johnston
E-mail: bryan.johnston@brewin.co.uk
General enquiries e-mail: info@brewin.co.uk
Web: www.brewindolphin.co.uk

Region: Scotland
Brewin Dolphin Ltd (Edinburgh Office)
Stocktrade Division
81 George Street
Edinburgh
EH2 3ES
Tel: 0131 240 0400
Fax: 0131 240 0423
Contact: Mike Graham
E-mail: mike.graham@brewin.co.uk
General enquiries e-mail: info@brewin.co.uk
Web: www.brewindolphin.co.uk

Region: Scotland
Brewin Dolphin Ltd (Dundee Office)
31–32 City Quay
Camperdown Street
Dundee
DD1 3JA
Tel: 01382 317 200
Fax: 01382 317 201
Contact: David Chalmers
E-mail: david.chalmers@blw.co.uk
General enquiries e-mail: info@brewin.co.uk
Web: www.brewindolphin.co.uk

Region: Scotland
Brewin Dolphin Ltd (Dumfries Office)
43 Buccleuch Street
Dumfries
DG1 2AB
Tel: 01387 252 361
Fax: 01387 257 288
Contact: Gordon McKerrow
E-mail: gordon.Mckerrow@brewin.co.uk
General enquiries e-mail: info@brewin.co.uk
Web: www.brewindolphin.co.uk

Region: Yorkshire & the Humber
Brewin Dolphin Ltd (Leeds Office)
34 Lisbon Street
Leeds
LS1 4LX
Tel: 0113 245 9341
Fax: 0113 243 5666
Contact: Martin Payne
E-mail: martin.payne@brewin.co.uk
General enquiries e-mail: info@brewin.co.uk
Web: www.brewindolphin.co.uk

Region: North West
Brewin Dolphin Ltd (Chester Office)
Liverpool House
47 Lower Bridge Street
Chester
CH1 1RS
Tel: 01244 353 900
Fax: 01244 353 901
Contact: Nicola Haughney-Carr
E-mail: nicola.haughney-carr@brewin.co.uk
General enquiries e-mail: info@brewin.co.uk
Web: www.brewindolphin.co.uk

Region: Scotland
Brewin Dolphin Ltd (Glasgow Office)
48 St Vincent Street
Glasgow
G2 5TS
Tel: 0141 221 7733
Fax: 0141 314 8142
Contact: Susan Stevenson
E-mail: susan.stevenson@brewin.co.uk
General enquiries e-mail: info@brewin.co.uk
Web: www.brewindolphin.co.uk

Region: Wales
Brewin Dolphin Ltd (Cardiff Office)
Sutherland House
Castlebridge
Cowbridge Road East
Cardiff
CF11 9BB
Tel: 029 2034 0100
Fax: 029 2034 4999
Contact: David Myrddin-Evans
E-mail: david.myrddin-evans@brewin.co.uk
General enquiries e-mail: info@brewin.co.uk
Web: www.brewindolphin.co.uk

Region: South East
Brewin Dolphin Ltd (Brighton Office)
Invicta House
Trafalgar Place
Brighton
BN1 4ZG
Tel: 0845 213 1190
Fax: 0845 213 1191
Contact: David Pegler
E-mail: david.pegler@brewin.co.uk
General enquiries e-mail: info@brewin.co.uk
Web: www.brewindolphin.co.uk

Region: Yorkshire & the Humber
Brewin Dolphin Ltd (Bradford Office)
Auburn House
8 Upper Piccadilly
Bradford
BD1 3NU
Tel: 01274 728 866
Fax: 01274 370 483
Contact: Rupert Fenton
E-mail: rupert.fenton@brewin.co.uk
General enquiries e-mail: info@brewin.co.uk
Web: www.brewindolphin.co.uk

Region: West Midlands
Brewin Dolphin Ltd (Birmingham Office)
9 Colmore Row
Birmingham
B3 2BJ
Tel: 0121 236 7000
Fax: 0121 212 0011
Contact: Stephen Jones
E-mail: stephen.jones@brewin.co.uk
General enquiries e-mail: info@brewin.co.uk
Web: www.brewindolphin.co.uk

Region: Northern Ireland
Brewin Dolphin Ltd (Belfast Office)
Waterfront Plaza
6th Floor
8 Laganbank Road
Belfast, Northern Ireland
BT1 3LY
Tel: 028 9044 6000
Fax: 028 9044 6001
Contact: Stephen Cartwright
E-mail: stephen.cartwright@brewin.co.uk
General enquiries e-mail: info@brewin.co.uk
Web: www.brewindolphin.co.uk

Region: Scotland
Brewin Dolphin Ltd (Aberdeen Office)
2nd Floor, Blenheim House
Fountainhall Road
Aberdeen
AB15 4DT
Tel: 01224 267 900
Fax: 01224 267 901
Contact: Bruce Angus
E-mail: bruce.angus@brewin.co.uk
General enquiries e-mail: info@brewin.co.uk
Web: www.brewindolphin.co.uk

Region: London
Brewin Dolphin Ltd (London Office)
12 Smithfield Street
London
EC1A 9BD
Tel: 0845 213 1000
Fax: 0845 213 1001
Contact: Sian Robertson
E-mail: sian.robertson@brewin.co.uk
General enquiries e-mail: info@brewin.co.uk
Web: www.brewindolphin.co.uk

Region: South West
Brewin Dolphin Ltd (Dorchester Office)
Hamilton House
6 Nantillo Street
Poundbury
Dorchester, Dorset
DT1 3WN
Tel: 01305 215 770
Fax: 01305 215 771
Contact: David Evans
E-mail: david.evans@brewin.co.uk
General enquiries e-mail: info@brewin.co.uk
Web: www.brewindolphin.co.uk

Region: South West
Brewin Dolphin Ltd (Truro Office)
CMA House
Newham Road
Newham
Truro
TR1 2SU
Tel: 01872 265 610
Fax: 01872 265 611
Contact: Jonathon Croggon
E-mail: jonathon.croggon@brewin.co.uk
General enquiries e-mail: info@brewin.co.uk
Web: www.brewindolphin.co.uk

Region: Scotland
Brewin Dolphin Ltd (Elgin Office)
26 Hay Street
Elgin
IV30 1NQ
Tel: 01343 548 344
Fax: 01343 543 084
Contact: Philip Gauld
E-mail: philip.gauld@brewin.co.uk
General enquiries e-mail: info@brewin.co.uk
Web: www.brewindolphin.co.uk

Region: Yorkshire
Brewin Dolphin Ltd (York Office)
Apollo House
Eboracum Way
York
YO31 7RE
Tel: 01904 435 600
Fax: 01904 435 601
Contact: Paul Widdicombe
E-mail: paul.widdicombe@brewin.co.uk
General enquiries e-mail: info@brewin.co.uk
Web: www.brewindolphin.co.uk

Region: East Midlands
Brewin Dolphin Ltd (Leicester Office)
2 Colton Square
Leicester
LE1 1QF
Tel: 0116 242 0700
Fax: 0116 253 6585
Contact: Chris Hailes
E-mail: chris.hailes@brewin.co.uk
General enquiries e-mail: info@brewin.co.uk
Web: www.brewindolphin.co.uk

Region: Yorkshire & the Humber
Brewin Dolphin Ltd (Teesside Office)
Progress House
Fudan Way
Teesside
Stockton-on-Tees
TS17 6EN
Tel: 01642 608 855
Fax: 01642 604 488
Contact: William Baker Baker
E-mail: william.bakerbaker@brewin.co.uk
General enquiries e-mail: info@brewin.co.uk
Web: www.brewindolphin.co.uk

Region: South West
Brewin Dolphin Ltd (Taunton Office)
2nd Floor, Ashford Court
Blackbrook Business Park
Blackbrook Park Avenue
Taunton, Somerset
RA1 2PX
Tel: 01823 445 750
Fax: 01823 445 751
Contact: Terry Leach
E-mail: terry.leach@brewin.co.uk
General enquiries e-mail: info@brewin.co.uk
Web: www.brewindolphin.co.uk

Region: Wales
Brewin Dolphin Ltd (Swansea Office)
Axis 6, Axis Court
Mallard Way
Swansea Vale
Swansea
SA7 0AJ
Tel: 01792 763 960
Fax: 01792 763 961
Contact: Richard Croydon
E-mail: swansea@brewin.co.uk
General enquiries e-mail: info@brewin.co.uk
Web: www.brewindolphin.co.uk

Region: West Midlands
Brewin Dolphin Ltd (Stoke Office)
1st Floor
Highpoint
Festival Park
Stoke
ST1 5BG
Tel: 01782 764 000
Fax: 01782 764 001
Contact: Richard Platt
E-mail: richard.platt@brewin.co.uk
General enquiries e-mail: info@brewin.co.uk
Web: www.brewindolphin.co.uk

Region: West Midlands
Brewin Dolphin Ltd (Shrewsbury Office)
Mutual House
Sitka Drive
Shrewsbury Business Park
Shrewsbury
SY2 6LG
Tel: 01743 399 000
Fax: 01743 399 001
Contact: David Hall
E-mail: david.hall@brewin.co.uk
General enquiries e-mail: info@brewin.co.uk
Web: www.brewindolphin.co.uk

Region: South East
Brewin Dolphin Ltd (Reigate Office)
45 London Road
Reigate
Surrey
RH2 7AN
Tel: 01737 223 722
Fax: 01737 224 848
Contact: Paul Cannons
E-mail: paul.cannons@brewin.co.uk
General enquiries e-mail: info@brewin.co.uk
Web: www.brewindolphin.co.uk

Region: South West
Brewin Dolphin Ltd (Plymouth Office)
Ashleigh Court
Ashleigh Way
Langage Business Park
Plymouth
PL7 5JX
Tel: 01752 334650
Fax: 01752 334651
Contact: Brian James
E-mail: brian.james@brewin.co.uk
General enquiries e-mail: info@brewin.co.uk
Web: www.brewindolphin.co.uk

Region: East Midlands
Brewin Dolphin Ltd (Nottingham Office)
1st Floor
Waterfront House, Waterfront Plaza
35 Station Street
Nottingham
NG2 2DQ
Tel: 0115 852 5580
Fax: 0115 852 5581
Contact: Mark Jones
E-mail: mark.jones@brewin.co.uk
General enquiries e-mail: info@brewin.co.uk
Web: www.brewindolphin.co.uk

Region: East Anglia
Brewin Dolphin Ltd (Norwich Office)
Jacquard House
Old Bank of England Court
Queen Street
Norwich, Norfolk
NR2 4SX
Tel: 01603 767 776
Fax: 01603 767 476
Contact: Richard Larner
E-mail: richard.larner@brewin.co.uk
General enquiries e-mail: info@brewin.co.uk
Web: www.brewindolphin.co.uk

Region: North East
Brewin Dolphin Ltd (Newcastle-upon-Tyne Office)
Time Central
Gallowgate
Newcastle-upon-Tyne
NE1 4SR
Tel: 0191 279 7300
Fax: 0191 279 7301
Contact: John Duns
E-mail: john.duns@brewin.co.uk
General enquiries e-mail: info@brewin.co.uk
Web: www.brewindolphin.co.uk

Region: South West
Brewin Dolphin Ltd (Marlborough Office)
Cross Keys House
The Parade
Marlborough
Wiltshire
SN8 1NE
Tel: 01672 519 600
Fax: 01672 515 550
Contact: Beverley McIlvar
E-mail: beverley.mcilvar@brewin.co.uk
General enquiries e-mail: info@brewin.co.uk
Web: www.brewindolphin.co.uk

Region: North West
Brewin Dolphin Ltd (Manchester Office)
National House
36 St Ann Street
Manchester
M2 7LE
Tel: 0161 839 4222
Fax: 0161 832 9092
Contact: Robert Race
E-mail: robert.race@brewin.co.uk
General enquiries e-mail: info@brewin.co.uk
Web: www.brewindolphin.co.uk

Region: South East
Brewin Dolphin Ltd (Lymington Office)
West Barn
Efford Park
Milford Road
Lymington, Hampshire
SO41 0JD
Tel: 01590 687 920
Fax: 01590 679 039
Contact: Robert Carroll
E-mail: rob.carroll2@brewin.co.uk
General enquiries e-mail: info@brewin.co.uk
Web: www.brewindolphin.co.uk

Region: Wales
Brewin Dolphin Ltd (Llandudno Office)
59 Madoc Street
Llandudno
North Wales
LL30 2TW
Tel: 01492 874 391
Fax: 01492 871 990
Contact: Helen Culshaw
E-mail: helen.culshaw@brewin.co.uk
General enquiries e-mail: info@brewin.co.uk
Web: www.brewindolphin.co.uk

Region: East Midlands
Brewin Dolphin Ltd (Lincoln Office)
Olympic House
Doddington Road
Lincoln
LN6 3SE
Tel: 01522 503 000
Fax: 01522 503 050
Contact: Peter Strange
E-mail: peter.strange@brewin.co.uk
General enquiries e-mail: info@brewin.co.uk
Web: www.brewindolphin.co.uk

Region: South East
Brewin Dolphin Ltd (Oxford Office)
4 King Edward Street
Oxford
OX1 4HS
Tel: 01865 255 750
Fax: 01865 255 751
Contact: Hans Price
E-mail: hans.price@brewin.co.uk
General enquiries e-mail: info@brewin.co.uk
Web: www.brewindolphin.co.uk

Region: Scotland
Brooks Macdonald Asset Management (Edinburgh Office)
10 Melville Crescent
Edinburgh
EH3 7LU
Tel: 0131 240 3900
Fax: 0131 240 3999
Contact: Alastair Wilson
General enquiries e-mail: edinburgh@brooksmacdonald.com
Web: www.bm-am.com

Region: South East
Brooks Macdonald Asset Management (Hampshire Office)
The Long Barn
Dean Estate
Wickham Road
Fareham
PO17 5BN
Tel: 01329552111
Fax: 01329552111
Contact: John Wallace
General enquiries e-mail: hampshire@brooksmacdonald.com
Web: www.bm-am.com

Region: London
Brooks Macdonald Asset Management (Head Office)
111 Park Street
Mayfair
London
W1K 7JL
Tel: 020 7499 6424
Fax: 020 7499 5718
Contact: James Keen
General enquiries e-mail: info-am@brooksmacdonald.com
Web: www.bm-am.com

Region: North West
Brooks Macdonald Asset Management (Manchester Office)
55 King Street
Manchester
M2 4LQ
Tel: 0161 861 4110
Fax: 0161 861 4119
Contact: Claire Bennison
General enquiries e-mail: manchester@brooksmacdonald.com
Web: www.bm-am.com

Region: South East
Brooks Macdonald Asset Management (Tunbridge Wells Office)
2 Mount Ephraim Road
Tunbridge Wells
Kent
TN1 1EE
Tel: 01892 554 900
Fax: 01892 554 999
Contact: Pam Beith
General enquiries e-mail: tunbridgewells@brooksmacdonald.com
Web: www.bm-am.com

Region: Isle of Man
Cayman National Bank and Trust Company Limited (Isle of Man Office)
Cayman National House
4–8 Hope Street
Douglas
Isle of Man
IM1 1AQ
Tel: 01624 646900
Fax: 01624 662192
Contact: Anita Gould-Davies
E-mail: anita.gould-davies@cnciom.com
Web: www.cnciom.com
A compelling range of banking and wealth management services including fund administration.

Region: West Midlands
Charles Stanley & Co. Ltd (Birmingham Office)
Civic House
156 Great Charles Street
Birmingham
B3 3HN
Tel: 0121 234 6700
Contact: Toby Carpenter
E-mail: toby.carpenter@charles-stanley.co.uk
Web: www.charles-stanley.co.uk
One of the UK's leading full service stockbroking and investment management groups. Member of the London Stock Exchange since 1852. Services: Discretionary and Advisory Investment Management, Share Dealing, ISAs, SIPPs, Charities, Financial Planning. Authorised and regulated by the Financial Services Authority.

Region: North West
Charles Stanley & Co. Ltd (Liverpool Office)
20 Chapel Street
Liverpool
L3 9AG
Tel: 0151 255 2680
Fax: 0151 255 2699
Contact: Derek Gawne
E-mail: liverpool@charles-stanley.co.uk
Web: www.charles-stanley.co.uk
One of the UK's leading full service stockbroking and investment management groups. Member of the London Stock Exchange since 1852. Services: Discretionary and Advisory Investment Management, Share Dealing, ISAs, SIPPs, Charities, Financial Planning. Authorised and regulated by the Financial Services Authority.

Region: Scotland
Charles Stanley & Co. Ltd (Edinburgh Office)
2 Multrees Walk
St Andrew Square
Edinburgh
EH1 3DQ
Tel: 0131 550 1200
Fax: 0131 550 1250
Contact: Ian Harley
E-mail: ian.harley@charles-stanley.co.uk
Web: www.charles-stanley.co.uk
One of the UK's leading full service stockbroking and investment management groups. Member of the London Stock Exchange since 1852. Services: Discretionary and Advisory Investment Management, Share Dealing, ISAs, SIPPs, Charities, Financial Planning. Authorised and regulated by the Financial Services Authority.

Region: South East
Charles Stanley & Co. Ltd (Eastbourne Office)
14 Hyde Gardens
Eastbourne
East Sussex
BN21 4PR
Tel: 01323 437 440
Fax: 01323 437 441
Contact: Paul Williams
E-mail: paul.williams@charles-stanley.co.uk
Web: www.charles-stanley.co.uk
One of the UK's leading full service stockbroking and investment management groups. Member of the London Stock Exchange since 1852. Services: Discretionary and Advisory Investment Management, Share Dealing, ISAs, SIPPs, Charities, Financial Planning. Authorised and regulated by the Financial Services Authority.

Region: South West
Charles Stanley & Co. Ltd (Dorchester Office)
1 Colliton Walk
Dorchester
Dorset
DT1 1TZ
Tel: 01305 251155
Fax: 01305 250188
Contact: Ian Brown
E-mail: ian.brown@charles-stanley.co.uk
Web: www.charles-stanley.co.uk
One of the UK's leading full service stockbroking and investment management groups. Member of the London Stock Exchange since 1852. Services: Discretionary and Advisory Investment Management, Share Dealing, ISAs, SIPPs, Charities, Financial Planning. Authorised and regulated by the Financial Services Authority.

Region: East Anglia
Charles Stanley & Co. Ltd (Cambridge Office)
Richmond House
16-20 Regent Street
Cambridge
CB2 1DB
Tel: 01223 316 726
Fax: 01223 310 078
Contact: Ian Hanson
E-mail: ian.hanson@charles-stanley.co.uk
Web: www.charles-stanley.co.uk
One of the UK's leading full service stockbroking and investment management groups. Member of the London Stock Exchange since 1852. Services: Discretionary and Advisory Investment Management, Share Dealing, ISAs, SIPPs, Charities, Financial Planning. Authorised and regulated by the Financial Services Authority.

Region: South West
Charles Stanley & Co. Ltd (Bristol Office)
58 Royal York Crescent
Clifton
Bristol
BS8 4JP
Tel: 0117 974 6565
Fax: 0117 974 6579
Contact: Wilf Blake
E-mail: wilf.blake@charles-stanley.co.uk
Web: www.charles-stanley.co.uk
One of the UK's leading full service stockbroking and investment management groups. Member of the London Stock Exchange since 1852. Services: Discretionary and Advisory Investment Management, Share Dealing, ISAs, SIPPs, Charities, Financial Planning. Authorised and regulated by the Financial Services Authority.

Region: South West
Charles Stanley & Co. Ltd (Bournemouth Office)
2 Westover Road
Bournemouth
BH1 2BY
Tel: 01202 317 788
Fax: 01202 317 754
Contact: Jason Winslow
E-mail: jason.winslow@charles-stanley.co.uk
Web: www.charles-stanley.co.uk
One of the UK's leading full service stockbroking and investment management groups. Member of the London Stock Exchange since 1852. Services: Discretionary and Advisory Investment Management, Share Dealing, ISAs, SIPPs, Charities, Financial Planning. Authorised and regulated by the Financial Services Authority.

Region: East Anglia
Charles Stanley & Co. Ltd (Bedford Office)
11 Grove Place
Bedford
MK40 3JJ
Tel: 01234 718888
Fax: 01234 718889
Contact: David Hill
E-mail: david.hill@charles-stanley.co.uk
Web: www.charles-stanley.co.uk
One of the UK's leading full service stockbroking and investment management groups. Member of the London Stock Exchange since 1852. Services: Discretionary and Advisory Investment Management, Share Dealing, ISAs, SIPPs, Charities, Financial Planning. Authorised and regulated by the Financial Services Authority.

Region: South West
Charles Stanley & Co. Ltd (Bath Office)
26 Queen Square
Bath
BA1 2HX
Tel: 01225 878999
Fax: 01225 878998
Contact: Chris Morgan
E-mail: chris.morgan@charles-stanley.co.uk
Web: www.charles-stanley.co.uk
One of the UK's leading full service stockbroking and investment management groups. Member of the London Stock Exchange since 1852. Services: Discretionary and Advisory Investment Management, Share Dealing, ISAs, SIPPs, Charities, Financial Planning. Authorised and regulated by the Financial Services Authority.

Region: London
Charles Stanley & Co. Ltd (Head Office)
25 Luke Street
London
EC2A 4AR
Tel: 0207 149 6437
Fax: 020 7739 7798
Contact: Ivy Pinner
E-mail: info@charles-stanley.co.uk
Web: www.charles-stanley.co.uk
One of the UK's leading full service stockbroking and investment management groups. Member of the London Stock Exchange since 1852. Services: Discretionary and Advisory Investment Management, Share Dealing, ISAs, SIPPs, Charities, Financial Planning. Authorised and regulated by the Financial Services Authority.

Region: South East
Charles Stanley & Co. Ltd (Guildford Office)
70–72 Chertsey Street
Guildford
Surrey
GU1 4HL
Tel: 01483 230 810
Fax: 01483 230 818
Contact: Gavin Brackenridge
E-mail: gavin.brackenridge@charles-stanley.co.uk
Web: www.charles-stanley.co.uk
One of the UK's leading full service stockbroking and investment management groups. Member of the London Stock Exchange since 1852. Services: Discretionary and Advisory Investment Management, Share Dealing, ISAs, SIPPs, Charities, Financial Planning. Authorised and regulated by the Financial Services Authority.

Region: South West
Charles Stanley & Co. Ltd (Exeter Office)
Broadwalk House
Southernhay West
Exeter
EX1 1TS
Tel: 01392 453 600
Fax: 01392 410 422
Contact: Christopher Harris-Deans
E-mail: christopher.harris-deans@charles-stanley.co.uk
Web: www.charles-stanley.co.uk
One of the UK's leading full service stockbroking and investment management groups. Member of the London Stock Exchange since 1852. Services: Discretionary and Advisory Investment Management, Share Dealing, ISAs, SIPPs, Charities, Financial Planning. Authorised and regulated by the Financial Services Authority.

Region: South East
Charles Stanley & Co. Ltd (Brighton & Hove Office)
24A Wilbury Grove
Eaton Road
Hove
East Sussex
BN3 3JQ
Tel: 01273 229 880
Fax: 01273 229 881
Contact: Alan Harris
E-mail: alan.harris@charles-stanley.co.uk
Web: www.charles-stanley.co.uk
One of the UK's leading full service stockbroking and investment management groups. Member of the London Stock Exchange since 1852. Services: Discretionary and Advisory Investment Management, Share Dealing, ISAs, SIPPs, Charities, Financial Planning. Authorised and regulated by the Financial Services Authority.

Region: East Midlands
Charles Stanley & Co. Ltd (Nottingham Office)
Parliament House
42/46 Upper Parliament Street
Nottingham
NG1 2AG
Tel: 01159 580 200
Fax: 01159 897 919
Contact: Rick Landucci
E-mail: riccardo.landucci@charles-stanley.co.uk
Web: www.charles-stanley.co.uk
One of the UK's leading full service stockbroking and investment management groups. Member of the London Stock Exchange since 1852. Services: Discretionary and Advisory Investment Management, Share Dealing, ISAs, SIPPs, Charities, Financial Planning. Authorised and regulated by the Financial Services Authority.

Region: East Anglia
Charles Stanley & Co. Ltd (Ipswich Office)
16 Northgate Street
Ipswich
IP1 3DB
Tel: 01473 297 700
Fax: 01473 225 736
Contact: Mark Marshall
E-mail: mark.marshall@charles-stanley.co.uk
Web: www.charles-stanley.co.uk
One of the UK's leading full service stockbroking and investment management groups. Member of the London Stock Exchange since 1852. Services: Discretionary and Advisory Investment Management, Share Dealing, ISAs, SIPPs, Charities, Financial Planning. Authorised and regulated by the Financial Services Authority.

Region: South West
Charles Stanley & Co. Ltd (Truro Office)
65 Lemon Street
Truro
Cornwall
TR1 2PN
Tel: 01872 263 131
Fax: 01872 267 949
Contact: Chris Bolshaw
E-mail: christopher.bolshaw@charles-stanley.co.uk
Web: www.charles-stanley.co.uk
One of the UK's leading full service stockbroking and investment management groups. Member of the London Stock Exchange since 1852. Services: Discretionary and Advisory Investment Management, Share Dealing, ISAs, SIPPs, Charities, Financial Planning. Authorised and regulated by the Financial Services Authority.

Region: East Anglia
Charles Stanley & Co. Ltd (Southend-on-Sea Office)
Hamilton House
12 Nelson Street
Southend-on-Sea
Essex
SS1 1EF
Tel: 01702 221 700
Fax: 01702 221 709
Contact: Tim Markham
E-mail: tim.markham@charles-stanley.co.uk
Web: www.charles-stanley.co.uk
One of the UK's leading full service stockbroking and investment management groups. Member of the London Stock Exchange since 1852. Services: Discretionary and Advisory Investment Management, Share Dealing, ISAs, SIPPs, Charities, Financial Planning. Authorised and regulated by the Financial Services Authority.

Region: South East
Charles Stanley & Co. Ltd (Southampton Office)
Latimer House
5–7 Cumberland Place
Southampton
SO15 2BH
Tel: 023 8038 1800
Fax: 023 8023 2307
Contact: Liam Pryce-Jones
E-mail: liam.pryce-jones@charles-stanley.co.uk
Web: www.charles-stanley.co.uk
One of the UK's leading full service stockbroking and investment management groups. Member of the London Stock Exchange since 1852. Services: Discretionary and Advisory Investment Management, Share Dealing, ISAs, SIPPs, Charities, Financial Planning. Authorised and regulated by the Financial Services Authority.

Region: South West
Charles Stanley & Co. Ltd (Wimborne Office)
Crown Court
6B The Square
Wimborne
Dorset
BH21 1JA
Tel: 01202 882 820
Fax: 01202 888 861
Contact: David Holmes
E-mail: wimborne@charles-stanley.co.uk
Web: www.charles-stanley.co.uk
One of the UK's leading full service stockbroking and investment management groups. Member of the London Stock Exchange since 1852. Services: Discretionary and Advisory Investment Management, Share Dealing, ISAs, SIPPs, Charities, Financial Planning. Authorised and regulated by the Financial Services Authority.

Region: South East
Charles Stanley & Co. Ltd (Reading Office)
Dukesbridge Chambers
1 Duke Street
Reading
RG1 4SA
Tel: 0118 902 2800
Fax: 0118 956 6611
Contact: Phil Dyson
E-mail: phil.dyson@charles-stanley.co.uk
Web: www.charles-stanley.co.uk
One of the UK's leading full service stockbroking and investment management groups. Member of the London Stock Exchange since 1852. Services: Discretionary and Advisory Investment Management, Share Dealing, ISAs, SIPPs, Charities, Financial Planning. Authorised and regulated by the Financial Services Authority.

Region: South East
Charles Stanley & Co. Ltd (Oxford Office)
Abbey House
121 St Aldates
Oxford
OX1 1EA
Tel: 01865 320 000
Fax: 01865 209 048
Contact: Simon Scott-White
E-mail: simon.scott-white@charles-stanley.co.uk
Web: www.charles-stanley.co.uk
One of the UK's leading full service stockbroking and investment management groups. Member of the London Stock Exchange since 1852. Services: Discretionary and Advisory Investment Management, Share Dealing, ISAs, SIPPs, Charities, Financial Planning. Authorised and regulated by the Financial Services Authority.

Region: South East
Charles Stanley & Co. Ltd (Tunbridge Wells Office)
43 Dudley Road
Tunbridge Wells
Kent
TN1 1LE
Tel: 01892 557 100
Fax: 01892 557 101
Contact: Katie Presland
E-mail: katie.presland@charles-stanley.co.uk
Web: www.charles-stanley.co.uk
One of the UK's leading full service stockbroking and investment management groups. Member of the London Stock Exchange since 1852. Services: Discretionary and Advisory Investment Management, Share Dealing, ISAs, SIPPs, Charities, Financial Planning. Authorised and regulated by the Financial Services Authority.

Region: East Anglia
Charles Stanley & Co. Ltd (Norwich Office)
3 St Andrew's Hill
Norwich
NR2 1AD
Tel: 01603 665 990
Fax: 01603 610 560
Contact: Willie Brownlow
E-mail: willie.brownlow@charles-stanley.co.uk
Web: www.charles-stanley.co.uk
One of the UK's leading full service stockbroking and investment management groups. Member of the London Stock Exchange since 1852. Services: Discretionary and Advisory Investment Management, Share Dealing, ISAs, SIPPs, Charities, Financial Planning. Authorised and regulated by the Financial Services Authority.

Region: South East
Charles Stanley & Co. Ltd (Newbury Office)
4 The Pentangle
Park Street
Newbury
RG14 1EA
Tel: 01635 553 700
Fax: 01635 553 710
Contact: Duncan Graham
E-mail: duncan.graham@charles-stanley.co.uk
Web: www.charles-stanley.co.uk
One of the UK's leading full service stockbroking and investment management groups. Member of the London Stock Exchange since 1852. Services: Discretionary and Advisory Investment Management, Share Dealing, ISAs, SIPPs, Charities, Financial Planning. Authorised and regulated by the Financial Services Authority.

Region: South East
Charles Stanley & Co. Ltd (Milton Keynes Office)
Witan Court
305 Upper Fourth Street
Central Milton Keynes
MK9 1EH
Tel: 01908 691681
Fax: 01908 691682
Contact: Michael MacDougall
E-mail: michael.macdougall@charles-stanley.co.uk
Web: www.charles-stanley.co.uk
One of the UK's leading full service stockbroking and investment management
groups. Member of the London Stock Exchange since 1852. Services: Discretionary
and Advisory Investment Management, Share Dealing, ISAs, SIPPs, Charities,
Financial Planning. Authorised and regulated by the Financial Services Authority.

Region: North West
Charles Stanley & Co. Ltd (Manchester Office)
2nd Floor
Sunlight House
Quay Street
Manchester
M3 3JZ
Tel: 0161 828 0200
Fax: 0161 828 0201
Contact: Jon Goldstone
E-mail: jon.goldstone@charles-stanley.co.uk
Web: www.charles-stanley.co.uk
One of the UK's leading full service stockbroking and investment management
groups. Member of the London Stock Exchange since 1852. Services: Discretionary
and Advisory Investment Management, Share Dealing, ISAs, SIPPs, Charities,
Financial Planning. Authorised and regulated by the Financial Services Authority.

Region: South East
Charles Stanley & Co. Ltd (Cirencester Office)
14 The Wool Market
Cirencester
GL7 2PR
Tel: 01285 885311
Fax: 01285 646594
Contact: Richard Fowler
E-mail: info@charles-stanley.co.uk
Web: www.charles-stanley.co.uk
One of the UK's leading full service stockbroking and investment management groups. Member of the London Stock Exchange since 1852. Services: Discretionary and Advisory Investment Management, Share Dealing, ISAs, SIPPs, Charities, Financial Planning. Authorised and regulated by the Financial Services Authority.

Region: Yorkshire
Charles Stanley & Co. Ltd (Leeds Office)
14 King Street
Leeds
LS1 2HL
Tel: 0113 200 5230
Fax: 0113 200 5233
Contact: Jonathan Baker
E-mail: leeds@charles-stanley.co.uk
Web: www.charles-stanley.co.uk
One of the UK's leading full service stockbroking and investment management groups. Member of the London Stock Exchange since 1852. Services: Discretionary and Advisory Investment Management, Share Dealing, ISAs, SIPPs, Charities, Financial Planning. Authorised and regulated by the Financial Services Authority.

Region: South East
Charles Stanley & Co. Ltd (Isle of Wight Office)
1 Langley Court
Pyle Street
Newport
Isle of Wight
PO30 1LA
Tel: 01983 520 922
Fax: 01983 520 897
Contact: Sean Mylchreest
E-mail: sean.mylchreest@charles-stanley.co.uk
Web: www.charles-stanley.co.uk
One of the UK's leading full service stockbroking and investment management groups. Member of the London Stock Exchange since 1852. Services: Discretionary and Advisory Investment Management, Share Dealing, ISAs, SIPPs, Charities, Financial Planning. Authorised and regulated by the Financial Services Authority.

Region: South West
Charles Stanley & Co. Ltd (Plymouth Office)
1A The Crescent
Plymouth
Devon
PL1 3AB
Tel: 01752 666 661
Fax: 01752 253969
Contact: Judith Cook
E-mail: judith.cook@charles-stanley.co.uk
Web: www.charles-stanley.co.uk
One of the UK's leading full service stockbroking and investment management groups. Member of the London Stock Exchange since 1852. Services: Discretionary and Advisory Investment Management, Share Dealing, ISAs, SIPPs, Charities, Financial Planning. Authorised and regulated by the Financial Services Authority.

Region: Midlands
Deutsche Bank Private Wealth Management (Birmingham office)
Baskerville House
Centenary Square, Birmingham B1 2ND
Tel: 0121 232 5700
Fax: 0121 627 6288
Email: enquiries.dbpwm@db.com
Web: www.dbpwm.co.uk

Region: Scotland
Deutsche Bank Private Wealth Management (Edinburgh office)
25 Melville Street, Edinburgh EH3 7PE
Tel: 0131 243 1000
Fax: 0131 220 4199
Email: enquiries.dbpwm@db.com
Web: www.dbpwm.co.uk

Region: Scotland
Deutsche Bank Private Wealth Management (Glasgow office)
130 St Vincent Street, Glasgow G2 5SE
Tel: 0141 227 2400
Fax: 0141 221 5962
Email: enquiries.dbpwm@db.com
Web: www.dbpwm.co.uk

Region: North
Deutsche Bank Private Wealth Management (Liverpool office)
Royal Liver Building, Pier Head, Liverpool L3 1NY
Tel: 0151 255 3000
Fax: 0151 236 1252
Email: enquiries.dbpwm@db.com
Web: www.dbpwm.co.uk

Region: South
Deutsche Bank Private Wealth Management (London office)
1 Great Winchester Street, London EC2N 2DB
Tel: 0207 54-58000
Fax: 0207 54-56155
Email: enquiries.dbpwm@db.com
Web: www.dbpwm.co.uk

Region: London
EBS Management Plc (London Office)
25 Luke Street
London
EC2A 4AR
Tel: 0207 149 6560
Fax: 020 71496960
Contact: Kate Ragnauth
E-mail: info@ebsmanagement.co.uk
Web: www.ebsmanagement.co.uk/
Pensions administration, SIPP and SSAS specialists.

Region: South West
Farley & Thompson LLP (Head Office)
Pine Grange
Bath Road
Bournemouth
Dorset
BH1 2NU
Tel: 01202 295000
Contact: Colin Chalkly-Maber
E-mail: chalkly-maber@farleyandthompson.co.uk
Web: www.farleyandthompson.co.uk
Farley & Thompson offers personal investment advice and the opportunity to deal in stocks and shares.

Region: East Anglia
Finansec Green (Head Office)
223–225 High Street
Epping
CM16 4BL
Tel: 01992 570840
Fax: 01992 579966
Contact: Martyn Woodland
E-mail: info@finansec-green.co.uk
Web: www.finansec-green.co.uk
Holistic ethical financial advice for individual and corporate clients.

Region: North West
GAEIA Partnership Ltd (Head Office)
1 The Arcade
829 Wilmslow Road
Manchester
M20 5WD
Tel: 0161 434 4681
Fax: 0161 445 8421
Contact: Brigid Benson
E-mail: brigid@gaeia.co.uk
General enquiries e-mail: office@gaeia.co.uk
Web: www.gaeia.co.uk
We are a firm of Independent Financial Advisers authorised through the Financial Services Authority specializing in ethical investment. We are not tied to any investment company or stockbroker, therefore our advice and recommendations are completely independent and impartial.

Region: Yorkshire
Garrison Investment Analysis Limited (Beverley Office)
5–7 Landress Lane
Beverley
Yorkshire
HU17 8HA
Tel: 01482 861455
Fax: 01482 889828
Contact: John Shires
E-mail: john.shires@charles-stanley.co.uk
Web: www.garrison.co.uk

Region: East Anglia
Griffiths & Armour (Financial Services) Limited (Watford Office)
34 Clarendon Road
Watford
WD17 1JJ
Tel: 01923 804 911
Fax: 01923 294 329
Contact: Paul McGuckin
E-mail: pmcguckin@griffithsandarmour.com
Web: www.griffithsandarmour.com/Financial_Services
Corporate and employee Wealth Management. Company benefits packages, pensions, financial planning, long-term care plans.

Region: North West
Griffiths & Armour (Financial Services) Limited (Liverpool Office)
20 Chapel Street
Liverpool
L3 9AG
Tel: 0151 255 2662
Fax: 0151 227 1655
Contact: Paul McGuckin
E-mail: pmcguckin@griffithsandarmour.com
Web: www.griffithsandarmour.com/Financial_Services

Region: North West
Hargreave Hale Ltd (Lancaster Office)
Stockbrokers
25 Brock Street
Lancaster
LA1 1UR
Tel: 01524 541 560
Fax: 01524 541 569
Contact: Andrew Garstang
E-mail: Lancaster@hargreave.com
General enquiries e-mail: Lancaster@hargreave.com
Web: www.hargreave-hale.co.uk
Share dealing and portfolio management services; telephone calls may be recorded.

Region: West Midlands
Interface Financial Planning Ltd (Head Office)
122 Hamstead Hall Road
Handsworth Wood
Birmingham
B20 1JB
Tel: 0121 554 4444
Fax: 0121 554 7444
Contact: Alan Moran
E-mail: alan.moran@interfacefp.co.uk
Web: www.interfacefinancialplanning.co.uk
Life planning and financial planning.

Region: South East
Kleinwort Benson (Newbury Office)
3 Northcroft Lane
Newbury
Berkshire
RG14 1BT
Tel: 01635 265100
General enquiries e-mail: enquiries@kleinwortbenson.com
Web: www.kleinwortbenson.com

Region: London
Kleinwort Benson (London Office)
30 Gresham Street
London
EC2V 7PG
Tel: 020 3207 7000
Fax: 020 3207 7001
Contact: Derek Wright
General enquiries e-mail: enquiries@kleinwortbenson.com
Web: www.kleinwortbenson.com

Region: West Midlands
Kleinwort Benson (Birmingham Office)
1 Victoria Square
Birmingham
B1 1BD
Tel: 0121 644 4850
General enquiries e-mail: enquiries@kleinwortbenson.com
Web: www.kleinwortbenson.com

Region: Scotland
Kleinwort Benson (Edinburgh Office)
18 Charlotte Square
Edinburgh
EH2 4DF
Tel: 0131 260 5900
Fax: 0131 260 5909
General enquiries e-mail: enquiries@kleinwortbenson.com
Web: www.kleinwortbenson.com

Region: Yorkshire & the Humber
Kleinwort Benson (Leeds Office)
1 City Square
Leeds
LS1 2ES
Tel: 01132 048 300
General enquiries e-mail: enquiries@kleinwortbenson.com
Web: www.kleinwortbenson.com

Region: East Anglia
Kleinwort Benson (Cambridge Office)
Wellington House
East Road
Cambridge
CB1 1BH
Tel: 01223 454 560
General enquiries e-mail: enquiries@kleinwortbenson.com
Web: www.kleinwortbenson.com

Region: Channel Islands
Kleinwort Benson (Guernsey Office)
Dorey Court
Admiral Park
St Peter Port
Guernsey
GY1 3BG
Tel: 01481 727111
General enquiries e-mail: enquiries@kleinwortbenson.com
Web: www.kleinwortbenson.com

Region: Channel Islands
Kleinwort Benson (Jersey Office)
Wests Centre
St Helier
Jersey
JE4 8PQ
Tel: 01534 613000
General enquiries e-mail: enquiries@kleinwortbenson.com
Web: www.kleinwortbenson.com

Region: North West
Kleinwort Benson (Manchester Office)
Peter House
Oxford Street
Manchester
M1 5AN
Tel: 0161 200 1630
General enquiries e-mail: enquiries@kleinwortbenson.com
Web: www.kleinwortbenson.com

Region: London
M&G Investments (Head Office (UK))
Laurence Pountney Hill
London
EC4R 0HH
Tel: 020 7626 4588
Contact: Richard Miles
E-mail: info@mandg.co.uk
Web: www.mandg.co.uk

Region: Scotland
Murray Asset Management (Head Office)
1 Glenfinlas Street
Edinburgh
EH3 6AQ
Tel: 0131 220 8888
Fax: 0131 225 7307
Contact: Ruthven Gemmel
E-mail: info@murrayasset.co.uk
Web: www.murrayasset.co.uk
Murray Asset Management is an independent investment management and financial
planning firm.

Region: London
Natwest Stockbrokers Ltd (Head Office)
Premier Place
2 1/2 Devonshire Square
London
EC2M 4BA
Tel: 0808 208 4400
Web: www.natweststockbrokers.com
Execution only sharedealing, ISAs, fund supermarket, CFDs & FX trading with free
online education

Region: South East
Premier Asset Management (Head Office)
Eastgate Court
High Street
Guildford
Surrey
GU1 3DE
Tel: 0845 230 9033
Fax: 01483 300 845
Contact: Simon Weldon
E-mail: simonweldon@premierfunds.co.uk
General enquiries e-mail: marketing@premierfunds.co.uk
Web: www.premierassetmanagement.co.uk

Region: South West
Principal Investment Management Ltd (Bath Office)
5 Miles's Buildings
George Street
Bath
BA1 2QS
Tel: 01225 460 010
Fax: 01225 446 434
Contact: Paul Hastings
E-mail: paul.hastings@pimltd.co.uk
General enquiries e-mail: sales-support@pimltd.co.uk
Web: www.principalinvestment.co.uk
Principal is a leading private client investment company specializing in discretionary
portfolio management.

Region: South East
Principal Investment Management Ltd (Registered and Head Office, Sevenoaks)
16 South Park
Sevenoaks
Kent
TN13 1AN
Tel: 01732 740 700
Fax: 01732 740 287
Contact: Paul Hood
E-mail: paul.hood@pimltd.co.uk
General enquiries e-mail: sales-support@pimltd.co.uk
Web: www.principalinvestment.co.uk

Region: London
Principal Investment Management Ltd (London Office)
10 King William Street
London
EC4N 7TW
Tel: 0207 280 8700
Fax: 0207 280 8701
Contact: Kevin Long
E-mail: kevin.long@pimltd.co.uk
General enquiries e-mail: sales-support@pimltd.co.uk
Web: www.principalinvestment.co.uk

Region: Wales
Pritchard Stockbrokers Ltd (Cardiff Office)
Unit 6, Charnwood Court
Heol Billingsley
Parc Nantgarw
Cardiff
CF15 7QZ
Tel: 02920 022799
Contact: Bill Hunt
E-mail: bill.hunt@pritchard.co.uk
Web: www.pritchard.co.uk
We provide risk-controlled wealth management and investment services to
individuals, companies, trusts and professional intermediaries

Region: Isle of Man
Ramsey Crookall & Co Ltd (Head Office)
Securities House
38/42 Athol Street
Douglas
Isle of Man
IM1 1QH
Tel: 01624 673171
Fax: 01624 677258
Contact: Joanna Crookall
E-mail: joanna.crookall@ramseycrookall.com
General enquiries e-mail: dealers@ramseycrookall.com
Web: www.ramseycrookall.com
The Isle of Man's longest established and most experienced firm of stockbrokers and
investment managers. Licensed by the Isle of Man Financial Supervision Commission.

Region: London
Redmayne Bentley (London Office)
Finsbury House
23 Finsbury Circus
London
EC2M 7UH
Tel: 020 7614 4800
Fax: 020 7614 4830
Contact: Nick Bettison
E-mail: nick.bettison@redmayne.co.uk
Web: www.redmayne.co.uk

Region: South East
Redmayne Bentley (Henley on Thames Office)
Market Place House
43 Market Place
Henley on Thames
Oxfordshire
RG9 2AA
Tel: 01491 570 700
Fax: 01491 579 353
Contact: Carole Anderson
E-mail: henley@redmayne.co.uk
Web: www.redmayne.co.uk
Award winning private client investment management and stockbroking.

Region: South West
Rowan Dartington (Head Office)
Colston Tower
Colston Street
Bristol
BS1 4RD
Tel: 0800 1411 2244
E-mail: info@rowan-dartington.co.uk
Web: www.rowan-dartington.co.uk
Rowan Dartington is one of the South-West's leading independent stockbrokers, providing clients with a wide range of tax-efficient investment products and services including Portfolio Management, Discretionary and Advisory Managed, Advisory Dealing, Execution Only, ISAs, SIPPs, Spread Betting and CFDs

Region: North West
Savoy Investment Management Limited (Stockport Office)
The Old Courtyard
103 Buxton Road
High Lane
Stockport
SK6 8DX
Tel: 01663 761980
Fax: 01663 767835
Contact: Nigel Carter
E-mail: ncarter@savoyim.com
Web: www.savoyim.com
Savoy Investment Management specializes in providing a stockbroking and investment management service for private clients, including ISA management, Trusts and Charities.

Region: London
Savoy Investment Management Limited (Head Office)
7 Hanover Square
London
W1S 1HQ
Tel: 020 7659 8000
Fax: 020 7659 8001
Contact: Christopher Jeffreys
E-mail: cjeffreys@savoyim.com
Web: www.savoyim.com

Region: West Midlands
Smith & Williamson Investment Management (Birmingham Office)
3rd Floor
9 Colmore Row
Birmingham
B3 2BJ
Tel: 0121 710 5200
Fax: 0121 710 5201
Contact: Mark Willis
E-mail: info@smith.williamson.co.uk
Web: www.smith.williamson.co.uk
Smith & Williamson provides investment services for private individuals, charities and institutions, and has over £10 billion of funds under management and advice (as at 31 October 2010).

Region: London
Smith & Williamson Investment Management (London)
25 Moorgate
London
EC2R 6AY
Tel: 020 7131 4228
Contact: Kate Harrison
E-mail: kate.harrison@smith.williamson.co.uk
General enquiries e-mail: info@smith.williamson.co.uk

Region: London
Smith & Williamson Investment Management (Head Office)
25 Moorgate
London
EC2R 6AY
Tel: 020 7131 4000
Fax: 020 7131 4001
Contact: Peter Fernandes
E-mail: info@smith.williamson.co.uk
Web: www.smith.williamson.co.uk

Region: South West
Smith & Williamson Investment Management (Bristol Office)
Portwall Place
Portwall Lane
Bristol
BS1 6NA
Tel: 0117 376 2000
Fax: 0117 376 2001
Contact: John Erskine
E-mail: info@smith.williamson.co.uk
Web: www.smith.williamson.co.uk

Region: Ireland
Smith & Williamson Investment Management (Dublin Office)
Paramount Court
Corrig Road
Sandyford Business Park
Dublin 18, Ireland
Tel: 00 353 (0)1 614 2520
Contact: Chris Kenny
E-mail: info@swf.ie
Web: www.swf.ie

Region: Scotland
Smith & Williamson Investment Management (Glasgow Office)
206 St Vincent Street
Glasgow
G2 5SG
Tel: 0141 222 1100
Fax: 0141 222 1101
Contact: Stephen Quaile
E-mail: info@smith.williamson.co.uk
Web: www.smith.williamson.co.uk

Region: South East
Smith & Williamson Investment Management (Guildford Office)
No 1 Bishops Wharf
Walnut Tree Close
Guildford
GU1 4RA
Tel: 01483 407 100
Fax: 01483 301 232
Contact: Mark Garnett
E-mail: info@smith.williamson.co.uk
Web: www.smith.williamson.co.uk

Region: East Anglia
Southgate Financial Services Ltd (Head Office)
Independence House
14a Nelson Street
Southend-on-Sea
SS1 1EF
Tel: 0333 577 2400
Fax: 01702 680 333
Contact: David Tickett
E-mail: hpw@ifa.cc
Web: www.ifa.cc
Independent financial advice from a CERTIFIED FINANCIAL PLANNER[CM] professional

Region: London
Standard Life Wealth Ltd (London Office)
30 St Mary Axe
London
EC3A 8EP
Tel: 0845 279 8880
Contact: Richard Charnock
E-mail: richard_charnock@standardlife.com
Web: www.standardlifewealth.com/
Standard Life Wealth – The Private Client Investment Specialists. Our business is to provide tailored discretionary investment management using investments from the whole of the market. Standard Life Wealth focuses on investment excellence and brings to private clients a number of investment strategies and techniques previously restricted to institutional investors.

Region: Scotland
Standard Life Wealth Ltd (Head Office)
Standard Life House
30 Lothian Road
Edinburgh
EH1 2DH
Tel: 0845 279 8880
Contact: Richard Charnock
E-mail: richard_charnock@standardlife.com
Web: www.standardlifewealth.com/

Region: West Midlands
Standard Life Wealth Ltd (Birmingham Office)
24–26 Calthorpe Road
Birmingham
B15 1RP
Tel: 0845 279 8880
Contact: Richard Charnock
E-mail: richard_charnock@standardlife.com
Web: www.standardlifewealth.com/

Region: London
Taylor Young Investment Management Limited (Head Office)
Tower Bridge Court
226 Tower Bridge Road
London
SE1 2UL
Tel: 020 7378 4500
Fax: 020 7378 4501
Contact: Peter Thomson
E-mail: peter.thomson@tyim.co.uk
General enquiries e-mail: invest@tyim.co.uk
Web: www.tayloryoung.com
Taylor Young Investment Management Limited is an independent house with a thematic approach to investment, offering good old-fashioned service with a genuine empathy towards our clients' needs.

Region: National
The Ethical Partnership (Channel Islands and Southern England Office)
180 Woodlands Road
Southampton
Hampshire
SO40 7GL
Tel: 08456 123 411
Fax: 2380293928
Contact: Jeremy Newbegin
E-mail: jeremyn@the-ethical-partnership.co.uk
General enquiries e-mail: enquiries@the-ethical-partnership.co.uk
Web: www.the-ethical-partnership.co.uk
Ethical and socially responsible investment specialists.

Region: South East
Thesis Asset Management Plc (Lymington Office)
48 High Street
Lymington
Hampshire
SO41 9ZQ
Tel: 01590 625 841
Fax: 01590 677 346
Contact: Giles Marriage
E-mail: giles.marriage@thesis-plc.com
Web: www.thesis-plc.com
Investment Management – discretionary, advisory and execution-only services.

Region: London
Troy Asset Management Ltd (Head Office)
Brookfield House
44 Davies Street
London
W1K 5JA
Tel: 020 7499 4030
Fax: 020 7491 2445
Contact: Fritz von Westenholz
E-mail: fvw@troyasset.com
Web: www.taml.co.uk
At Troy, we seek to preserve and build our investors' wealth by constructing conservative portfolios for the long term, while maintaining competitive fees, tax efficiency and transparency.

Region: London
Turcan Connell (London Office)
12 Stanhope Gate
London
W1K 1AW
Tel: 0207 491 8811
Fax: 0207 409 0811
General enquiries e-mail: enquiries@turcanconnell.com
Web: www.turcanconnell.com
Leading provider of legal and financial advice for private individuals, charities and the owners and managers of land.

Region: Scotland
Turcan Connell (Edinburgh Office)
Princes Exchange
1 Earl Grey Street
Edinburgh
EH3 9EE
Tel: 0131 228 8111
Fax: 0131 228 8118
Contact: Alex Montgomery
E-mail: alex.montgomery@turcanconnell.com
General enquiries e-mail: enquiries@turcanconnell.com
Web: www.turcanconnell.com

Region: Channel Islands
Turcan Connell (St Peter Port Office)
Borough House, Suite 7
Rue Du Pre
St Peter Port
Guernsey
GY1 1EF
Tel: 01481 710 867
Fax: 01481 710 578
Contact: Martin Conlon
E-mail: martin.conlon@saltiretrustees.com
General enquiries e-mail: enquiries@turcanconnell.com
Web: www.turcanconnell.com

Region: London
Williams de Broë Ltd (Head Office)
100 Wood Street
London
EC2V 7AN
Tel: (020) 7072 7500
Fax: (020) 7072 7501
Contact: Andrew Butler-Cassar
General enquiries e-mail: london.office@wdebroe.com
Web: www.wdebroe.com

Region: West Midlands
Williams de Broë Ltd (Birmingham Office)
Colmore Plaza
Colmore Circus
Birmingham
B4 6AT
Tel: (0121) 232 0700
Fax: (0121) 232 0701
Contact: Adrian Quin
General enquiries e-mail: birmingham.office@wdebroe.com
Web: www.wdebroe.com

Region: South West
Williams de Broë Ltd (Bath Office)
24 Gay Street
Bath
BA1 2PD
Tel: (01225) 341 580
Fax: (01225) 341 581
Contact: Michele Rogers
General enquiries e-mail: bath.office@wdebroe.com
Web: www.wdebroe.com

Region: South West
Williams de Broë Ltd (Bournemouth Office)
Midland House
2 Poole Road
Bournemouth
BH2 5QY
Tel: (01202) 208 100
Fax: (01202) 208 101
Contact: Scott Jones
General enquiries e-mail: bournemouth.office@wdebroe.com
Web: www.wdebroe.com

Region: Scotland
Williams de Broë Ltd (Edinburgh Office)
Donaldson House
97 Haymarket Terrace
Edinburgh
EH12 5HD
Tel: (0131) 460 4000
Fax: (0131) 460 4001
Contact: Murray Mackay
General enquiries e-mail: edinburgh.office@wdebroe.com
Web: www.wdebroe.com

Region: South West
Williams de Broë Ltd (Exeter Office)
16 Dix's Field
Exeter
EX1 1QA
Tel: (01392) 204 404
Fax: (01392) 426 176
Contact: Michele Rogers
General enquiries e-mail: exeter.office@wdebroe.com
Web: www.wdebroe.com

Region: South East
Williams de Broë Ltd (Guildford Office)
39 Epsom Road
Guildford
GU1 3LA
Tel: (01483) 207 650
Fax: (01483) 207 659
Contact: Martin Vanstone
General enquiries e-mail: guildford.office@wdebroe.com
Web: www.wdebroe.com

Region: London
Heartwood (London Office)
12 Henrietta Street
Covent Garden
London
WC2E 8LH
Contact: Guy Hudson
E-mail: guy-hudson@heartwoodgroup.co.uk
General enquiries e-mail: info@heartwoodgroup.co.uk
www.heartwoodgroup.co.uk
Independently owned, Heartwood provides stand-alone, funds-based investment management, complemented by a truly integrated private wealth management service, combining investment, pensions, retirement and tax planning advice.

Region: South East
Heartwood (Tunbridge Wells Office)
77 Mount Ephraim
Tunbridge Wells
Kent
TN4 8BS
Tel: 01892 701 801
Fax: 01892 701 804
Contact: Guy Hudson
E-mail: guy-hudson@heartwoodgroup.co.uk
General enquiries e-mail: info@heartwoodgroup.co.uk
www.heartwoodgroup.co.uk

INDEX

INDEX OF ADVERTISERS